# THE QUIET KID

Michael Scarlett

Copyright © 2020 Michael Scarlett
ISBN: 9798668587094
Library of Congress Control Number: 2020913929
Published in the United States of America

All rights reserved as permitted under the U. S. Copyright Act of 1976. No part of this publication may be reproduced, distributed, or transmitted in any form or by any means, or stored in a database or retrieval system, without the expressed written permission of the author and publisher.

www.BurkhartBooks.com

Bedford, Texas

For Zachary, because you wanted to know more.

# Contents

| | |
|---|---|
| Prologue | 7 |
| 1. Genesis Part I | 9 |
| 2. Genesis Part II | 12 |
| 3. Sherry | 16 |
| 4. Cal Johnson Rec Center | 17 |
| 5. New Neighbors | 19 |
| 6. Summer – 1972 | 21 |
| 7. Hide 'n' Seek | 23 |
| 8. Kings of the Playground | 25 |
| 9. Legos | 28 |
| 10. Seventh Grade | 29 |
| 11. Early 1974 | 34 |
| 12. Summer 1974 | 41 |
| 13. Summer 1974 Part II | 49 |
| 14. Summer 1974 Part III | 54 |
| 15. Late Summer 1974 - Prequel to a Tragedy | 56 |
| 16. End of the Innocence Part I | 58 |
| 17. LSD | 62 |
| 18. End of the Innocence Part II | 65 |
| 19. Tragedy on Christmas Eve | 67 |
| 20. End of the Innocence Part III | 69 |
| 21. Don Lance | 70 |
| 22. Reason to Believe | 74 |
| 23. Afterlife | 76 |
| 24. Spacey Tracy | 77 |
| 25. Cody | 80 |
| 26. If Beavis and Butthead | 82 |
| 27. Shirley | 84 |
| 28. The Park | 91 |
| 29. Shirley Part II | 96 |
| 30. Clearwater | 99 |
| 31. Bobbi Spencer | 104 |
| 32. Control | 106 |
| 33. A Quiet Rebellion | 108 |
| 34. Grounded | 114 |
| 35. Busted on the Bus | 116 |

| | |
|---|---|
| 36. Halloween 1975 | 119 |
| 37. Blaine | 120 |
| 38. LSD Part II | 124 |
| 39. Grade 9 and Summer | 127 |
| 40. Ted | 133 |
| 41. South Young | 137 |
| 42. Carrie | 144 |
| 43. Prayer Meeting/Fall Creek Falls | 146 |
| 44. Art | 151 |
| 45. Watertown | 158 |
| 46. Valerie | 162 |
| 47. Valerie/Ted Part II | 169 |
| 48. Skynyrd | 174 |
| 49. Wheeler | 176 |
| 50. Molly Chambers | 180 |
| 51. Penny Marks | 185 |
| 52. Watertown Part II | 189 |
| 53. Blaine Part II | 193 |
| 54. Senior Year | 197 |
| 55. Janet | 202 |
| 56. Cameron | 210 |
| 57. Hannah | 214 |
| 58. Keely | 219 |
| 59. Hannah Part II | 222 |
| 60. Cameron II | 223 |
| 61. Hannah Part III | 228 |
| 62. The Breakup | 231 |
| | |
| Epilogue | 235 |
| Endnotes | 237 |
| Thanks | 243 |
| About the Author | |

# Prologue

*The following events are true. Some of the names have been changed to protect the innocent (or sometimes guilty).*

The view was great from where we were sitting, but until that night, I never noticed how horrible the acoustics were in the Knoxville Civic Coliseum. At the floor level, you didn't experience the echo bouncing through the upper structure like a yodel in the Swiss Alps. After the opening act, I slipped off to the restroom with a rolled-up dollar bill and a make-up mirror I'd borrowed from Amber to snort lines. It was time to find out what kind of devilry was in this Angel Dust. By the middle of Ted Nugent's set, I was beyond the point of no return.

I had never felt so helpless in all my life. Even on LSD, I had held onto a thread of coherency. It might've been as frail as a spider's web, but a connection with reality, nonetheless. That strand snapped with the animation of the concrete and steel structure around me. At first, it pulsated. Then it breathed, expanding as it sucked in oxygen. Exhaling, compressing, constricting my breath. Gremlins hidden behind the columns conspired against me, slipping behind the seats, melting into the walls. They plotted to bring down the house, seeking to entomb me. The outer shell began to separate from the superstructure, rivets popping loose as the concrete skin pulled away from the supports.

When it drew breath, it drained the spirit from within me. When it exhaled, I could feel its crushing pressure. The steel support columns were shifting all around me—the concrete walls sliding off like the putrid hide of some rotting animal carcass, the skeleton caving in, threatening to bury me beneath a pile of debris. The volume of its respiration grew louder and louder. The droning echo in my head was no longer audible as music. *Stranglehold* became nothing more than an amplified *wah-wah-wah-wah*, over and over and over. I wanted it to go away. If there had been a ledge with a clear shot to the escape of death, I probably would've thrown myself off. I could no longer feel my arms and legs. My entire body went numb.

# 1. Genesis Part I

Stained glass, in vibrant blues, yellows, greens, and reds, hindered the radiant brilliance of the sun from bursting into the sanctuary to fill every void. No one seemed to notice—not even my parents. Perhaps my baby sister noticed, but to ask Kristi out loud would have been a violation of church conduct. I was trying not to fidget in the unpadded wooden pew at Immanuel Baptist Church on Sunday morning, a week before my seventh birthday. Gray old men in three-piece suits, pious and holy, sat in the front pews, sparkling representatives of the Baptist faith. Half an hour earlier, they had been outside smoking cigarettes. Reverend Lowe was just reaching the boiling point, sweat forming in little beads on his forehead like condensation on a glass of iced tea on a sweltering afternoon. At the tender age of six years, eleven months and twenty-four days, I imagined the Almighty Himself must have looked something like the heavy set, white-haired man pacing back and forth in a whirlwind of fury, countenance aglow, a fire smoldering in his eyes conveying wrath from on high.

"The wages of sin is death. Oh, believe me, brothers and sisters, if you sin, you will die! Make no mistake! When you were born into this world, Adam was with you already. He was a part of you … born into your flesh. The flesh must die!"

Hellfire and damnation. Fire and brimstone. The unquenchable fire. And so it went for another twenty minutes. It seemed as if it would drag straight on into eternity.

But that Sunday morning, something was different. Something in the words made them come alive as the message reached its destiny at a crossroads. A choice. A choice, which even at the age of not quite seven, I understood. I perceived with crystal clarity the pretty colors of the stained glass no longer hindering the light. The Spirit of God bore witness with mine, and I understood. Jesus Christ is the SON of God. HE died for me so that I wouldn't have to pay the price for my sins. That was the truth I understood at the age of not quite seven.

Then as if He knew the precise second when this truth entered my heart, I heard a whisper, a voice, whether audible or internal I can no longer discern, but I heard Him call my name. *Michael, it's time. Come.*

I took the long, awkward walk down the aisle, answering the altar call.

A circle of doubt formed. The deacons of the church questioned. Was I old enough to understand? They could scarcely fathom that someone who had been on this earth a mere 2,551 days (including leap years) could grasp a concept to which they had devoted most of their adult lives. It caused everyone else to question.

Ted Rector interceded on my behalf. He was the smiling man with the flat top that always called me Superman. That was all I knew of him, but I loved him for that.

When at last, they were convinced, I was to be baptized after my seventh birthday. The idea that I would turn seven years old appeased them. Apparently, six was the cutoff. It's odd that in other religions, an infant can be baptized without the slightest knowledge of salvation.

That day, I gained knowledge that surpasses all understanding. I met Jesus, a man I would never forget. He would never leave or forsake me.

I was sure that Reverend Lowe was cast from the same mold as the Lord —that God himself must have looked something like this man. On the day I was baptized, the image was shattered. In white briefs and a wife beater with garters holding up his black socks, just before he slipped on the robe that would make him appear holy before the congregation, Reverend Lowe became just a man. God, in His infinite wisdom, used him—a common man—as a vessel to do the work of His choosing. I was buried in baptism with Christ, my Savior, rising again into newness of life.

I believed it. I still do—although at times, I must strive with reasoning to believe it with the unquestioned faith and simplicity of someone who is not quite seven. I responded to the altar call. But that's not what saved me.

*The shepherd called to the lamb. Little more than an infant, a wobbly kneed babe lifted his head in response to a voice he'd never heard before, yet somehow was uncanny in its familiarity. The little lamb scampered unsteadily toward his master, whom he trusted without reservation. The shepherd lifted him up into his bosom and held him tightly.*

Faith.
That was the ticket.

Standing in line to sharpen my pencil in the second grade, Jeff Cox changed everything that I knew to be true in the world with a statement and a simple question.

"I'm a Presbyterian. What are you?"

In the weeks that followed, I began to take note.

*Why are there so many different churches?*

*Methodist, Lutheran, Episcopalian, Presbyterian, Catholic ...*

Those were just the churches on our drive to Immanuel Baptist.

*Why so many? Isn't there just one God?*

# 2. Genesis Part II

JFK and Jackie had taken up residence in the master suite of the White House. Jack had a lot on his plate with Castro and the Cubans, Communism, nuclear weapons in the Bay of Pigs, and the impending decisions regarding Ho Chi Minh and Indochina. The year was 1961.

In a smaller world, my parents had their own issues.

They had just left Knoxville for a place unfamiliar.

My dad was a salesman for Ragland Wholesale Grocers. East Tennessee had been the only place that he and Mom had ever called home. But when his job offered a promotion, they moved to Augusta, Georgia, bringing with them Sherry, my dad's daughter, and the product of his first marriage.

I was born in April at St. Joseph's Hospital in Martinez, a suburb of Augusta.

Augusta's claim to fame is the Masters tournament, held annually at Augusta's National Golf Club, where the best professional golfers in the world compete for the privilege of donning what may be the ugliest green jacket ever to disgrace the world of sports fashion. While Gary Player was subtracting his way to victory that year, my mother was preparing to take the baton that had been passed down through the ages.

Eve was generous in sharing the sufferings of her curse. Six thousand years had done nothing to diminish the pain – or so I'm told. And now, ten days after the conclusion of the Masters, on the twentieth day of April, in the year of our Lord nineteen hundred sixty-one, I was about to bring pain into my mother's life like she had never known. Unfortunately, it would not end there.

The teenage years were still ahead.

Ragland relocated Dad again, and the family moved to Greenville, South Carolina. Dad became somewhat disgruntled. Mom felt as if she would die of loneliness so far away from home and friends and family. Then, a change of jobs brought them back home to Knoxville before I was three.

We weren't rich, but if anything was lacking, I was unaware. The one thing I always had was stability. My parents stayed together, which was nothing out of the ordinary in those days. I don't recall the arrival of my baby sister, Kristi (I was only three). She was just

## The Quiet Kid

always there. We got along most of the time, as well as can be expected of cats and dogs.

A couple of examples:

Kristi snuck up behind me once and smacked me open-handed between my shoulder blades. I wasn't wearing a shirt at the time. I ran her down as she tried to escape my room up the flight of stairs. When I caught up to her, she'd just cleared the top riser. I rudely introduced the front of her skull to the drywall in the hallway. The red mark she left imprinted on my back did little in my defense after she went crying to Mom. It seemed her crime was undeserving of the punishment I'd dished out.

Another time, we were alone in the house, waiting for a ride to school. Kristi went out to fetch the newspaper from the mailbox. I locked her out. Determined to get back inside, she broke a window, slicing the side of her hand (fortunately not deep enough to require stitches), while simultaneously landing me in hot water once again. We were both too stubborn for our own good, but most of the time, we managed to coexist without incident.

Then there was the time she wrecked her bicycle and scraped her knees bloody. I scooped her up and carried her half a block home, leaving her bike behind in the grass.

The seemingly flawless stability of life in our house wasn't without its disruptions. It never entered my mind that Sherry was half or any less my sister than Kristi, but she would occasionally decide that she wanted to go live with her biological mother. Without adequate warning, she would disappear from our lives for a while. I never quite got used to it.

Our neighborhood was full of kids, so a game of two-hand touch street football wasn't out of the question. Inevitably, a car would come along, halting the action mid-play. "Car!" Someone would yell, which would result in a do-over.

Sometimes, Dad would get involved. Dad was a sports nut. He would play catch with a ball of any kind—be it football, baseball, or even a Frisbee in the street. He did this trick that all the neighborhood kids would stand in line for. It was a kind of judo flip. The kid would bend over, sticking his or her arms between their legs. Dad would grab their wrists and, with one quick jerk, send them somersaulting and like a cat always landing on their feet. He had an old Ford truck and would often let us ride for short distances in the bed. Sometimes, if it was only a trip to the IGA market a few blocks away, my cousin Mark and I could talk him into letting us ride on the sideboards. "Hold on tight," he'd say, believing that we had the good sense to do it.

Mom was forever trying to protect us from the world. Dad always gave us a little leeway, letting us go out—perhaps a little too far out on a limb sometimes. He was certain we'd always land on our feet.

I don't remember any hugging or actual verbalizing of the phrase, "I love you." I would like to think they were present when we were younger. But as we came to the age where we began to suspect that our parents were the enemy and that we should separate ourselves from them, they simply allowed it. I don't think they really knew what else to do. (It's a shame that teenagers don't come with a troubleshooting manual).

There was plenty of caring that my parents showed us in their own ways. Dad let us be who we were. Mom doted and worried. And she prayed—a lot.

God bless them both.

I never knew much of my Mom's parents. There is a vague recollection way back somewhere of visiting her dad in a nursing home. Holidays were always spent with my dad's parents.

On my dad's side were eight siblings, netting thirteen cousins. My aunts, Beth and Angie, and my Uncle Zane were close enough to the ages of the rest of us that it reinforced our numbers even more whenever we assembled at Christmas or Thanksgiving.

On Christmas Eve, the grandkids all received the same present every year: a one-dollar bill and a book of LifeSavers candy. The consistency of Papaw and Mamaw's annual gift-giving took away any possibility of suspense. The same could be said of my Papaw's stoic prayer on any holiday or any given Sunday. He was a tall, sturdy rail of a man, lean, but not skinny. At 6'2", he towered over most everyone else in the family (Uncle Jim being the exception). He reminded me of a white-haired Abe Lincoln minus the top hat and the beard.

## The Quiet Kid

*Our heavenly Father, we give thee thanks for the many blessings that Thou hast bestowed upon us. Bless this bounty that thou hast set before us that it may nourish our bodies and bless the hands that have prepared it. Forgive us, Oh Lord, where we have failed thee. And help us now to do thy will. For it is in the name of your precious Son that we do pray. Amen.*

Okay, maybe I missed a word or two in the paraphrasing. But you get the gist.

I always thought that it was a bit rehearsed. There was something comforting and reassuring in its dependability. Now, looking back, I realized what I missed. They were the same words—more or less—spoken with the same inflection, year after year, and yet they always sounded heartfelt—like he meant every word.

# 3. Sherry

The upper platform of the high dive at Alcoa Municipal Swimming Pool didn't seem all that high from the water.

"You can do it," Sherry encouraged. "Just don't think about it. Don't look down. Just jump." My big sister's instruction seemed so simple when I was still looking up at it, hanging onto the security of the concrete turtle head protruding from the northeast wall.

I was nine years old, watching from the bottom of the ladder as she plodded carefully up each rung. Beyond the concrete tower of the platform, the shallow end of the pool looked like it was a mile away across the wide expanse of cyan-tinted H2O. The time Sherry disappeared from my vision was mere seconds. On top of the platform, she bee-lined out to the end of the narrow board, and bounced once, the springboard hoisting her into the air. I saw her plunge straight down into the chlorinated water with a white, foaming splash. Just as she resurfaced, I hopped on the ladder, hoping she would reach the turtle's head before I got to the top. I wanted her to be looking when I jumped. Once there, I heeded her instruction.

No hesitation.

Focusing only on the path to the end of the board, I ignored the sunspots reflecting off the crystal-clear surface. One foot in front of the other until the board ceased to exist.

Then I just stepped off.

# 4. Cal Johnson Rec Center

In between Dolly Parton and the Everly Brothers on Cas Walker's Farm and Home Hour, Cas promoted his local food markets airing a commercial that featured two boys, black as carbon with beaming, white smiles. They grinned from ear to ear and nodded their heads as they gorged on watermelons, which could be purchased at Cas Walker Supermarket. Accompanying the scene was a song with these words:

*Thumpin' good, thumpin' good,*
*Cas Walker Melons are thumpin' good.*

I was nine when my dad took me to Cal Johnson Recreation Center, where he played a shirts-and-skins basketball game with some of his buddies. Other than the men on the hardwood court, I was the only white person in the building. I pretended to be OK with that, but on the inside, I trembled like the aftershock of an earthquake. On another court, some teenage boys were playing hoops. They were black, so I was confused when they tossed the "n" word at each other carelessly, aggressively, and as often as they tossed the ball. It didn't ease my discomfort any. I had heard the word before, but never in a context that made it seem in any way acceptable.

Mostly, I had heard black people referred to as "colored." The Magnolia area surrounding the fairgrounds was referred to as the colored part of town. In our ignorance, we imagined that to be polite. Never had I heard the word—the one that started with an "n"—uttered in our house, except when my uncle Charles came to visit. I would always cringe whenever we were told he was coming. He used lots of colorful words that I wasn't allowed to repeat.

After a while, I spotted a boy around the same age as me bouncing a basketball off the block wall by some folded bleachers. When I ventured closer, he extended an offer. "You can play if you want." Other than his dark skin, I could see little difference between us. In fact, I saw a glint of what might have been fear in his eyes, telling me that we had plenty in common. So I accepted his offer.

Feeling at ease in his company, I asked him why the other boys called each other that name—the one starting with an "n"—only I said the word.

His reaction wasn't one of shock caused by what I had said. And it wasn't anger. I didn't know any better, and he perceived it. Raising a finger to his lips as if to shush me, he said, "Don't let them hear you." He was genuinely concerned for my safety.

He never gave an explanation for my query. I'm not sure he knew the answer. We were both content to let the question go for the moment. Maybe we were too young for such deep wisdom.

# 5. New Neighbors

Mark Lee lived next door. We were cousins, but more like brothers joined at the hip. We did everything together. We were cowboys with hats and the holstered silver six-shooters we'd gotten for Christmas. Climbing the mimosa tree that had been split at the core by a bolt of lightning, we played Lost in Space. Three empty wrappers from any Tom's product granted us free entry to the Tom's Club Saturday movie matinees at the Tennessee Theatre. We walked to the IGA for Icees and Odd Rod trading cards, rode our bikes through the neighborhood, spent the night at each other's house, rummaged through his sister's 45's, belting out our best falsetto imitations of Frankie Valli and the Four Seasons, or taking another fatal cruise with Jan and Dean never to return from *Dead Man's Curve*. We lived in similar houses—compact three-bedrooms with asbestos siding. (You read that right). His was lime green. Ours was pink. (You're thinking about John Mellencamp now, right?)

He was slightly pudgy with dark hair and blue eyes. I was the skinny one, with dusty blonde hair and eyes of hazel. We rarely fought, but when we did, the results weren't pretty—a flurry of wild flailing arms. Whoever connected first would send the other home crying. We'd be separated for a couple of days, having to beg our mothers to, at the very least, let us talk at the fence. We would make up, shaking on it over the top rail of the chain link, and soon, life would go back to normal.

Mark and I went outside one day to find a new family had moved in across the street. A spindly kid with curly, orange hair as brilliant as a burning fire and thick, black-rimmed Buddy Holly glasses was standing at the edge of the grass facing my house. It was doubtful that his toes could have been any closer to the street without touching the pavement. His legs were spread apart slightly, and he rocked, shifting his weight back and forth. It would have been impossible to ignore this kid whose posture seemed to suggest that he had been waiting all morning for one thing: Us. Either that, or he thought he was a dog trapped in the confines of an invisible fence seeking an escape route. The latter never occurred to us, seeing that that invention had not yet made its way to the yard. Truth be told, the unseen force holding him back was probably just beyond the front window somewhere within a few short steps of checking up on him.

"What's your name?" We asked.

"I'm poo-poo face."

Not knowing how to respond to this, Mark and I looked at each other, shrugged, and went about the business of our day.

The next day we returned to find the kid swaying like an orange Q-tip with legs in the exact same spot.

"I'm mud pie face," was the reply we got that day.

"I'm clown face," the day after.

He was a weird little kid. And I liked him from the start.

Pretty soon, our routine was established. Every day, Mark and I would venture out to see what kind of face was staring out across the street in our direction. Eventually, he warmed up to us enough to give out his real name. David, we soon discovered, had a severe stutter, probably the reason for his many faces, enabling him to respond to us in short, premeditated spurts. After a while, his mom must've reached the conclusion that we weren't going to pick on him because she allowed him to slip beyond the borders of their yard.

One summer afternoon, David and I attempted to execute mass genocide on the ants in his back yard using a mixture of household cleaning chemicals. His little sister was appalled and mortified at our complete disregard for their lives. "Oh, Bay-eth," David would sing as he heaped a batch of our homemade brew on another anthill.

Beth's lip began to quiver as her green eyes welled up with tears. "You're just trying to make me cry."

# 6. Summer – 1972

It was summer again—three months of glorious sunshine and unrepentant lolly-gagging sandwiched in between Memorial Day and Labor Day and fifth and sixth grade. I was crossing the front lawn of Southwood Garden Apartments zigzagging on my bike. To keep from getting too far ahead of James Underhill and his girlfriend, Sophie, I kept doubling back, riding in circles around them as they walked.

My secret mission: To steal her away from James. He had no idea. And she wasn't aware that the stunt I was about to attempt was intended solely to impress her. What is she doing with him, anyway? The way he fanned his bangs up in what he called a bird's nest was completely ridiculous. Maybe I was just jealous because, after all, he had cute little Sophie with her brown pixie haircut for a girlfriend. I was out to remedy that.

After all, what are best friends for?

They were walking hand in hand.

The circus horns of Blood, Sweat, and Tears blared from the open door of a balcony apartment as we ducked into the alleyway between the front units. *Spinning Wheel.*[1a]

An elevated tenant parking lot in the back forty was accessible by a flight of concrete steps, dividing a grass embankment, twenty feet high, that bottomed out into the courtyard. James and Sophie took a seat on the sidewalk, where I promised they would have the best vantage point for the show. "Wait here. I'll be right back."

I could have walked my bike up the steps. But instead, I peddled around to the parking lot entrance via Baker Street. I had wanted to be close to her, even if it was only in intermittent spurts each time that I had passed close enough to smell her sweet perfume. And this way, the anticipation would be greater while they waited for me to reappear. So I left them, riding off to take the long way around.[1b]

"Up here!" I shouted down to them when I had reached the top. Then I peddled quickly back to the top of the parking lot. The paving sloped hard before leveling off into the lot. It would be no problem picking up enough speed to clear the steep slope after jumping the concrete curb.

My one big mistake was not pulling up hard enough when I hit the curb.

In the air, I was somewhere between consciousness and delirium. Drifting in slow motion, I watched the scene unfold, tumbling end over end, the green grass in front of me, and then the blue sky. I floated upside down to the bottom.

I had been right about one thing. My acceleration was adequate. With a loose grip on the handlebars, I landed flat on my back. There was probably a dull thud, but I never heard it. The bike recoiled away from me after the impact as I rolled. The near loss of consciousness kept my body from tensing up, a rag doll landing unscathed in the grass.

Far away, it seemed from some remote planet, I heard a scream. Sophie ran to see if I was alive. Milking it for all it was worth, I played possum, wanting to pounce as she bent over me, wanting to surprise her by slipping my hand behind her neck to pull her in for a kiss. That thought was mortifying beyond any intimidation the drop presented as I had looked down at them from the top of the parking lot. Instead, I cracked a smile, peeping out through one squinted eye.

"Oh, thank God you're okay!"

Even in failing, the jump had accomplished some of its original intent. I didn't get the girl, but for a moment, I had her undivided attention. I didn't steal her from James, but it had still been worth it.

# 7. Hide 'n' Seek

"Let's hide in the graveyard."

"Nuh-uh. No way." Mark wasn't having it.

"David will never look for us there."

"What about Bill Zachary?"

"You don't really believe that, do ya?"

Mark's older brother Robbie antagonized us at every given opportunity. We had recorded ourselves doing a sing-along to Partridge Family songs on a cassette tape. Robbie overdubbed parts of it with snarky remarks. He often teased Mark with his version of the Cracker Jack ditty.

*Rolly Polly fat boy, peanuts and a prize ...*

The legend of Bill Zachary was Robbie's latest thing. According to Robbie, Bill Zachary's tombstone had been removed from the graveyard at the turn of the century. He was still pissed about it, now haunting the cemetery at the edge of the Lee's property. As if it wasn't creepy enough already.

A raggedy wooden fence was still standing like a sentinel in front of the moss weathered monuments which dated back to the 1800s. A giant, dead oak tree arose from the midst of the headstones like something right out of a horror movie. At dusk, the sky was peppered with bats emerging from the hollow oak.

Mark gnawed his bottom lip, deciding.

"C'mon, b'fore David gets to a hundred."

"All right."

We made a mad dash, outrunning our uncertainties to hide from the living behind the markers of the dead forgotten by time. Crouching low, we peeked over the shoulders of the headstones.

"See 'im?"

"Not yet."

We whispered softly not for fear of being heard by David but from fear born of anxiety, a deep dread founded in respect, not wanting to disturb the sleeping dead all around us.

Home base was the mimosa tree in our front yard. We were unable to see when David reached the end of his count. He had to be there by now, but we were stuck until we could see the flame of his red hair. At last, we spotted him, moving through the backyard of my house. He was too close to base to make a run for it, but we were poised for flight, ready to depart from this dark decision.

He ventured deeper into the yard, getting close to the field in the back forty. We were just about to go when David spied Beth and Kristi. He caught Beth easily but had to chase Kristi as she fled toward home base.

"Crap! Now we have to wait again."

"I knew this was a bad idea." Mark's worry was rising in his voice.

"Naw, we'll be fine." I tried to hide my concern.

We were there for a long time. Way too long. But we waited it out, not seeing David again until at long last we heard him calling.

"Ollie, ollie oxen free."

# 8. Kings of the Playground

To my left stood the two-story brick school building where I had spent the better part of the last six years of my life. Giffin Elementary. Behind me lay the woods where we weren't allowed while school was in session.

Jeff Cox and Dusty Hurst were in the outfield just beyond the edge of the blacktop.

I couldn't look at Jeff without envisioning him on our safety trip jumping up and down on the bed in our hotel room, holding his whitey tighties in front of his pelvis, chanting, "I'm a Panda Bear, I'm a Panda Bear." We'd just gotten back from the Washington Zoo. It was a visual I doubted I'd ever eradicate from my memory banks.

The White House, The Lincoln Memorial, The Washington Monument, Arlington Cemetery, and The Eternal Flame at Kennedy's Tomb hadn't gone completely unnoticed. But at every given opportunity, I was off with Dusty to infringe upon the personal space of a couple of giggling girls. Lori Smith was the object of Dusty's affection. I had a longstanding joke with her counterpart, Joyce Avans. "Are you stoned or drunk?" we would ask each other, neither of us having ever been stoned or drunk. It made me a shoo-in for wingman. Both girls were smoking hot by sixth grade standards. "Let's go to the vicinity," Dusty would say, as if the vicinity was an actual place, like Cleveland.

At the moment, my focus was on the real estate over the heads and just out of reach of my two buddies at the perimeter of the playground. It was their turn to pay.

James Underhill and Rodney Caldwell were on my team. Everyone else on the opposing side was irrelevant. None of them were engaged in our private little game within the game. Besides, I knew none of them would be involved in making a play.

Every elementary school playground game invented—Dodge Ball, Four Square, Kickball—employed the use of a red ball made from the rubber of some tree that must have been cultivated for this specific purpose. We were playing Kickball with a twist. The rules were simple. Try to kick the ball beyond the edge of the blacktop and out of the defender's reach. The defender could thwart the effort by simply catching the red, rubber orb before it bounced off the dirt. Succeeding in the first meant collecting compensation—a nickel each from the defending team. If one of them caught the ball, then the kicker had to pay that individual. So, the advantage always went to the offense. Either way, the victor of the moment would celebrate by singing out the theme song borrowed from the jingle of a Pepsi advertisement.

James Underhill and I had long been at a disadvantage to the other boys, lacking the athletic prowess that they seemed to possess naturally. I had made up for some of it with speed and sheer tenacity, running down a fair percentage of the airborne spheres that had appeared to have been launched into no man's land.

"Go crank!" Dusty would yell in disgust whenever I ran one down. Or, "Cut your face!" when I taunted him with the mocking Pepsi ditty.

The pitcher rolled the ball.

Today was my day. I met the ball with a forceful, fluid motion that raised a distinct, hollow sound that can only be extracted from the sweet spot of that particular type of rubber.

The ball sailed, not so much high as it did long. Jeff was closest, but he had no chance, running to chase the ball down as it bounced away over the cracks in the sun-hardened clay.

"Nickel, Nickel ah doody ah dah da." I sang triumphantly, galloping leisurely toward first base.

"Watch out for the gooshie!" Dusty hollered, attempting in vain to distract me as I rounded second base, hoping at least to have a shot at relaying the ball in for an out before I made it home.

"Go crank, you cranker!" I hollered back, running with even less urgency as I glanced back to see Jeff finally catching up with the errant, bouncing ball just I as stepped on third.

We were the kings of the playground.

We had it made. We were in our own little world, and no one else could touch it. The rules of life were whatever we decided. Never caring what anyone else thought, we were just enjoying life as it came. Everyone else looked on, wanting in our little circle. We never noticed, nor did we care. The close of school that spring would change all that.

Home was four blocks from Giffin Elementary School. Mark and I had walked the same route every weekday for six years. For every mile, that school pulled us apart—different classes, new friends—those four blocks reeled us back in. The park at the corner of McClung

## The Quiet Kid

Avenue and South Haven marked the halfway point. On our last day of sixth grade, we were mindful of another halfway point: six years down and six more to go. The next six would separate us a little more, at least in terms of the choices we made.

That summer, Richie Barrett and I took up smoking cigarettes. At the edge of the woods behind Giffin Elementary, we were spotted by Big John, the school janitor. It was probably the sun beaming bright on Richie's blonde hair that caught his eye. We thought we were up the creek, but he didn't seem to mind. We were moving on. We weren't his responsibility. Besides, we had our own Marlboro reds. Daddy's stolen Winston's just didn't cut it anymore.

*Winston tastes bad like the one I just had*
*No filter, no flavor, just waded up toilet paper ...*

Dressed in bib overalls, Big John possessed a smile that made you feel like everything would be okay no matter what, comforting like a big stack of warm pancakes, his bright pearly white teeth against his dark skin, so black it was blue. He laughed at us like someone was tickling him. "Hee, hee, hee. Lawd chile, yo mommas catch you, she gone tan yo hide."

Perhaps he was reliving the days when he himself was molting the first layer of his innocence.

# 9. Legos

It was a warm afternoon in the summer of 1973. A gentle breeze kicked up often enough to pacify the heat. The day was too nice to stay indoors. So we hauled David's Lego set out to the front porch—all 4,788 pieces, including windows, doors, fences, roof tiles, and miscellaneous green base platforms.

Absorbed in the search for the correct red, beveled roof pieces to top off my house—a three-story monstrosity complete with multiple balconies—an unexpected voice moving through the yard broke my concentration. "Still playin' with little kiddie toys." It was Ian Bradford.

Ian lived on Dodd Street on the other side of the block. I could see the back of his house from my front porch. He was taking the shortcut to Mark's. A section of top rail was missing from the fence in the back corner of his yard, allowing him to bend down the chain link to hop over. He had followed the fence line along with David's backyard and out between the houses. He was a friend of Mark's, but I didn't really see any need for his company. I found him kind of goofy and annoying. Squatty, with a big head, big lips, and buck teeth. Anyway, he never made much effort in my direction.

*A-hole.*

"Je-je-jerk," David said out loud after Ian was safely out of earshot.

# 10. Seventh Grade

The halls of South High School[2] were enormous, comparatively speaking. Giffin Elementary had been a small pond. Now, I was a guppy in the belly of some great behemoth, lost in a sea of students, swimming in an ocean, wave after wave of school spirit red and white football jerseys and psychedelic tie-dyed T-shirts and tank tops and denim and ... and spaghetti straps and halter tops—*gotta stay focused* ... too preoccupied with locating the correct rectangular gap in the seemingly endless walls of lockers to concern myself with the thought of where I fit in the overall scheme of things.

Funny how that thought had consumed me: How to fit in? I wanted nothing more than to be accepted, to be noticed, to be liked, and I had picked out what I thought was the coolest shirt ever when mom took me shopping at JC Penney a week earlier. Multi-colored, one sleeve cyan, one orange, the collar trimmed in yellow, the main body of the shirt was lavender. Centered at the breastplate on the front of the shirt was a cartoon pair of bell-bottom pants with eyes. In retrospect, I couldn't have done much more to make myself a target. But for some reason, I got overlooked.

It was the beginning of the school year, 1973. The war was finally over. Or so they told us.

*Maybe the bullies have other things on their minds—Watergate, inflation, Dark Side of the Moon. Maybe the troops coming home had called off the dogs?*

Not that I had ever been bothered with bullies before. Walking home from Giffin, Mark and I had befriended a dark-haired, gentle giant. Bunky Nelson, a grade above ours, had overseen our safe passage as he walked in close proximity with us most every day.

"Let it all hang out, let it all hang out," he would always sing.

To which I would reply, "I can't do that, baby. I won't have no blood left," which seemed logical as a second-grader. As stupid as it was, Bunky found it hilarious, ensuring our safe passage home for a long time. By the time he moved on, it no longer mattered, as we were then the superlative sixth graders.

Now, Bunky was nowhere to be found. The thought of being at the bottom of the food chain had me a little on edge. Between that and the occasional flashes of distracting bare skin leftover from summer, finding my first-period class was becoming quite the task.

*If only Sherry was here.* She had always helped me out in times like these.

I blended well enough, despite the blaring, neon shirt. Skating past the barbershop as often as I could hadn't been easy, but somehow, I'd managed to maneuver around Mom's constant reminders and, Dad pretending, as he did, that he hadn't heard them. My sandy blonde hair parted left to right, had snuck over my ears. All the upperclassmen, jocks included, had hair longer than mine. But I was on par with the rest of my class.

*There it is.*

MR. GARDNER.

White letters on a black, plastic sign hung below the glass portion of the mahogany door, informing me that I had arrived at the right location.

*At last, Gardner's first period Health.*

I swung the door open, slinking into the room.

*No wonder they call him rat face.*

It would be easier to find on the second day, as would the remaining five classes. Homeroom had been a breeze: first door on the left from the Moody/Tipton entrance. In time, I would know the place like the back of my hand, which, by the way, I could tell you relatively nothing about. Who really looks at the back of their hand?

First-period Health is where I met Don Colter. The classroom's fluorescent lighting cast an unnatural white luster on his blonde hair, which happened to be a little too thin for someone his age. At first, I thought he was albino. He could've been the long-lost brother of Johnny and Edgar Winter. He had asthma and Coke bottle-thick, black rimmed glasses that gave his eyes a comic book appearance that reminded me of a mosquito. I don't know why exactly. What do mosquito eyes even look like? Being skinny further reinforced this image. Crazy Jane would later dub him Mo-squeeto. And it would stick. He was kind of peculiar. Maybe that's why we hit it off.

"What's hap-o-ning?" he would always say.

He was to be the first person in whose company I would experiment with conscious altering, hallucinogenic drugs. But let's not get ahead of ourselves.

It was probably three weeks or so into the school year when I noticed him swallowing a small blue tablet at the water fountain.

## The Quiet Kid

Back in class, when I asked him about it, he said they were for his asthma. He also said I could try one if I wanted. Of course, I did. Yawning and feigning a stretch, he reached back toward my desk, turning his fist over to drop three pills into the palm of my hand.

"What are the yellow ones for?" I whispered.

"In case you get too hyper. It'll bring you back down, man."

"Do I take them together?' I was a little apprehensive, but more than ready to experiment.

"No, man. Take the blue one first. Wait about an hour, until the first one kicks in. Then take both of the yellow ones."

"What are they?"

"Valium."

I followed his instructions to the letter. Looking both ways before crossing the hall, I discreetly popped the blue tablet in my mouth as the bell rang, making a beeline for the water fountain. The two yellow tablets were stashed away in the coin pocket of my Levi's. In exactly one hour, the bell ending second period would tell me when it was time.

Forty-five minutes into second period, my heart was racing. I was feeling acutely alert. My senses were operating at supreme performance level, blood rocketing through my veins. Mr. Phelps' head was down in his office. He was probably reading "Woodworking Monthly" or some other such nonsense. As long as I took care not to hack off a finger on his new band saw, he would be none the wiser. I was gearing up for the second phase, anxious for the next new experience.

Just as Don had described, the Valium brought me back down to earth. The roller coaster, having run through its gamut of twists and curves and downward spirals, coasted back into the loading bay. From there, I proceeded through the turnstile to the floating river raft ride, still alert, but much more mellow. Every note I had blown through my trumpet had been a revelation—crisp and clean and bright—melodious harmonies blending with the leads of the first and second chairs. And now that band was over, the sun radiated warmly inside the halls of South High School, smiling down on me.

It was about that time that I happened upon a sight that had me reluctant to pinch myself. I didn't want to risk being awakened from this exquisite dream. Serendipity in hip hugger bell-bottom jeans, black converse tennis shoes, and a burgundy smock top adorned with a pear right about where her forbidden fruit was concealed, Amber Barrett was strolling my way with a huge grin on her face. Her golden hoop earrings swung freely in front of her wheat brown hair, which was parted down the middle, tucked behind her ears and floating just above her shoulders. Her blue eyes sparkled, accentuated by the powder blue on her eyelids. The crowd seemed to part for her, allowing her slow-motion passage. *My day just got even better.*

Girl crazy had plagued me at a very young age. My parents have video evidence to support that statement. Vacationing in Daytona at the age of three, I was in hot pursuit of some cute little blonde at the motel swimming pool. I scarcely believed my own eyes when I saw it, but there it was, me—showing my true colors in glorious eight-millimeter black and white. Now, in vivid Technicolor, the warm and fuzzies were compounded by the effects of diazepam.

"Scarlett! How've you been?" she said, bear hugging me. Taking a step back, she held onto to me at the shoulders and visually drank me in like I was something she needed to retain in the event of a pop quiz.

"Great. Never better. How you likin' junior high?" The Valium had removed any need to feel self-conscious. I reciprocated, examining her from bottom to top, forcing myself not to hold onto the pause I took at the pear, a patch sewn as conspicuously as a bullseye on a target. Her eyes revealed no unease that I might've stared a bit too long. She was still smiling. A straight horizontal line, a slight defect, indented the enamel across her front teeth. *I wonder what that's from?* It didn't matter to me. It did nothing to detract from her vibrant cuteness. *If anything, it makes her unique.*

"I think the real question is, how does it feel to be a punky little seventh grader?" she said.

"Yeah, well ..."

"I'm just joshin' ya. It's great seein' ya. I gotta run, but we should catch up sometime. Tell your mom and dad I said hi," she said as she started backward down the hall. "I'll be seein' ya around," she added before turning to go.

I stood there in a daze for an undetermined amount of time, thinking about her skin, like light brown sugar from a lingering summer tan. When I had finally gathered my senses, I started toward the cafeteria, glad for the forty-five minutes of lunch before having to be in Cheatham's fourth-period math class, remembering the last thing she had said with a smile on my face. I considered the improbability. *Naw. No way. She couldn't possibly ... but you never know.*

# 11. Early 1974

Ronnie Montrose left the Edgar Winter group to form his own band, seeking his own sound. I think he found it. Guitars crunching, grinding, soaring through spectacular riffs accompanied by powerhouse vocals from a kid named Sammy Hagar. Kismet smiled on their future. And they were coming to town in early March of '74.

One way or another, I was going.

The penchant I carried for music was an Olympic torch traveling hand to hand from artist to artist toward the inevitable lighting of some glorious eternal flame. It dated back to the days when Mark Lee and I would help ourselves to his sister's 45's, listening to Frankie Valli and the Four Seasons. From there, we went on our own musical quest, passing through the likes of the Osmonds, the Partridge Family, and the Jackson Five, before the torch was re-ignited by something a little more substantial.

In the summer of 1970, when I was nine, I owned a copy of Johnny Cash Live at San Quentin on vinyl, sparking the core of my misguided rebellion. All the curse words were dubbed over with an annoying *beeeep* that was long enough to censor the first and last consonant sounds of the word. I had to use my imagination.

By the time I was in the sixth grade, modern technology introduced the portable cassette recorder/player. With this advancement, I was able to bring my favorite songs to school, ranging anywhere from The Chi-Lites, *Have You Seen Her* to David Bowie's, *Space Oddity*. Much like the sense of smell, music is a catalyst for memory – at least for me. There are certain songs that evoke memories of events or people, tying the two together, inseparable without fail every time I hear them. When I hear the opening line preceding the eminent countdown of *Space Oddity* …[3]

I will always think of Dorothy Ravo …
She wasn't strikingly beautiful …
She had that certain something …
… you couldn't quite define …
… je ne sais quoi …

I stumbled into the lightless void of my Uncle Zane's bedroom makeshift photographic developing lab on a Sunday afternoon to discover the meaning of the term "gooseflesh" when he flipped the light switch down, dropped Black Sabbath on the turntable, and Hell's Bells enveloped the cataclysmic blackness. It scared the hell out of me at first. At the same time, I found it impossible to run away. Something compelling about the darkness goads our curiosity until we finally descend the stairs to see what is in the basement.

Deep Purple followed with *Smoke on the Water*, indubitably the song most attempted by novice guitar players across the rock 'n' roll globe. I was no exception, picking out the individual notes at first before learning how to transpose the progression into power chords on my pearl white Jimi Hendrix imitation Stratocaster, maximizing the distortion through a Crate Amplifier.

The guitar and the desire to learn how to play came after I had been bitten by the rockstar bug. It happened at my first real concert. (David Cassidy doesn't count, does it? Even though Sherry, who had to accompany Mark and me because we weren't quite old enough, would never let me live that one down).

My buddy Gary Reed had an extra ticket. We were barely tall enough to see over the edge of the stage, neither of us imposing enough in stature to present any kind of threat. Security paid us little mind when we hoisted ourselves up on top of the side-turned, foldable metal tables, set up as a barrier between the audience and the stage.

The show featured Dr. John, the Cajun Zydeco "night tripper" popular for the song *Right Place, Wrong Time*, and opened with blues guitarist Freddie King, both of which were enthralling. There was a world of difference between the back row at the Keith Partridge bubble gum experience and sitting on the edge of the stage where you could see the sweat fly. But it was the band in between that was incendiary. Jimmy Hall took the stage with Wet Willie and *Keep on Smilin'*.[4]

Bathed in blue lights, guitars and harmonicas wailed. That's when the bug bit.

I made haste to purchase the album, learning the words to every song. Within a week, I had sketched a pretty good rendition of the front cover, featuring the Reverend Pearly Brown playing guitar. Strapped around his neck were a harmonica and a sign which read: "I Was Born Blind. God Loves a Cheerful Giver."

Subsequently, I was intent on being at every live show that rolled through town from that night forward. I had already missed the Stones. I wasn't about to let another big one slip by.

His palm up, doing an imitation of a nomadic divining rod, Jeff Yancey chanted like a Hare Krishna seeking higher consciousness. "Penny, nickel, diiime, quata. Penny, nickel, diiime, quata." Stretching the "i" in dime gave the mantra a sense of rhythm. But all he was searching for was some spare change.

Jeff Yancey was short and squirrelly. By squirrelly, I mean, if he had accidentally run out in front of a car, you wouldn't have known what to expect. Would he bolt straight ahead? Stop on the road and try to make it back? Or would he dive headlong underneath the moving vehicle, attempting to roll out between the front and rear tires, banging his head on the undercarriage in the process? His thick mop of dirty blonde hair sat in a long heap, mostly on top, and parted to one side. He took a breather from his chanting as a somewhat frail and nerdy seventh-grader questioned Jeff's motive.

"Why do you need it?" The kid in glasses asked timidly.

"Cos fool, I'm 'bout to go see Ronnie Montroes." It didn't take much to throw Jeff into confrontational mode.

"So why should I give it to you?"

"Look, Carl Cream, if you got spare change, you bes' give it and live another day. If not, skee-daddle and stop wassin' my time." Jeff fanned his hand at the kid as if he was dirt that needed to be swept out of sight.

The kid retrieved a quarter and three dimes from the pocket of his plaid knit slacks and slapped them into Jeff's palm before making a frenzied retreat.

"Run home to yo momma." Jeff's implied threat chased the kid down the hall.

We were drifting about, loosely anchored to the cafeteria's main entrance. The clattering of lunch trays, clanking of silverware, and the homogenized drone of everyday teenage conversation spilled out into the hallway ebbing and flowing in waves.

I was working a slightly different angle.

Scissors had not touched my hair since the beginning of the school year. The part in my blondish locks now flirting with my shoulders had shifted to the middle of my head. A silver dog chain I had lifted at a five-finger discount from the Family Pantry had been converted into a belt as a fashion accessory to my Levi's. The geeky preschool colors had been ditched in favor of flannel and T-shirts.

## The Quiet Kid

Underneath the unbuttoned plaid, I wore my Freddy Fudpucker, a light maroon cotton T featuring a cartoon Bandito in an oversized Sombrero toasting the ingredients printed next to him, presumably the contents of his glass.

- 1 1/2 oz TEQUILA
- 1 oz NEAPOLITAN LIQUEUR
- POUR OVER ICE, ADD ORANGE JUICE

I had never had one. No matter. It was good advertisement for the crowd I was scoping out, the ones who could identify with my cause: the non-conformists.

I was conforming, rapidly becoming a part of that order.

"Spare change? Humble Pie and Montrose ... you goin', man? Gonna be great ..."

I was getting a lot of feedback and loads of sympathy, but not much in the way of recompense. *A lousy dollar and forty-two cents.* That's all I had to show for two days of diligence. If it didn't get any better, I was going to have to skip some lunches.

"Who let all these freaks out in the hall, man?" Don Colter always sounded like he'd learned to speak English by listening to Cheech and Chong records. His voice echoed in the antechamber, which was all but empty now.

"He-ey, Don. 'Sup?" I said, stuttering intentionally on hey, giving extra emphasis to the "a" sound.

"What's hap-o-ning?" he said as he approached.

"We're just tryin' to scrap up the dough to see Montrose."

"Yeah, but these fools don't e'en know who Montroes is," Jeff chimed in.

"Or Humble Pie, for that matter," I finished. "You goin'?"

Don already had a ticket for the show. And he had a couple of crisp new George Washington's to spare before making his way into the cafeteria, one for Jeff and one for me.

Mom had told me I could go if I could raise the money on my own. She wasn't about to give it to me, probably hoping I'd fall short. She'd rather I didn't go. She hadn't actually witnessed firsthand the crowd's attending rock concerts, but she had her suspicions as to what they were like. In reality, they probably weren't as scary as her darkest fears. At any rate, I was starting to feel a little better about my chances.

Or maybe I just didn't care as much in the moment.

From somewhere inside the cafeteria, a familiar laugh erupted, almost braying. I might have found it annoying had I not known the source: an Amazon of a brunette girl named Laura McNeil, cute in spite of an aquiline nose and eyes that appeared somewhat beady behind her wire-rimmed glasses. As the laughter grew nearer, my heart leaped in my chest, hoping that Laura's best friend would be with her. And then I distinguished the giggle that belonged to Amber Barrett as they stepped out into the hallway.

"Hey, ladies," I sang out.

"Hey, Michael." Amber had stopped calling me Scarlett and had started using the formal version of my first name. Only a handful of people – the ones closest to me—called me Michael.

Laura McNeil was another. "Hey, Michael! Whatcha doin'?"

"Me and my good buddy Jeff are holding a private fund-raiser for the: *I don't have enough cash to go to the Montrose show.*" I nodded toward Jeff, who had wandered down to the corner, sponging off a couple of cute little girls from our grade.

"How much do you need?" From the right pocket of her olive drab Army Jacket, Amber procured a leather wallet. She never carried a purse.

"Let's see; I have two dollars and forty-two cents." I pretended to punch numbers into an invisible calculator, looking up as if drawing numbers out of the air before punching in more numbers. "That would be three fifty-eight." I grinned smugly. I wasn't much of a mime, but to my satisfaction, both girls appeared to be amused.

Laura wiggled a small pack of neatly folded green free from the tight pocket of her hip-hugger jeans and was extracting a couple of ones. "I'll give you two bucks."

I reached for the two dollars, but she jerked them away. "Not so fast, hotshot," she said." On one condition."

Laura loved being a tease.

"And that is...?"

"Weeell ... Amber hasta give you the rest."

"I sure will," Amber said. "In exchange for your chain."

Without hesitation, I slipped it through my belt loops, having second thoughts as I dangled it in front of her, still far enough away that she had to make the effort. "How 'bout a loan?" I said.

"Okay." Leaning in to take it, her palm slid over the back of my hand, where it rested, not exerting any effort to take the chain nor exhibiting any intention of letting go.

Rolling my hand over to relinquish control, I let her have it, watching her blue eyes twinkle as the tips of her fingers raked lightly over my wrist and palm.

"Thanks." She smiled, glowing and looking like I'd just given her the Hope diamond. "I'll wear it proudly."

Amber pulled the chain through her belt loops, letting it drag across her hips. I was trying not to stare. "But you gotta give it back."

"When?"

"How 'bout … after the concert?" It was two weeks away, but I figured what the heck? It wasn't like I paid for it.

"Deal." Extending her hand, we shook on it, holding on a little longer than necessary.

Then she laughed. "Sucker. It's mine now."

She snatched back her hand and ran off down the hall, leaving me with little else to do but give chase.

"Hey!" Jeff snapped as we blew by him. "Where you goin'?"

"I'm done," I offered over my shoulder. Amber had slipped around the corner, and I sped up to keep from losing ground.

"Don't make me break up with you again." I hollered down the hall. (We weren't going together.)

Amber stopped in her tracks and grinned, freezing me momentarily. "Then we'll just have to renew our relationship," she said, just before she disappeared beyond the forbidden threshold of the ladies' room.

Closing slowly with a soft hiss, the languid door goaded me, daring me to come inside. If I could've been sure it was only her on the other side, there would've been no hesitation. For a moment, I contemplated the risk. Deflated, I turned back toward the cafeteria, disheartened not because she'd gotten away with my dog chain, but because she had gotten away, period. On the other side of that avocado green door was the girl that crept into my thoughts more often than I cared to admit. No one knew, except yours truly.

"Chin up, Michael, you'll get it back."
Laura had just rounded the corner.
I looked up, grinning a good façade. "I know. And ya know what?"
Her expression beckoned a response.
"I'm goin' to Montrose! Thank you very much."
"Yea!" Laura laughed at me as she passed.

I turned to watch her go in, spying Amber, who peered through the crack in the open door.

"I'll deal with you later," I threatened idly.
"I'll be waiting," she sang out into the hall.

# 12. Summer 1974

On the last day of school, every student from grade seven to the senior class at South High was free to roam the halls. It was annual signing day. By 2:30 pm, most of the building had emptied out. All was quiet, save the random slamming of a locker echoing in the hall. I was in the cafeteria with Laura McNeil and Amber Barrett. Redolence of baked yeast rolls lingered pleasantly from lunch, occasionally overpowered by the acrid tang of Pine-Sol.

Amber was signing my yearbook and taking her sweet time about it, making sure she didn't leave anything out when Brenda Flanders walked in. "Hey Amber, know what I mean, jellybean?"

"No way. I do not know whatcha mean. Understand, rubber band?" Amber replied.

Laura chimed in. "Take a dip, paperclip, 'cause I don't neither."

The three of them giggled in unison, Brenda being completely unaware that I knew exactly what they were talking about.

I looked up with a perfunctory smile, pretending to be clueless. Brenda's silky blond mane cascaded halfway down her back. I gave her the once over. *She's cute, but not really my type. Amber, on the other hand ... I love the way she bites her lower lip when she's concentrating ...* and then went back to signing Laura's annual.

Amber had told me a few weeks before. And Laura had no qualms about letting me in on the secret, which apparently wasn't all that secret. "Know what I mean?" was code for "are you on your period?" as was "Understand, rubber band?" And two possible negative responses (or positive, depending on how you look at it) had just been demonstrated by Amber and Laura. The jellybean part was thrown in simply for their amusement. I felt like I'd been inducted into some secret society, a silent partaker to some highly privileged information. I knew little about the menstrual cycle beyond the basic concept. That was enough. Who needed all the gory details?

Brenda had come for her yearbook, which Laura had just finished signing. "See you all at the tower field tonight," she said on her way out. She was one of the ones who got it right. The tower field, now officially named Maynard Glen Field, was nicknamed for the radio towers that once occupied the turf owned by TVA, an obscured piece of South Knoxville history which rendered it to be commonly referred to as the "tire field," or as some would say in South Knoxville speak, "the tar field."[5]

"So, when are you and Amber gonna renew your relationship?" Laura inquired.

To date, we still had no relationship other than friends, but our ongoing flirtations were urging us closer and closer to taking a walk down that path.

"When I get my chain back," I replied.

She still had it. Not the whole time, mind you, but since March, the thirty-two-inch silver chain had been in Amber's possession the majority of the time. The frequent exchange of it linked us together. Also, it had been the habitual reason for breaking up and renewing our "relationship." I would snatch it away when she least expected, and invariably she would sweet talk me out of it.

"Well, you're just a punky little seventh-grader. If you want it, you'll have to come and get it"

"Oh, I'll get it."

"Oh, you're gonna get it, all right," Laura added. The innuendo sailed right over my head.

"There. All finished," Amber said with a satisfied smile as she stood to give my yearbook back.

I returned the smile and then winked at Laura before turning to leave. "I've had enough of this place for one year."

"Are you coming to the field tonight?" Amber wondered, hopefully. "We're playing Stansberry."

"Oh, I'll be there … and I'm coming for it."

Amber's voice followed me out into the hall. "We'll see about that. I'm still a foot taller than you."

She wasn't actually a foot taller. As the year progressed, I had almost caught up to her. But she was still taller, maybe by an inch or so.

Tucking my yearbook under my arm, I chuckled and thought about the night ahead. And then, stepping out into the courtyard facing Moody Avenue, I opened the yearbook, elated. Amber had scribbled enough to fill the entire front bookplate.

Marijuana is a gateway drug. Or so they say. If you would have asked me, I would have said that's a big load of hooey. I don't think it works that way. Certain individuals feel it necessary to taste everything at least once—maybe twice if they like it. No one or no thing has to open the gate for them. These individuals will crawl through the mud on their bellies under barbed wire to get to the gate and then kick it down when they arrive. It's like saying bungee jumping is the gateway to sky diving, or walking is the gateway to crawling. Wait. Wouldn't that be backward? My point exactly. One might try smoking hooch and then decide to move on to something more powerful, but don't kid yourself. It makes no difference which came first. Poor Mary Jane is simply the patsy.

I was wired that way, having to taste everything at least once. I took asthma medication and Valium over the course of nine months before kismet gave birth to opportunity, and I smoked weed on a summer band field trip to Fort Dickerson.

Hip deep in kudzu, the drop overlooked Chapman Highway. The golden arches seemed a mile away. Even so, I could almost smell the quarter pounders and fries. Rick Brady whipped out two carefully rolled joints. After we smoked them, Merle Britton and Noel Coffey, crawled out of the undergrowth into the park, still professing their inexorable highness.

I had known Rick since fourth grade. He was a spastic kid with a sailor's vocabulary and thick blond hair in a style that reminded me of Peppermint Patty's. He was always chewing on things or pounding on them. He had introduced me to black lights, motorcycles, and soundproofing. Every square inch of his bedroom had been covered in egg cartons to muffle the booming sound of his drum kit. At the age of ten, he had already mastered *Hawaii Five-O* as well as *Wipe Out*.

We developed a fetish for wild things, which resulted in his acquiring an alligator as a pet. Then we got permission from our teacher to take it on a class-to-class tour of Giffin Elementary school. (We were always looking for any excuse to get out of class). Al E. Gator was just a baby and barely sixteen inches in length. But still, it was best to keep your fingers away from those teeth. Ouch!

Mom didn't trust him from the get-go, but when she picked us up on the Henley Street Bridge after we had taken it upon ourselves to walk home from a West Knoxville movie theatre, well, that was the straw that put the icing on the camel's back—or something like that.

Now, according to Merle Britton and Noel Coffey, Rick had just gotten me high as a kite. Funny thing, though—I didn't feel any different.

"Those guys are idiots," Rick said, producing a third joint. "They just got high on oregano. Now we're gonna smoke the real thing." The flame from the match bowed into the end of the joint, igniting a glowing cherry as he drew it in, fire flaring up in between puffs. Tightlipped, he smiled, holding the smoke in as he passed the joint to me. Rick was proud of himself for having duped the others.

It tasted different. And yet, I still didn't feel anything. Apparently, this is a common phenomenon amongst first-timers.

It was June 11, 1974.

Amber's legs were bent at the knees, forcing her butt to stick out. From behind the backstop, I could see a streak of dirt across her tight and otherwise white denim shorts. She had lifted her shiny orange pinhole jersey, wiping her hand off, leaving behind a trail of evidence. East Tennessee orange clay tarnished the purity of white. My eyes were drawn to the curve of her derrière like a lighthouse beacon cutting through a heavy fog to guide the ships home. I gazed down the length of her tan thighs. Her brown sugar skin drew a sharp contrast between the white denim and the white tube socks with three horizontal orange stripes stretching over her calves. She wasn't exactly what you would call thin. She was thick in all the right places. I didn't care that I was staring. Everyone else was concentrating on the game. Locking in on the first pitch, her elbow cocked high in the air just like her daddy had taught her (to keep it level). Amber swung hard, driving it down the third baseline. She scored a double, bringing a runner home from second. Unfortunately for George Barrett's Big Orange team, they were no match for Stansberry's Roadrunners in baby blue. Few teams ever were.

After the game, Laura McNeil and Gerald Barrett waited for us at the concession stand. In pursuit of Laura, Richie's older brother, Gerald, had become my newest running mate. Gerald and Richie were in no way related to Amber, though they all hailed from the state of Ohio, and their dads shared the same first name. Small world.

Amber emerged from the pep talk taking place in a circle of orange and white by the team's dugout. She seemed none the worse for wear after the loss, and I was glad to see the huge grin on her face as she approached.

## The Quiet Kid

"You don't look like someone who jus' took a beatin'," I said, suddenly realizing how insensitive it sounded and wishing I could take it back. We turned to walk toward the block building painted in white and red, representative of the Baby Rockets organization. I shoved my hands in my pockets, focusing on our feet, which were moving in sync as we walked, my right with hers and then the left, right, left, right, left. Neither of us talked for a minute.

Amber broke the silence. "I'm just glad they didn't shut us out this time."

"I heard that."

"Anyway, I'm with friends now, right?" The soreness was rising to the surface, and I could see she was covering her disappointment under a blanket of smiles.

"Hey, I was jus' kiddin' about ..."

"Forget it," she reassured me, flashing a smile. Her upper lip dipped down slightly, forming a "V," interrupting the defective line across the enamel of her front teeth.

She paused and then said, "Punky little eighth-grader."

Gerald and Laura greeted us at the concession stand. I offered to buy Amber a coke.

"We can share one," she said.

"What's your poison?"

"It doesn't matter. You pick."

I bought a large suicide: half 7Up, and half RC Cola. We leaned against the block wall, trading drinks from the same straw. Gerald and Laura wandered ahead, walking arm in arm through the gravel parking lot.

"We'll catch up," Amber said.

During the school year, Amber and I had cut-up, flirted, and engaged in our pretend off-again, on-again relationship routine, but we hadn't had much in the way of serious conversation, not when it was just the two of us. I made a lame attempt at small talk. "So, what're you doin' for the rest of the summer ... besides this, I mean?"

"Lucky me. After softball ends, I'm goin' with Laura and her parents to Naples, Flor' da for two weeks."

"That sucks."

Amber scrunched her eyebrows, looking serious. "Why?"

"Because I won't be there to see how good you look in a bikini."

"You still might."

"What? Are ya gonna stow me away in the trunk?"

"No, silly," she laughed. "I mean, you might see me in a bikini." Then she smirked, adding, "If you're lucky."

Our cup was empty, so I removed the straw to chew on it, dropping the wax-coated paper cup into a rusted, fifty-gallon barrel, and we went to catch up to the other lovebirds.

Spotting them at the upper field, they were leaning against the chain-link fence watching the game. It wasn't hard to pick out Gerald's buzzed head. Even the old men there had longer hair than he did. I noted that he still had his arm draped over Laura's shoulders.

Taking a cue from him, I stretched my arm across Amber's shoulder only to be reminded she was a little too tall. Adjusting quickly, I lowered to reach around her waist. I was relieved when she tucked her arm under my arm, sticking her thumb through my belt loop as she rested her hand on my hip. We crunched across the gravels, dragging our feet a little as we went. Having gotten to know her fairly well over the past few months, I felt like it was time like she probably wanted me to. Still, the slightest hint of uncertainty lingered. *What if she wants to keep it this way? What if she just wants to be friends?* The tightness with which she gripped my side erased any doubts. I sensed the direction of our relationship and where it was heading.

The field lights began to warm up slowly, becoming visible as the last of sunlight faded from the sky. Concrete bleachers and lawn chairs were occupied by parents consuming popcorn or hotdogs or Royal Crown colas and rooting for their kids' teams. The chanting of their teammates filled the dusk. "Batter, batter, batter, batter, swa-wing batter," or "We need a pitcher, not a belly itcher."

A chain-link fence seemed to stretch endlessly, enclosing the adjacent ball fields. We loitered around the perimeter for a while before relocating to a more remote area of the ball field, seeking to escape the din of the crowd.

Crossing the practice fields, the four of us walked closer together now. Then it surfaced: the silver dog chain. I hadn't thought much about it, having been preoccupied with more pressing matters. Laura flashed a smile and the chain as she attempted to slip it to Amber. I intercepted, running through the freshly mowed grass. On the far

# The Quiet Kid

side, I descended the steep embankment leading down to the old abandoned house. Amber would know exactly where to find me.

The back door was already open, and I slipped inside. The ball field's halogen lights breached the panes of the windows. It was dark inside except for the projected rectangles of light framed in shadows. As long as the lights remained on, no one would come looking for us. The floor in the kitchen had been stripped down to the plywood, and each step I took provoked a creaking echo throughout the empty shell of a house. I ducked around a corner to gather a breath from the musty air and waited.

"Michael, where are you?" Amber's voice searched the house timidly. "No punky little eighth-grader can hide from meeeee!" She shrieked as I jumped out to grab her with both arms around her waist. Holding tightly, I pulled her close as she slipped around to face me. She clutched my face in both hands and kissed me. I was caught a bit off guard, but I wasn't complaining, submitting to her, letting her lead.

The dog chain clanked loudly on the plywood floor.

She didn't care. The silver chain had served its purpose. It was of no use to her now. We were no longer just friends. The glow from the ball field lights softened and then evaporated, leaving us enveloped in the darkness, holding one another close, our mouths still in a tangle. Neither of us wanted to go. But we both knew it was no use trying to fight it. They would come looking. Eventually, they would find us.

Before fleeing back to the field, I asked her to "go" with me. She said yes as she slipped away.

Softball season had ended. Amber was in South Florida with Laura. I received a letter from her saying there had been a big hullabaloo around their hotel. A drug bust had gone down. I jokingly conveyed my disappointment in a letter back. "It could have been a connection," I wrote. I was more than half-serious.

*Boo cops. Go, bad guys.*

Amber would still be there for another week, working on her tan.

In the middle of the afternoon, the ball fields formerly occupied by the towers were unoccupied. We were taking full advantage. Sitting on the concrete bleachers warmed by the sun, Gary Reed was toking hard on a fat joint.

Gary had turned me on to my first live rock show (that's my story, and I'm sticking to it). So, I thought it only right that I should return the favor. After experiencing alterations in time and space from my second attempt at smoking marijuana, I was on a mission to tell all my friends about it. Gary's name was the first on my list. And after a couple of attempts, I succeeded in helping him expand his horizons on a higher plane of consciousness. For the record, this wasn't the first time Gary had smoked. It wasn't even the first time that week.

Gary's Saint Bernard, Bruno, wandered over to us inquisitively. Up to then, he had been nosing around the stench of a fifty-gallon trash barrel by the backstop. But apparently, the aroma from the smoke tugged at his attention. Just then, Gary got a crazy idea.

"Let's get Bruno high."

Who was I to argue?

Gary straddled the huge dog as if he were riding him. I turned the joint backward, inserting the cherry in my mouth, blowing "shotguns" in Bruno's face. Gary was holding on for dear life. The massive dog struggled mightily, causing me to wonder how long Gary could hold him back, but hold him he did. After Bruno had gotten at least three good hits, Gary let him go.

Bruno bolted … at first. After putting twenty yards between him and us, he stopped in his tracks. With his nose to the ground, he wandered erratically from side to side, following the scent of something in no particular direction. We were pretty sure the dog was high. We couldn't stop laughing. Gary's upper lip kept sticking to his gums from the cottonmouth. And we laughed even harder.

Eventually, we got back to smoking and lost track of Bruno's whereabouts. About the time we started getting concerned, Bruno came sniffing around for more. We were happy to oblige, and this time, he didn't struggle.

# 13. Summer 1974 Part II

The year prior, I had thought Ian Bradford was a complete—as David had put it—je-je-jerk. I now felt an enigmatic need to prove to him how grown up I was. With Mark as a hub, we started hanging out in the summer of '74. Ian had been second on the Mary Jane list. Strange how we became almost inseparable at times. He seemed a whole lot cooler when he started getting high and letting his hair grow.

Wading through crumpled newspapers, molested magazines, earmarked TV Guides, empty Coke cans, pizza boxes, McDonald's bags, and other assorted trash that rendered the hardwood floor virtually invisible, Mark and I navigated our way toward the source of the pulsating beat.

Ian's mom was never known for her housekeeping. We never cared. She had so many other respectable attributes. For instance, based on the advice of the family doctor, she condoned the viewing of Playboy magazine because it was a healthy and perfectly normal activity for boys our age. Secondly, she seemed to be oblivious (or at least pretended to be) to the fact that the smoking of a smelly benign weed had as of late become our primary source of entertainment.

Sammy Hagar was coming through loud and clear from beyond the wooden door of Ian's bedroom. *Rock Candy*.[6]

I gave the door a gentle two-finger push and let it swing open. Ian was thrashing out rhythm on an air guitar. Big Nasty was passed out on a bean bag chair in the corner.

Ian had his back turned to the door. I had to shout to get his attention. "Get your little sister, and let's do this."

"Scarlett. Hey man, you made it. C'mon in." We shook hands, wrapping thumbs around opposing thumbs.

Ian's little sister, Stacy, and her best friend Kelly Carmichael had been waiting anxiously in the bedroom across the hall. Having heard me shouting at Ian, they manifested like ants at a picnic.

"It's nice to be so loved." I smiled over my shoulder at the two cuties slipping in behind me with tails wagging, Kelly grinning, showing a mouthful of braces, Stacy twitching at the knees like she was binging on caffeine.

This would be Stacy's first time.

She and Ian had pitched in five bucks each on top of my five to buy a lid. It was a pretty fat sack, considering, but a better deal could have been had on an O-Z if I could've gotten my hands on five more.

Ian turned the volume down a few notches so we wouldn't have to yell. I took a seat on the edge of the bed, which in contrast to the rest of the house, was neatly made. Ian's room was always immaculate. Mark plopped down on the bed to my right. I patted the vacant spot to my left and motioned for Stacy to come and fill it. "You should get first dibs," I said.

"Hand me that Yes album, sweetie," I said to Kelly, who was closest to a stack of albums towering over the top of the massive stereo speakers. She handed it to me, still smiling. I winked at her, and she took a seat cross-legged on the floor next to Ian. Big Nasty still hadn't stirred, enveloped in the comfort of the bean bag. I pulled the baggie from my pocket for public inspection. It was three fingers deep with marijuana. Holding the top edges, I let the weight of the contents unroll the clear plastic bag and took a deep whiff. "Mmm. Smells like Jamaican."

We never knew where the stuff was really coming from. But if it was good, it was always tagged with some exotic name – Acapulco Gold, Blue Hawaiian, Maui Wowie, Panama Red.

"Ian said he didn't get high the first time. You think I will?" Stacy asked, raking her dark brown bangs behind her ears apprehensively. She had a cartoonish, nasally little girl voice and pouty lips. She was too cute to face any such disappointment.

"With the size of this bag, I'd say you got nuthin' to worry about." Opening the album cover, I dumped half of the weed out over Roger Dean's stunning depiction of a lake cascading over cliffs in all visible directions and started breaking out the stems.

Relieved, she smiled. "Can I do anythin'?"

"Pass this around." I held out what was left in the baggie for everyone to examine, while I completed the task of breaking up the buds into a fine little pile. With a pack of JOB 1.5's, I pushed the crumbled buds up the inclined side of the opened album sleeve, sifting the seeds which rolled down into the crease.

When the first joint was rolled, I offered it to Stacy. "Here. You do the honors."

## The Quiet Kid

"You gotta let some air in with it," Kelly offered when she saw Stacy struggling to get it lit. "Yeah, that's it."

I continued to roll one fat joint after another with Kelly's assistance. She kept getting up off the floor to hold the joint for me so I could smoke without having to stop. I barely knew her, but she wasn't at all uneasy, slipping a hand under the album cover to palm my thigh for support as she leaned over me when I took a hit. Smoking pot had a way of creating an unspoken intimacy between partakers.

Before the first joint was out, I handed a second to Mark to put into circulation. A nice little pile of plump doobies was collecting in the valley of *Close to the Edge*. I lit a third one and passed it. "Are you feeling anything yet?" I directed the question to Stacy, but looked to Kelly as well, not wanting her to feel left out.

Kelly grinned exuberantly, flashing her braces again. "I've got a confession to make," she giggled. "This ain't my first time."

Ian snickered, sounding like air being forced out of a tire stem in short little spurts.

It made sense now, why Kelly was so comfortable with all this, taking hits like a pro, even instructing Stacy, before watching to see how it was done. But it did little to explain why she had offered, along with her aide, an unobstructed view down her loosely buttoned shirt when she was holding the joint for me.

*Maybe she's just naïve.*

"I ain't feelin' a thing." Stacy looked disheartened.

"Hey, don't worry, you will. Just don't concentrate on it so hard. It'll come." I turned to the human pile of refuse dumped in the beanbag chair, hoping to distract her. "What's up with Big Nasty? He still breathin'?" He seemed unaware of our presence in the room.

We called him Big Nasty because apparently, he didn't deem it necessary to bathe on a regular basis, or maybe he just wasn't able to. I really didn't know anything about his home life. He was the teenage version of Pigpen from Peanuts, with long, nappy hair. He was usually wasted. And today was nothing out of the ordinary. It had to be more than just weed.

"He showed up stoned and then just passed out there." Ian filled us in. "He's been that way for the last hour."

"Yeah, well, we should wake him up."

I crouched down, putting the cherry in my mouth, and blew a rivulet of smoke in George's face until his head was engulfed in a cloud. He awoke in a coughing fit. "Hey man, that ain't funny!" He wasn't amused, but it was choice entertainment for the rest of us.

Ian started again. "Ssss. Ssss. Ssss," but couldn't contain it. "He he he he he he heeeeeeeeee!" The room erupted in laughter, continuing long after Big Nasty slipped back into his coma.

"Oh yeah. I'm feelin' it now," Stacy said just as the howling laughter subsided, causing it to start all over again.

We were all looking at each other through slits when Trip showed up. He found a place in the loosely formed circle, sitting cross-legged on the floor. His wavy, black hair hung well past his shoulders, framing his unibrow. The whites of his eyes were still untainted. We replenished the cloud of smoke, which had dissipated slightly when the door opened. No one could say exactly how many we smoked, but I had little doubt about Stacy's state of mind at this point.

"So Stace, how you feelin' now?" I had to ask.

She peered at me with what little of her eyes where visible behind the heavy lids and grinned a sheepish grin. "I ain't feelin' a thing."

Having fallen out of the popular crowd, I was still okay here. Here on the Island of Misfit Toys, I always fit right in. I took a good look around at everyone, never guessing that any of us even had a future. Who knew?

Trip and Stacy would one day marry.

Kelly Carmichael would unofficially be my girlfriend for a weekend plus seven minutes times four.

Ian would soon vow his life to Christianity, juggling his commitment to this dilemma: Is smoking pot a sin?

I had recently claimed Atheism. I was only lying to myself.

This would be one of the few times I would see Mark looking glassy-eyed with a crooked grin. He decided later that he didn't care for getting high even though he continued to hang out with us throughout our remaining school years.

I would dabble deeper and deeper into drugs, experimenting until it nearly killed me. And who knew if I would ever cross paths with Big Nasty down the road. We were living in the moment, oblivious to pretty much everything else.

## The Quiet Kid

Trip hung around until we put on Frank Zappa just for kicks. The schizophrenic *Don't Eat Yellow Snow* proved to be more than he could handle. He left the room with his hands strapped behind his head, and his forearms closed around both ears, repeating, "It's freakin' me out, man. It's freakin' me out." He was the only person I had ever known to have that kind of reaction from the combination of weed, electric guitars, and xylophones.

For a while, we got pretty silly. We weren't hurting anyone. We didn't go on a murderous rampage. We didn't steal a car and run over little kids at the McDonalds' drivethru. We did, however, get a serious case of the munchies. We were only getting warmed up. The real madness would come much later.

# 14. Summer 1974 Part III

Whenever I heard Roger Daltrey deliver Pete Townsend's lyric from *My Generation*[7] putting an expiration date on life, it resonated as my own voice inside my head. Never trust anyone over thirty. I fully intended to be gone before I became one of them. I wasn't thinking about offing myself at thirteen, nor was I even considering the possibility of a life-threatening mishap resulting from my lifestyle.

Gary Reed and I were always unwittingly dreaming up the necessary means to get the job done. In a weed-deprived effort to get high, we had taken to sniffing vapors from a Pam-soaked paper towel, never realizing in our fleeting hiatus from reality we had ding-dong ditched the Grim Reaper's front door.

I looked at Gerald, trying not to laugh.

He was still snickering about having pissed in Gary's beer. Gary had scowled, saying, "This tastes funny," and looked straight at Gerald, shifting to Richie. "What'd you do to it?" Nobody fessed up, but Gary had sense enough to pour it down the drain.

Then somebody got this birdbrained idea.

Now, it was hard for me to keep a straight face, but looking at Gerald was better than the alternative. If I watched the knife when Gary threw it, I would be sure to recoil.

*Thunk.*

I looked down to see the heavy pocket-knife, four inches when folded, stuck upright in the hardwood a hand's width to the left of my foot.

*Not even close.* Smiling, I tried to conceal my relief.

Plucking the erect knife from the hardwood floor, I took careful aim. We had been practicing with it for days. Getting it to stick was no problem. Placing it close to the target but not too close, that was the challenge. I picked out a spot in the grain of the wood.

*Thunk. Pdudududdtttt.* The knife stuck hard, and the deflection of it vibrating to a stop sounded like a diving board launching a fat man.

*Two inches.* I was satisfied with the placement but troubled because Gary had watched and not batted an eye when the blade whizzed by his barefoot.

The poor man's version of Russian roulette continued. Again, Gary threw. Again, I refused to look. At least I had on tennis shoes—not that the thin canvas material would've slowed down the momentum of the slicing blade driven by the weight of the handle. It was only a matter of time.

It was my turn again. And just as every time before, I picked out the spot in the grain of the hardwood. End over end, the knife somersaulted.

*Chunk.*

It stuck with a thick, sickly, wet sound—metal penetrating flesh. Gary never flinched. It must've taken a full two seconds—a long time considering the knife was sticking straight up out of his foot—before his brain caught up. It was like looking at a surreal painting. We couldn't believe it, couldn't quite process what we were looking at, but we couldn't look away. When it finally registered—*yes, this is really happening*—he didn't act rationally, as one might expect given the situation. No, he didn't reach down and yank the daunting object from its imposition. Instead, he began flailing about wildly, hopping on one leg, trying to kick the knife loose. We watched, frozen in helpless amazement. After what seemed like forever, the knife fell to the floor with a harmless thump.

It didn't occur to us until later. If the blade had struck an artery, it could have been disastrous. As it was, Gary sustained only a minor wound, with minimal bleeding. The hardwood floor survived with only a few nicks. We hoped his parents wouldn't notice.

# 15. Late Summer 1974 – Prequel to a Tragedy

It was unlikely you would see a girl any cuter than Terri Mayfield strolling through the park. It was Terri who introduced me to her boyfriend, Larry Ward. He had an identical twin brother named Barry, also Ward. They were both in the service of the United States Armed Forces, along with a friend of theirs named Mogen. The three of them allowed me in their little circle for a brief moment in time.

At the park, inside the wooden plank walls of the fort, smoke trailed behind a joint we were passing. The three soldiers were partially dressed in their fatigues. I was in my usual civilian attire: a T-shirt and jeans. Mogen was grilling me on the phonetic code they used.

"Easy one. M."
"Mike."
"N."
"November."
"O."
"Oscar."
"P."
"Papa."
"Q."
"Quebec."
"R."
"Romeo."

"Come on, Mogen, he's been through it three times already. I think he's got it," Larry complained.

"Yeah, but he still got hung up on … S." Mogen turned to me for a response.

"Sierra."

"See, he knows it, man. Let him have a go at shotgunnin' the beer."

"Do you really think we oughtta? He ain't but thirteen." Barry added the voice of reason.

"Dude, he ain't gonna tell nobody." Larry pleaded my case.

Mogen continued. "T."
"Tango."
"U."
"Uniform."

# The Quiet Kid

"I know he ain't gonna tell, but what if …"

"I swear. I won't breathe a word." I looked at Barry convincingly.

"V."

"Victor."

"Aw … all right." Barry gave in.

"Yes! Now you can stop." Larry pulled a Budweiser free from the plastic rings banding the six-pack.

"He's almost done. W."

"Whiskey."

Larry poked a hole in the aluminum can with a pen. "Get ready." He handed me the can with the pen still in it. "Pull it out when you get to the end."

"X."

"X-ray."

"Remember, gullet open, or you're wearin' it," Larry instructed.

"Y."

"Yankee."

"Z."

"Zulu."

"Perfect!" Mogen exclaimed.

I slid the pen out, covered the hole with my mouth opened wide, tilted my head back, and popped the tab. Every drop went straight down my open throat without swallowing until the very end—a feat I never attempted to duplicate.

"Whatta man!" Larry bragged.

"If you was old enough, you'd be going back with us." Mogen was referring to their return to Fort Campbell after the weekend.

Barry popped the tab on another beer and handed it to me. "Here. You earned it."

I welled up with pride at the accomplishment. I felt like one of the troops.

Mogen held up his beer in a toast. "To Mike."

"Here, here! To Mike." Larry and Barry toasted in unison as we bumped the tops of our beers together.

I took a long drink and another toke when it came my way.

# 16. End of the Innocence Part I[8]

In early October, the leaves had just begun to turn auburn, gold, orange, and red, drifting lazily from the trees. Caught up in a whirlwind, they waltzed around one another in a swirling, cascading loop, inches above the sidewalk.

Walking home from school with Donny Rupe, I received a stunning revelation.

"Have you done it yet?" he asked.

"Done what?"

"It."

"Wha–? Oh. You mean, Amber and me?

"No. You and Tina Turner. Yeah, you and Amber, dumbass."

I was so naïve. Trying anything with her hadn't even occurred to me. *Would she? Is she that kind of girl? Is she ... promiscuous?* I hadn't really considered it. *She's not a jock. Although ... she is an assistant to the girls' basketball team. Like that means anything. She plays softball on a team. Still, the shoe doesn't fit.* I thought of her wearing that drab green army jacket, and then instantly transitioned (smiling) to last summer, picturing her in denim cut-offs and a halter top. *She cusses like a truck driver. She's not preppy and for sure not a goody-two-shoes. She smoked weed with me twice this past summer. She is a bit on the wild side. Which I like. Maybe she wo ...*

"Earth to Mike." He made a sound like static feedback and repeated. "Earth to Mike. So, have you or what?"

Clueless, I asked, as if the outcome rested solely on his response. "Do you think she would?"

"You gotta be kiddin' me, man." Donny stopped. We were standing on the sidewalk in front of the corner park about to cross South Haven. He tucked his hair behind his ear on one side and gave me a look of incredulity. "Have you just not been payin' attention? Have you seen the way she looks at you? That girl is crazy about you, man. She'd do anything for you. Anything."

I digested the thought as we crossed the street.

Sex was a foreign language to me. I had heard a few of its words and phrases tossed about, mostly slang. Having not yet spoken, I understood very little. Some things get lost in translation.

## The Quiet Kid

I was with Mark Lee at Cal Johnson Rec Center in a predominately black neighborhood when I first heard the all-too-often misunderstood slang. We were around twelve years old—two scared white boys safeguarding wire metal baskets, which housed the possessions of boys only a couple of years older than we were as they played basketball. Locked inside the steel cage, we sat on bar stools, enjoying the stench of sweaty socks and other gym paraphernalia. The baskets stacked high on metal shelves were tagged with a number that corresponded to the one on the safety pins worn by their owners. Tennis shoes squeaked on the lacquered hardwood floor beyond the block walls. The faint sound of cheers rose and faded. Occasionally, someone would toss up a brick, punctuated by the clank of the ball against the iron rim.

Four black boys about our age followed the door that flew open into the smelly locker room. One of them grabbed a broom and poked the wooden stick end through diamond-shaped openings in the wire cage.

"Give us the money!" His demand stabbed at us with a force rivaling the broomstick. The other boys poked their fingers inside the cage, shaking it to stir a rattling reverberation from the metal. Their intimidation shook us to the core.

"We don't got any money."

"In the baskets." Agitated, he raised his voice, stressing each word as if it pained him greatly to say them. "IN THE BASKETS! GET-THE-MONEY-OUT-THE-WALLETS-IN-THE- BASKETS!"

I glanced nervously at the clock. The game should be over soon. Any minute … If we can just stall them. I hoped. We squirmed away, pressing our backs against the block wall, away from the jabbing broomstick. If we stayed against the wall, we remained just out of reach.

The chatter of the ballplayers filled the room before we saw them. Relieved, we knew that the Cavalry had arrived. They were also black, but black and white wasn't the issue. It was all about the green. The riff-raff was quickly removed from the locker room.

"Hey man, thanks fo' not givin' up our stuff to them punks," one of them said to us.

"No problem." He set me at ease enough to joke. "What took you so long?"

"We jes' wanted ta see if ya'll'd give up the goods." He laughed.

After a change of clothing, the team was on their way out. The same guy asked an enigmatic question. "Y'all gittin any?"

"Any what?" I truly did not know.

He used a word I had never heard in that context. Yet somehow, I knew he was not talking about a cat. Intuitively, I made the connection between the word and his intended use, describing an apparently particularly desirable part of the female anatomy. "Tell me y'all gittin' some. 'Cause if you ain't, y'all don' know what you missin'. Best thang in the world." He threw his head back, laughing like a hyena on his way out.

Enhancing the mystery further, I was at River Park in the Island Home community with my dad and my little sister. Kristi found a used condom on the ground. Dad told her it was a balloon, but it was nasty. And then he threw it away. Later, he came in privacy to enlighten me. That's when I got "the talk." I feel certain his explanation was complete in his own mind. For me, it left a lot to the imagination.

Seeing the movie *Love Story* shortly after only muddied the water. The less than graphic sex scene with Ali McGraw on her belly unearthed more questions. *It goes where, exactly?*

Parents, when you explain these things to your kids, you might have to draw a picture. Or two. Whatever it takes. Sometimes ignorance is not bliss.

Okay, so my introduction to the foreign language of sex wasn't exactly sophisticated. This was the beginning of my Rosetta Stone. It would now take some hands-on experience and much trial and error. But at least I knew what I was after. And that was all that mattered.

Being thirteen with no driver's license had a way of slowing down the quest. My most intimate moments with Amber were shared with the rest of the school as they passed by in the halls. The South High School rulebook prohibiting PDA had been duly noted and promptly ignored.

We went to school dances where we could at least sneak outside, engaging in a game of tonsil hockey with some similitude of privacy. The first order of business: getting our picture taken to prove we had been there. We never bothered to pause at the dance floor before slipping outside.

I wasn't about to dance anyway. Amber had shot down any hope of that before we were even an item. It had taken place at South's rec hall in the spring before our relationship was an actual thing. A dance was held there. To what purpose I can't recall. Nor do I remember exactly how I ended up there. We hadn't even planned to meet. Amber just happened to be there. Bachman Turner Overdrive came over the P.A. system. When *Takin' Care of Business* played, I seized the moment and asked Amber out on the floor. I was so self-conscious, asking her afterward how I did. In so many words, she politely told me I sucked. Eventually, I improved. I could feel the rhythm. That wasn't the problem. I just had to learn how to apply it. But I never recuperated from her comments enough to dance in public again at any high school function.

We posed together in our flannel shirts (we were grunge way before Nirvana) and exited out into the darkness. Pressed up against the brick wall, we kept each other warm. Eventually, we would figure out how and where we could be alone.

# 17. LSD

Why we were smoking in the boys' restroom was anyone's guess. Perhaps we didn't want to brave the cold. Maybe, it was just a fulfillment of that Brownsville Station song which, incidentally, should be heard playing in the background right about now. When the door opened, I reacted before I even saw Mr. Ridinger. I flipped my cigarette, watching it sail end over end. And somehow it cleared Don Colter's head, landing in the toilet water with a sizzle. A lucky shot. *I couldn't do that again if I tried. Not in a million years.* Don, knowing that the news wasn't good, disposed of his smoking gun as quickly as I had. Since I was already on my way out the door, I never saw where it went.

When we were safely down the hall, I turned to him. "Man, if that had been Coach Warpath, we'd both be getting' three licks right now."

"Yeah, man, no kiddin'." Don pulled his hand from his back pocket, producing the snuffed out cigarette butt still crushed between his charred forefinger and thumb.

"Holy crap, man. That musta hurt like hell."

"It still does. Better than gettin' busted just on principle. But tonight I'll be feelin' no pain. You still comin'?"

"Oh yeah. No way I'm missin' out."

1974 was winding down. The final bell rang out on a Friday afternoon, releasing the hounds. Instead of going home, I was spending the night at Don's. The ride home with his brother Earl was Heinz-ketchup-thick with anticipation.

In Don's bedroom, I stared at the poster of the girl who, by implication, was a native of the country she was representing. Had that been true, I imagined she would have been a much darker brown. This girl looked more like a native of the Dominican Republic. Her wet T-shirt revealed much more than just her supposed home in Jamaica. Like it mattered to me. I just liked the clinging shirt, and the water, and those eyes—mostly, the clinging, wet shirt.

Don dropped Rush on the turntable and followed the instructions printed clearly on the back. *Best results achieved when played at maximum volume.*

John was the exact middle of the five Colter brothers, Don being the youngest. He had a long scar across his cheek and a metal plate in his head. Other than that, he was as normal as anyone else. He produced four minuscule brown squares from a sandwich baggie, dealing them out to Earl, Don, and me, placing the remaining piece on his tongue. Then he grinned like someone had smacked him upside the head with the idiot stick. Don and Earl followed suit. I examined mine for a moment. It was about an eighth of an inch square and looked as though it had been cut from an undeveloped roll of film.

As I ingested it, John cautioned me. "No matter what happens, remember ...." He paused for effect. "It's only the drugs."

Forty-five minutes later, we were outside smoking cigarettes and joints, when the urge to laugh swept over like a wave dragging us into a riptide. None of us knew exactly what we were laughing about. It really didn't matter. It was just. Damn. Funny. My face hurt, but I couldn't make it stop. All I could do was swim in the direction the tide was pulling. We laughed on and on. The joint went out. It became irrelevant. The effect of Tetrahydrocannabinol was overtaken by Lysergic acid Diethylamide.

*Lucy in the Sky with Diamonds.*

Time became irrelevant. Reality became irrelevant, escaping through the cage door, or rather, passing through the bars. Not between the bars, right through the steel. Or whatever it is enclosing reality.

*Marshmallows? Yes, soft pink marshmallows, pliable and dripping like wax hand grenades exploding in brilliant bursts of music and life that tastes just like: Blue Jean Blues. When did we come inside? I love this song. And it really does taste blue. You taste that?*

I didn't need to ask these questions out loud. We were all on the same plane. I could see it their faces, but I wanted to be sure.

"Why is your face glowing?"

"It's the molecules, man. The music is feeding them."

"Oh yeah, man. I feel it."

Anything was possible.

After a while, the drug saturated us completely. We began to mellow. The lines of transition were blurry and skewed, sharp and fuzzy all at the same time. Sometime during the still-dark morning hours, when most sane people were sawing logs or dreaming of giving speeches in front of their peers in their underwear, I found myself on the top bunk of a bed, in a room illuminated by only a black light, which of course was actually violet and fluorescent. The Jamaican girl was looking down at me. She was smiling now.

Roger Waters was laying down life lessons about *Time*.[9]

David Gilmour's guitar splashed a fresh coat of warm, bright orange on the canvas of my new reality. Its taste and texture were unlike anything I had yet imagined.

Perception evolved into lucidity and then regressed back into meaninglessness. I peeled my skin away to reveal my inner tranquility, only to have it swallowed up by complete and utter madness. Months passed by, or perhaps only seconds. Who could be certain? My hand melted into the floor as I stared in disbelief. I flew down to scrape it up again and then floated back to where I had started. Space was infinite, time eternal. Music developed color, which in turn yielded to taste. I breathed in deeply and could hear its flavor. Swimming in a primordial ooze, I approached the brink of insanity. If it apprehended me, there would be no returning.

Suddenly, the rebel flag hanging in the open doorway swooped back, and Don's old lady entered the room. And then it happened again. The image flashed like a strobe, repeating over and over and over again in rapid succession until she became a skeleton and then vanished as swiftly as she had appeared. I recalled what John had said to me before. "No matter what happens, remember it's only the drugs."

My countenance turned inside out, smiling back at me.

Sleep never came that night. The residual effects lingered for days. I floated on a higher cosmic plane when I entered school the following Monday.

# 18. End of the Innocence Part II

I ducked my head to avoid the biting wind, absorbing the jolt of the railroad tracks through the handlebars of my bicycle. I could see Gerald ten feet behind me. His face was red from the cold. Still, he managed a toothy grin when he saw me looking back at him underneath my armpit. He must have been reading my mind. *The girls are home alone.* Christmas break had given us an early present. All of the little kiddies were off for two weeks while mommy and daddy were obliged to work. This thought motivated us, pressing us onward, enduring the chill of December.

When we got there, the girls were still in their bedclothes. Gerald and I had no trouble finding a place to warm our hands. He disappeared with Laura, heading up the stairs to her bedroom, leaving Amber and me to the couch ….

Before heading back to our neighborhood, Gerald and I took a detour to the tiny airport on Dickinson Island. Had it been summer, we might have taken the long way from my house, walking along the railroad tracks, focusing our strides over every other wooden tie, trying not to step in the rocks between them. Or we would've teetered along on the steel rail, seeing who could stay on the longest before losing their balance and falling off. When we came to the trestle spanning Baker Creek, looking twenty-eight feet down at it through the ties, we would've been on high alert for the constant threat of an approaching train, constantly reevaluating which direction would be the best to run, depending on the distance and from which direction the train was coming. We would have vacated the steel rails at Fisher Place on our way to the bridge at Spence Place.

Where the road veers left, the bridge crosses over to Dickinson Island. A steep wooded embankment towered over the right side of the road. At the top was a meadow. Across that was the campus of Tennessee School for the Deaf. But we weren't going there today. We rode our bikes past the veer in the road, down a makeshift dirt road where pick-up trucks frequently backed their boats in for launching. Pulling our bikes off into the woods there, we hid them out of plain sight. Then we walked quickly to the bridge. Each of us threw a leg over the cold guard rail, put our backs toward the frigid river, and lowered ourselves underneath. Hanging from a cable between the guardrail posts, our feet found the flat a spot on top of a concrete beam that spanned the width of the bridge, offering plenty of room for two people to sit.

Had it been summer, we might have been in shorts, or maybe we would have stripped down to our skivvies and launched high over the guardrail into the chilly current below. The pressure from the deepwater felt as though it might crush our skulls. But we would fight through it, snatching a rock or beer can or whatever we happened upon, surfacing with proof that we had been to the bottom. We discovered that climbing up the concrete pier to the beam and over the railing was easier than the alternative, which would have been swimming over to the boat ramp and walking back up to the bridge. It was much less hassle and reduced the risk of coming face to face with a water moccasin. Had it been summer, we might have stood against the railing, sun in our faces, still dripping the river onto the hot pavement.

It wasn't summer. Now we were sitting on top of cold concrete, watching reflections of light dancing to the rhythm of the current as it made its way west toward downtown Knoxville.

Gerald lit a joint. He passed it and sniffed at his middle finger, scrunching his eyebrows as if he'd caught a whiff of something peculiar.

"Shoo-wee. Laura Lou got a stinky poo." His raspy voice, attempting to hold his smoke as he said it, made it seem funnier than it was. We both laughed, choking on the smoke, which burst from our lungs in clouds.

We traded sordid details of our escapades void of romantic sensitivity. His were better than mine since he consummated the deed. I was only slightly envious. I was too busy being pleased with the bridges I had crossed.

We stayed under the shelter of the bridge for a while, listening to the single-engine planes coming in for a landing, getting stoned until we wondered if we would have trouble climbing back up. When we finally resurfaced on top, we watched a small white Beechcraft with red stripes taxi down the runway and take to the sky. I followed it out of sight, but my mind wandered elsewhere, drawn to flights of its own by the thought of next time ....

# 19. Tragedy on Christmas Eve

I was way past too old to believe in Santa Claus. That illusion had been shot down when I was in second grade. Scott McClain and his older brother had somehow managed to hide under couch cushions and watch as their parents did the job that was supposedly carried out by the jolly old fat man while the good little kiddies slept.

Yet it had only been a year since I had prayed for snow on Christmas Eve. I still found hope in the season.

It was Christmas Eve again. Barry Ward was hitchhiking home from Fort Campbell, Kentucky for the holiday. Someone picked him up, shot him once in the stomach, and left him bleeding to death beside I-40. The day before Christmas. What kind of heartless person does something like that? And why? I mean really: How can anyone be so cold? It probably wasn't for money. Barry was found with money in his possession. Was it for the thrill of taking someone's life? I can't imagine. All I know is judgment day is coming.

The anguish his family must have experienced, I can't begin to fathom. Lying awake in bed late at night, they might have wondered if they could have possibly done anything to prevent it. *Why didn't he take a bus?* He had money. *Someone should have been there to pick him up.* If they slept at all, they would awake and wonder if it was a dream. *How could God let this happen?* Maybe they questioned His existence. *How could a merciful God allow this unspeakable act of senseless violence?* The reality setting in at last brought no rest, no relief, no answers, only grief ... and after that, more grief, leaving an unfillable void. It must have been unrelenting torture for them.

I think of these things now, but at the time, I could only see my own inability to cope with the sadness at the loss of my friend.

I was thirteen and unable to believe there was a human being on the planet where I lived that could be so ruthless, and on the day before Christmas, no less. I had no clue how to deal with the loss of hope I suddenly felt toward all humanity. We were a sad and pathetic species. There was no way I could be festive. There was no way my parents could understand or help. So, I did the only thing that seemed logical at the time. I ran away from home on Christmas Day.

Seeking refuge with my peers, I spent most of the day at the Colters. Then, fearing I would be found there, I relocated. Jackie and

Janis Pratt were more than accommodating, but I couldn't stay there all night. They found a place for me at John Burdett's. He was older, living in his own apartment at Southwood Gardens. I was thoroughly stoned by the time I went to sleep on his couch. When I awoke to the sound of knocking at three a.m., I was still sufficiently numb. My sister Sherry and her boyfriend took me home to my distraught mother. It was the first time in—I couldn't remember when—that I found comfort in her arms. Her sobbing was enough for both of us.

# 20. End of the Innocence Part III

Opportunities being rare as they were, it was some weeks later before I was alone with Amber again. We were in Hurley Farmer's basement in his older brother's bedroom. The only access was the door, which led out to the back of the house. It could be secured from the inside with a deadbolt. Amber knew why we were there. Hurley smoked us up and then left us alone. I locked the door behind him. The look in her powder blue eyes confirmed what she expected.

She flipped the light switch down with one finger. Pitch Black. The stereo was playing low, the needle extracting a melody from the grooves of vinyl. Robert Plant crooned *Thank You*.[10]

It was 1975. I was thirteen; she was fourteen. We were too young—yet every bit old enough. I was petrified in the darkness, exhilarated by the heat of her bare skin. We fumbled awkwardly in the absence of light, but we didn't go the distance. The reason for hesitation was hard to define. Perhaps I was afraid of doing it wrong. I'd stood on the platform a little too long, now fearing the unknown lurking just beyond the edge. I should've known all I needed to do was step off. Gravity would've taken care of the rest. She was head over heels. I don't think she would have been having any of it if she didn't believe in her heart of hearts that we would someday vow our eternal love before God and assorted witnesses. I respected her. We put Visine in our eyes and walked back to my house.

A week later, we did it, the late afternoon sun playing voyeur, peeping in the window of Amber's upstairs bedroom. Downstairs, her mom and dad were oblivious, having fallen under the hypnotic spell of the idiot box.

From there, we took advantage of every moment, unobstructed by adult supervision.

# 21. Don Lance

Don Lance planted his size eleven Converse in the pane of glass at the back door, the full weight of his tall, lanky frame behind it. The tempered safety glass caved easily, staying more or less in one piece. We removed it and reached inside to push down the long cylindrical crossbar, releasing the lock. And just like that, we were in.

It was cold again. For the second time in as many weeks, Don and I had just broken into Giffin Elementary School.

On our previous visit, we had only gone inside as a means of escape from the wind, searching for a warm place to smoke. But this time we were just bored, looking for something to do. It was dark, and the streetlights outside the brick building didn't do us any favors. In the near darkness, we searched the long closets between classrooms. Not finding much, other than some assorted textbooks and a stray coat or two, we were about to give up when I came across something interesting. In a hard-shelled case with metal hasps, I figured it right away to be a musical instrument.

Outside where there was adequate light, we uncased a saxophone. Some poor kid had left it there over the weekend with no intention of practicing. Now, it belonged to us. We really didn't know what we were going to do with it, but I announced on a whim, "I'm gonna learn how to play it."

We had been there for what started to feel like way too long and decided it was time to go. Not wanting to be seen toting our newly acquired possession down the street, we took a safer path through the woods. From there, we could cut through the park and then across South Haven. The yards of resident homeowners would provide stealth as we navigated the last two blocks to my house. It seemed simple enough.

It wasn't going to be that simple.

The light of the moon was enough to guide us along the familiar path through the woods and into the park. We had just crossed the bridge and were looking up the gradual rise toward South Haven Road. Apparently, someone living in the vicinity had alerted the local authorities of our presence at the school. The police, being all too aware of the shortcut, were doing the drive-by. We heard the four-barrel Holley kicking in, their spotlight scanning our general direction.

"Cops!"

## The Quiet Kid

We dove headlong in the grass. The spotlight floated ineffectively over us, shining on the bridge. Unmoving and undetected, we laid on the ground. If not for the pounding of my own heart in my ears, all would've been quiet. Neither of us spoke for several seconds. Then Don broke the silence.

"They're gone."

"Do you think we're safe?"

We were both unsure if we were ready to move just yet.

"Yeah. They're prob'ly headed for the school. We should get outta here while we can."

The voice of reason galvanized us, and we ran the entire two blocks through the yards to my house, leaving the saxophone ownerless in the grass.

Rising early the next morning, we went seeking the stolen instrument. It was still there. We stashed it in my basement, where it would eventually be discovered and turned over to the proper authorities. When Mom asked, it seemed (with shrugs all around) that no one knew exactly how it got there.

We didn't have the good sense to stay away. Sometime later, after the broken window had once again been replaced, Don and I were at the backdoor facing the playground of Giffin Elementary. Fourteen concrete stairs eight feet wide led to the porch in an alcove. The double doors were ten feet back from the top step. It was chilly in the middle of a sunny afternoon. After what had happened the last time we were there, Don and I opted to sit on the cold concrete platform at the top of the stairs to smoke the two joints we had. The risk factor deterred us from breaking in again.

After the first joint was gone, Don was about to light the second one. He raised it to his lips. A split second more, and his thumb would've spun the metal wheel, releasing a spark from the lighter's flint. A man uniformed in dark blue appeared over Don's shoulder. Don, who had his back toward the playground, must have detected the cop in the look on my face. Deer in the headlights. With an urgent but calm efficiency, Don stuffed the joint inside his tube sock and swallowed the roach from the first joint. By the time he had accomplished this, the officer and his partner were towering over us.

"What are you boys doin' here?" The sternness of his voice demanded a good answer. We didn't have a good one.

"Nuthin', sir." It was the best Don could muster. At least he said, sir. I said nothing.

"Did you know you're trespassing on city property?"

"No, sir."

"We've had reports of some break-ins over the past few weeks. Do you know anything about that?" The first officer on the scene was the one doing all the talking. His partner stood silent with arms folded.

"No, sir," Don replied, answering the question, but offering nothing else.

He looked hard at me. "Do you?"

"No, sir," I answered, knowing that we had one thing in our favor. There was no broken glass.

The second officer spoke. "You boys could get in a lot of trouble just by being here." His voice did not possess the same edge. It seemed a little kinder somehow, given the circumstance.

Good cop, bad cop.

"Empty your pockets," Bad Cop commanded. "Slowly."

Rising to our knees, we extracted the contents of our pockets, depositing each item one at a time on the concrete surface.

I had a pack of cigarettes, a BIC lighter, two one-dollar bills, and some assorted change. Don was carrying a small pocketknife, his lighter, some Visine, six ones, and no change. For some odd reason, he was holding no incriminating paraphernalia. (A roach clip would've done the trick.) He didn't even have rolling papers. The two joints were rolled before he left home.

Bad Cop spoke again. "Get up." He was getting annoyed at the lack of evidence. He was intent on finding some. Taking out his aggression, he proceeded to search me violently, at the same time commanding, "Search the other one."

Good Cop patted Don down, though it was plain to see that he wasn't being as thorough.

When Bad Cop got to my socks, he pulled them up, stretching them tight, carefully feeling every inch from my ankles to my calves. To say I was nervous would've been a colossal understatement as I watched Good Cop kneel to raise a leg of Don's jeans. When the search was over, it came as a complete surprise to me that we were not being escorted in handcuffs to the back of the patrol car, which

## The Quiet Kid

I knew without seeing had to be parked in front of the school. I was still in shock when Bad Cop said, "Get out of here and don't let me catch you anywhere near this school again."

"Yes, sir," we said in staggered unison and with gratitude as we walked carefully down the stairs, not wanting to seem too anxious, and Don not wanting to shake anything loose.

On the way home, I asked Don, "How did he not find the joint? Whad jew do with it?"

"I pushed my socks down and hid it in the rolls."

Good Cop never bothered stretching them tight.

Secretly, I thanked God. He had been kind to us that day, kind beyond merit.

When we got to the park, we made our way down to the bridge. No one else was around, and we smoked the remaining joint. Every hit felt like a small victory.

# 22. Reason to Believe

The gloves were off. We had gone all the way, and now nothing was taboo. I could tell her anything. I could tell her everything. We were transparent. All uncertainty had vanished, washed away in a wave of bliss. Drunk in love, overwhelmed in the completeness of our union, my guard dropped, both hands dangling at my sides, leading with my chin, inviting the knockout punch.

Sex ruins a good friendship, or so they say. Amber and I had attended school dances, getting our pictures made in standard poses. We had talked late, late into countless nights, sometimes falling asleep on opposing ends of the telephone line, neither of us wanting to be first to hang up. I had spent a summer watching her play softball at the field of the towers. She took my dog chain. I took it back. June 11th had been declared our official anniversary. When we met, she had been (according to her) a foot taller than I was. And now the "punky little eighth-grader" had caught up to her. At every given opportunity, we had fused ourselves together at the fingers, palms, arms, shoulders, midriffs, hips, pelvic bones, and faces. By the fluorescent light in the halls of South High, my back disposed to the porcelain tile; Amber pressed tightly against me. My fingers long and reaching, dug deep into her back pockets, groping for something they'd already found.

"Gettin' somma that tongue," Alan Morton had observed in passing.

She taught me the secret code of her menstrual cycle, as well as schooling me on the hallowed parts of her anatomy. There were still things about her body only she knew, and I was unaware that I didn't. I knew what I needed to. I had ventured into the holiest of holies. She blew me away. Experiencing the most intimate way two people can be together had been a first for both of us ... as far as I knew.

If she was a virgin, shouldn't there have been blood? I became suspicious. Many telephone conversations dragged beyond midnight, stretching into the early morning hours, with Amber convincing me time and time again that it was perfectly normal. But I knew better. I was naïve, but not that naïve. A month and a half had passed since the first time we did it, but still, I kept wondering, obsessing every time we did it again over the thought of another getting there first.

Finally, she told me the truth. The bliss ended with a horrific crash. I had been on a joyride, failed to heed the crossbar, and absorbed the impact of the oncoming train. I might have been able to withstand the blow had she not misled me, insisting that I was the first.

There had been another before me. Rick Brady. Salt in the wound. The reality of it set in, torturing me.

Borrowing some of Sherry's records, I fed the burning flames of my torment listening to Rod Stewart as he searched for a *Reason to Believe*,[11] lamenting about betrayal, over and over and over and over.

The following night was more of the same. I was devastated. How could I make the pain go away? I wrestled with circumstance. It was what it was, and I couldn't change it. I didn't understand love and yet was consumed by it and the jealousy from my perceived betrayal. She said she loved me, and yet, she lied. Maybe she knew I couldn't handle the truth. And then finally, it surfaced. *Could she be trusted now?* I didn't know how to play the hand I was dealt. And then, in a moment of clarity, the solution was staring me in the face. All I had to do was even the score.

It was brilliant!

I was such an idiot.

I didn't know it at the time, but I was about to tear out a page from Ross Gellar's (not yet written) rulebook. You know, the one that says: *It's okay. We were on a break.*[12]

The plan was simple: break up long enough to throw down with another girl, get back together with Amber, and everything would be copasetic.

Again, I was such an idiot.

# 23. Afterlife

By mid-March, the afternoon temperatures were starting to warm. But in the early morning, I could see my breath when I rolled out of the gray Galaxy 500 and bid adieu to my old lady. I trudged to the top of the ramp by the smoke pit, waiting until the Ford disappeared beyond the brick corner of the shops wing before striking a wooden match on the metal railing. I lit a Kool. The railing layered in years of bad paint jobs was cold even through my jacket, but it was nothing compared to the hollow iciness I housed in my chest. I really didn't care. My emotions had been turned off. It's like they say: Mind over matter. If you don't mind, then it don't matter.

Ten minutes later, Amber arrived, and I put my plan into action, explaining to her how I felt. "I just need some time to sort through all of this," I told her. And also: "I love you. I just don't know if I'm in love with you." I honestly thought I had invented that one.

It seemed to be going well, and then the wheels came off. I hadn't prepared myself for her reaction. When I got to the actual part about breaking up, the water welled up in her eyes. Her chin quivered just before the flood came. She bawled. Amidst the sobs, she said she couldn't deal with school that day, not after this. She started walking away. Not knowing what else to do, I followed her. I couldn't bear what I had done. We walked the familiar road to my house, ultimately ending up in my bed.

Yeah, that went well.

We got into all kinds of trouble when our parents found out we had skipped school. But after the dust settled, the whole truth had been revealed. I told her my true motive for breaking up. She wasn't going to hinder my pursuit of getting some strange if that was going to make me feel better. All she cared about was that I came back to her when I had fulfilled my mission. We could still see each other on the side. This would set the tone for the next four years. From time to time, she would set me free to prowl, and like a stray cat, I would come wandering back home when the hunger drew me. Amber never cared, as long as I came back.

Again, mind over matter.

# 24. Spacey Tracy

Two days after our break-up was official, I was approached by this petite girl who asked me to "go" with her. She was cute with dark kinky hair and dimples, possibly of Mediterranean descent. If you had fished her out of the Tennessee River fully clothed and put her on a scale before she had a chance to dry out, I would've bet she'd have come in under eighty pounds. And though she was a year younger, I couldn't find it in my heart to turn her down. Did I mention she was cute? Her name was Lisa, but I nicknamed her after the T-shirt she often wore with an image of a cartoon fox and the word "Foxy."

After lunch, we would walk the halls together down toward the shop classes. There wasn't much foot traffic in that part of the building in the forty minutes that proceeded fifth period. Secretly, I was trying to avoid being seen by any of Amber's friends. I figured I could save her that much. Lisa and I were in a recessed area at the end of the hall, getting tongue-tied one afternoon when Alan Morton strolled by.

Alan was a couple of years older. I considered him one of the coolest guys in our school. Though my hair could never (without peroxide) be as blonde as his, I was determined to grow mine every bit as long. The straight tips of his locks reached down his back between the shoulder blades. He had on a denim shirt. His jeans wear scruffy and faded, almost completely worn through at the knees, with only the white threads preventing the holes from gaping.

"Son, do you have a hall pass?" Alan did his best Vice Principal, Cunniff imitation.

"He-hey, what's up, Mr. Morton?" I reached over Foxy's shoulder to shake his hand, thumbs wrapped around thumbs.

"Oooh, I like your bracelet." Foxy still had both arms stretched around my back, as she admired the bracelet with its huge triangular turquoise stone inlaid between two sterling silver strands that looped around his wrist.

"And who is this cute young lady? You been hidin' her from me, haven't you?"

"Alan, this is Foxy-uh- I mean, Lisa." She tore herself loose to shake his hand.

"Wow! You look just like this girl I know, only…smaller. Yep. A miniature Spacey Tracy."

Every time he saw us after that, which was almost every day for a while, Alan would address her that way. It caught on. She preferred Foxy, but I couldn't pass up teasing her with Spacey Tracy on occasion.

After a while, our conversations became thick with sexual innuendo. But there was only so much we could get away with in the halls at school. A late-night phone conversation led to a real-get-your- butt-over-here-and-get-some-of-this proposition from her. All I had to do was show up at her house. But I had no transportation. And even if I had, I came to the realization that I just couldn't. Not with her. She was too young. It just didn't feel right. I felt like I would be taking advantage of her sweet naivety. So, I turned her down. Shortly after, I ended it. I had officially become a heartbreaker. Not something you want on your resume.

On a weekend trip to Atlanta, I trespassed across the boundaries of friendship with Kelly Carmichael. Mostly we held hands and kissed when no one was looking, sometimes when they were, but our sleeping arrangements restricted us. Ian and I had our own room. The girls were in with Stacey's parents and had a curfew. Had we believed Elvin Bishop, *We Fooled Around and Fell in Love.* We adopted it as our song, but neither of us was that naïve. We both knew it was only young lust.

The heat from that weekend smoldered like leftover embers from a campfire just waiting for morning to be stirred. Morning came when I wandered over to Ian's to find the girls there with no one else at home. We played a game called Seven Minutes in Heaven. Behind the closed door, Kelly stoked the fire with gasoline, but four hundred twenty seconds proved to be too short a time for a raging firestorm. The blaze was contained by controlled burns.

*Knock. Knock.*

Stacey's interruptions cooled things down at seven-minute intervals. The time with her was mostly awkward. She was Ian's sister for crying out loud. Kelly was more than willing, but then I had another attack of conscious. *She's too young*, the miniature angel in white perched on my right shoulder reasoned. The argument from the devil on my left might've been more persuasive had the intervals between the timed knocking been a little longer. Stacy's four hundred and twenty seconds became more and more uncomfortable. Eventually, I heeded the sounder of the two opinions. Whisking the tiny goateed red devil away, I called it quits.

As I crossed over the dilapidated chain link fence on my way home, I was reminded of my mission.

The good cherub had won the first round, perhaps because the name of the game itself implied it was being played on his turf. Satisfied with his small victory, he let his guard down. And then I heard the whisper in my other ear. *You just need to find someone older.*

# 25. Cody

I turned fourteen on a Sunday. Monday, it was back to school, Tuesday, the regular routine. I smoked cigarettes out back with Don Colter that morning. He got me started on Kools. But after I decided they were killing me (rumor had it the filters contained fiberglass), I switched again—this time to Marlboro Menthol. I said hello to Amber when I passed her in the hall on my way to class. U.S. History ... Art ... Phys Ed. At lunch, I hung out with Cody Farmer. He was Hurley's brother. Hurley was in my grade. Cody was a couple of years older. Freckles ran in their family, both of them redheads. Hurley had scarecrow hair, straight and straw-like. Cody's hair was a fiery wave. At sixteen, Cody was a lot bigger, stouter, and nicer. I liked Hurley just fine, but he could take some pointers on politeness from his big bro.

It wasn't the first time I had hung out with him. Cody was a good friend of Alan Morton's. We had gotten high together a few times. He was exuberant and bright. He was pretty cool in my book.

Algebra I ... English ... Study Hall. At last, the long walk home.

Wednesday, I got up to do it all over again. But things were different. Hurley wasn't at school that day.

Tuesday afternoon, Cody had gone swimming at Southwood Gardens Apartments pool. Someone saw him floating face down in the chlorinated water. Those who were present thought he was goofing. By the time they got him out, it was too late. He had drowned.

Nothing about this made sense. How could this happen? Was there more to the story that was covered up? When I heard the news, I thought immediately of Brian Jones and the mysterious circumstances surrounding his death. He had been found motionless at the bottom of the swimming pool at his farm in East Sussex, the former home of A.A. Milne, who had penned the original Winnie the Pooh.

How was it possible Cody couldn't make it to the side? I'd been there many times myself. The pool wasn't that big. I never heard a sound explanation. None was stated in the paper, and I didn't know any of the people who had been with him that afternoon well enough to ask. I was thoroughly confused.

## The Quiet Kid

All I knew was that I had just seen him yesterday. Today, he was gone. Something was horribly wrong. Storytime was over. Nothing would ever be the same at Pooh Corner.

# 26. If Beavis and Butthead

If Beavis and Butthead had been around in the seventies, I'd have accused Mike Judge of sneaking into our school and stealing the identities of two guys I knew. Only Maynard Wyndham didn't have braces. Beavis, the squirrely one, couldn't have been anyone other than Jeff Yancey. Much to the dismay of Mrs. Canton, they were both in the same English class as Don Colter and me.

Mrs. Canton's head weaved and bobbed like it was on springs, her black hair curled in disarray. She was a strange bird, to begin with. Her picture could've been in Webster's by the word "schoolmarm." Stiff and white, her collar might've been the only thing supporting the weight of her head, which seemed to have disconnected from the rest of her body.

She was finding it impossible to keep us quiet that afternoon. So, she split us up, placing one of us in each corner of the room— Don and I on the back row. Beavis and Butthead were stuck in opposing corners in the front.

It was no wonder she had developed the nervous condition. I'm sure we weren't the first to disrupt her class. And this wasn't the first day we'd made her life unbearable. Earlier in the year, I had refused to take my seat, claiming to be cold and standing up by the radiator. When she finally resorted to bringing in reinforcements in the form of the chorus teacher from down the hall, I simply sat down before he arrived.

The four of us were notorious for getting in trouble or least doing stuff for which we should've been in trouble. At lunch one afternoon, we were outside waiting for our favorite misfit to come by: a twitchy old guy, a grade-A weirdo, notorious for driving around with what looked like a handkerchief hanging out of his nose. We were in the habit of calling out the nickname we'd given him, a real original: "Ragnose." Whenever he'd drive by, we'd cap off the insult with an obscene gesture that involved spreading our legs apart and fanning a hand toward our crotches, uttering a single syllable, "Wah." This implied something along the lines of "Eat my shorts."

That afternoon, with Ragnose nowhere in sight, we began making the obscene wave at whoever happened by. The vice-principal, Mr. Cuniff—old crooked finger himself—witnessed the event and wanted to know, "Son, what does this (Cuniff making the gesture without aiming it at anything in particular) mean?"

We had no good explanation, and we figured he wasn't bright enough to deduce a good one. Our decided punishment was three days of detention to be served after school.

More recently, Jeff Yancey had mysteriously gone MIA when Mrs. Canton called role. Probably a bad case of spring fever.

She had just settled into her lesson when Jeff's head appeared in the window. Don and I were snickering and *psssting* Maynard to get his attention. Jeff would duck down every time Mrs. Canton turned her annoyed swivel head. When we saw what Jeff was up to, we restrained our laughter. He kept poking at a flowerpot, inching it closer and closer to the edge of the counter. Finally, he reached in and gave it a good shove. We watched in awe as it slid off into the floor. *Crash!* The ceramic shattered. Dirt splayed out on the linoleum tiles. We tried our best to look shocked. By the time Mrs. Canton could react, Jeff was long gone.

Now we had her in the crosshairs. I almost felt sorry for her, but not enough to break the stare I had fixed on her. After she had segregated us, we had somehow communicated through hand gestures or possibly telepathy, a silent plan. We would all stare at her. No other form of mischief could have been more effective or impossible to defend. She stood there helpless, staring vacantly through her glasses, burning a hole in the back wall of the classroom. The final minutes of class ticked away. Her empty gaze was fixed despite the furious wobble. She looked like a bobblehead doll propped against a concrete vibrator. For a while, I thought her head might break free and roll off into the floor, but the bell saved her.

We were all guaranteed a passing grade. There was no way she would have risked having any of us in her eighth grade English class again.

# 27. Shirley

*Smack!* The penny exploded off the wood panel wall less than four feet from the head of Coach Rice. Every ear in the auditorium was attuned to the sound it made as it rolled down along the slope of the concrete floor, students wondering if the minted presidential likeness might roll all the way down to the stage. Coach Rice searched for a suspect, his eyes magnified and bleary through thick, Coke-bottle lenses framed in black.

*Clink.* The penny came to a halt against the metal leg in a row of seats about halfway down.

In terms of inducing a desired effect, the throw was nearly flawless. After a quick turn-around, I was looking straight ahead, suppressing a guffaw, wanting to look but fighting the urge.

Jaime Tate, a Roger Daltrey doppelganger with a darker mane, was turned sideways with one leg in the adjacent seat. He just happened to be staring off in space in the general direction of the back wall when Abe Lincoln had announced his arrival.

"Tate!" The crusty voice of Coach Rice pierced the silence. "Come with me to the office!" He added, "Now!" after Jaime, looking a bit confused, didn't jump fast enough.

Nicknamed "Sunshine," Coach Rice became an erupting volcano whenever he overheard the term being used in his presence. He was a black man of a most unsunny demeanor. It was all I could do to refrain myself from belting out the chorus from John Denver's *Sunshine on My Shoulders*.

Instead, I watched with a tinge of guilt as Sunshine escorted Jaime Tate around the corner to the office.

No one else had seen me throw it. I tried not to think about it and went back to the list I had been making.

AC/DC
Aerosmith
Alex Harvey Band
Alice Cooper
The Allman Bros.
America
Argent
Average White Band
Atlanta Rhythm Section
Bachman Turner Overdrive
Bad Company
Badfinger
The Beatles
Black Oak Arkansas
Black Sabbath
Blind Faith
Blood Sweat and Tears
Blue Oyster Cult
Bob Dylan
Bonnie Bramlett
Brownsville Station
Bruce Springsteen
Buffalo Springfield
Canned Heat
Cat Stevens
Charlie Daniels Band
Chicago
Climax Blues Band
Cream
Creedence Clearwater
C, S, N & Y
David Bowie
David Essex
Deep Purple
Dobie Gray
Doobie Brothers
Doors
Dr. John
The Eagles
Edgar Winter Group
Elton John
Emerson Lake & Palmer
Electric Light Orchestra
Eric Clapton
Fleetwood Mac
Foghat

Freddy King
George Thoroughgood
Grandfunk Railroad
The Grateful Dead
Grinderswitch
The Guess Who
Head East
Heart
Hot Chocolate
Hot Tuna
J. Geils
Jackson Browne
James Taylor
Janis Joplin
Jefferson Airplane
Jethro Tull
Jim Croce
Jimi Hendrix
Joe Walsh
John Lennon
Johnny Winter
Kansas
The Kinks
Kiss
Led Zeppelin
Leon Russell
Leslie West
Linda Ronstadt
Little Feat
Little River Band
Lou Reed
Lynyrd Skynyrd
Manfred Mann
Marshall Tucker Band
Molly Hatchet
Mott the Hoople
Montrose
The Moody Blues
Muddy Waters
Pink Floyd
Queen
Rolling Stone
Savoy Brown
Slade
T. Rex
Uriah heep

*Riiiiiiiiiiiiiiiiiiiiing!*

It had to be one of the most annoying sounds ever imposed on human ears, but to every student (and probably most of the teachers), it was the single most highly anticipated noise. The bell rang, ending the last period of the day.

Marble panels, purplish in hue, extracted from the quarries of Candoro Marble Works, finished the interior lobby walls of South High School. Directly across from the auditorium was the final resting place for trophies won by champions past, locked, and displayed behind oversized panes of glass. I passed them without notice. It was a long way from the auditorium to the smoke pit, especially with a stop at my locker in between.

Books were tossed in carelessly, finding no time to situate themselves before being trapped by the slamming of the vented metal door. I palmed the lock, giving it a forceful shove and spun the wheel to reset it. Making haste through the locker labyrinth, I slowed just a bit at the end of the hall, where the walls changed into an alternating bond pattern of slick yellow tile just before reaching the back door. I didn't want to appear too anxious. Before I opened the door, I could see her through the window, seated on the railing. Shirley Wilson was already there, waiting.

Shirley was attractive in a way that most girls could only try to be. She wasn't cheerleader pretty. There was something wild and mysterious about her, something ravenous and lupine, and at the same time, lost and childlike in her pale brown eyes. She wore little makeup—if any—maybe a little eyeliner. It just came naturally for her. Her complexion was dark with an olive tone, her hair thick and brown and wavy, hanging past her shoulders. Plenty of girls could put forth twice the effort with half the results.

I pushed the metal lock bar on the heavy back door and stepped outside. A smile greeted me on the other side.

"Hey, Mike."

"Hey, girl."

We had planned to meet immediately after the final bell. Secretly, I had hoped to make tracks before the rest of the gang arrived.

No such luck.

*Hurley Farmer. Dammit!*

## The Quiet Kid

Figuring he would be too great a distraction, we lingered. I was hoping Crazy Jane and Debbie would show up.

I bummed a cigarette from Hurley. "You gotta light?"

"You wan' me to kick you in the ass to jump-start your lungs?" Hurley grinned smugly through threads of red hair that hung over his eyes. Freckles splotched his face, overlapping more splotches of freckles. He shook his hair back out of his eyes and lit my cigarette.

Jane and Debbie stepped out onto the cement porch.

*Good. Not a minute too soon. Maybe they can keep him entertained.*

Debbie Ford was petite and pretty with short brown hair. Jane was tall, blonde, and long-limbed, sometimes answering to the nickname Big Bird when she wasn't Crazy Jane.

Hurley was persistent in his efforts to yank the precarious cotton string securing Debbie's halter top. Jane rescued Debbie repeatedly, chasing Hurley away when he'd get too close. By the time we reached Rock City Ball Park, they had fallen behind, leaving a generous gap between them and us.

"Here. Hold this for a sec." I handed Shirley my Alice Cooper album. I had brought it to school for entertainment during Art class. Producing a slender, Instamatic camera from my shirt pocket, I stepped back just far enough to snap a quick frame. Her yellow shirt was bright in the sun, the contrast nice against her olive-brown skin. I slipped the camera back into my pocket.

"You gonna give that one to Amber?" Shirley's voice was deep, almost masculine, with a hint of softness. The query was laced with cynicism.

"We broke up." Ah, exactly the opportunity I was looking for.

"You did not."

"It's true." I knew it was a temporary situation, but at the time, it was true. There was no need to expound. I was surprised she didn't know already. Amber's friends and Shirley's friends didn't run in the same circles. Short-lived, my relationship with Foxy had barely lasted two weeks. Apparently, Alan Morton was no gossip. I had managed to keep it low key.

"I thought you two were lifers. What happened?"

Now came the tricky part. "Um...les' just say she wasn't totally honest with me about some stuff. I couldn't handle that, ya know? Anyway, we're done."

*"Can you say 'hypocrite?"*

"Wow. I didn't see that coming."

"Yeah, but it's okay now." I wanted to change the subject. We had arrived in front of the Family Pantry market.

"You want Pepsi or Mountain Dew?" I asked, pushing through the glass door.

"Mountain Dew, duh."

Sno-Balls, the Pantry's version of an Icee, were a daily ritual on the walk home from school, especially when it started heating up in the latter part of spring.

I took a twin pack of brownies at a five-finger discount for later, paid for two Mountain Dew Sno-Balls, stepped outside, and handed Shirley her frozen treat. We loitered against the brick ledge, waiting (because Shirley wanted to) for the others to catch up. From the storefront, we could see the wooden bleachers facing the baseball diamond at Rock City ballpark.

My dad pitched many a game from the mound of that field. During one of those games, I had left in a rush to get to the Pantry. I expounded the details to Shirley.

"I could've saved myself a hassle if I'd stayed on the sidewalk, but I was in such a hurry to get my Sno-ball, I jumped across right there." I pointed to the spot. "Landed on broken glass and sliced my hand pretty good. Blood everywhere." I held my right hand palm up to show off the scar. "See the little ridge right there?" I sat my cup down on the brick ledge to point at my ring finger just below the first knuckle. "I was still holdin' the dime when I ran back up the bleachers to show my mom."

"I bet she freaked." Her brown eyes were deep with concern, as if it had just happened.

"Um, yeah. My cousin Mike was there keepin' her calm. He tied my arm off with a bandana to slow the circulation, and they took me to Baptist.[13] That was the best part. He had this '68 Mustang ... copper colored... it was badass. He was driving like Steve McQueen in Bullet on the way to the emergency room."

Shirley parked her Sno-ball next to the Billion Dollar Babies album which she had leaned against the storefront glass. She ran her finger across the scar, examining it intimately.

"You two should get a room." Hurley stepped up on the sidewalk, stopping to see if he could stir it up a little more as

## The Quiet Kid

Debbie and Jane went inside. He had a face full of freckles and a head full of mischief. But he got distracted easily. ADHD had not yet been labeled as a diagnosis, but I'm pretty sure that he had it anyway.

In his nasally voice, he said, "Hey Scarlett, I thought you were gonna loan me that album."

"Take it. Only make sure I get it back." I laughed. "I know where you live."

Hurley leaned in as close as he could possibly get to Shirley when he reached for the LP. His red straw hair draped down, almost in Shirley's face.

"Get off." Shirley gave Hurley a shove backward, nearly landing him on the hood of a parked car.

Regaining his balance, he made an aggressive lunge toward her.

"Watch it," I said, rising quickly from the brick ledge.

Hurley stopped in his tracks and laughed. "What? Is she your woman now?"

I felt Shirley's fingers slide between mine, and I sat back down next to her. Our knuckles formed a snug bond.

"What if I am?" she defended.

He scoffed, shaking his head a little as he pushed the door open to step inside.

When we resumed our walk home, it was Shirley and me who were lagging. We sipped our frozen Mountain Dews held in opposing hands. Our other hands were tangled and swinging freely between us as we passed the little gray market.[14] Laughing carelessly, we waved goodbye to Jane and Debbie, who had turned off at Jane's street. Hurley had gone ahead, and we could see him ascending McClung on the other side of South Haven. We strolled by the park; my guilt now pushed back firmly out of reach. When we arrived at my street, I passed it by, walking with her to the far end of McClung Avenue. I didn't turn to go home until we were standing in front of her house. I wanted to kiss her, but not there ... not just yet. I wanted it to be somewhere a little more private. I walked away backward, our fingers sliding slowly apart.

"I'll see you soon," I promised, knowing it to be true, knowing school would be out for summer in a few more days.

"Look for me tomorrow," she paused, smiling. "You better come find me."

"I will. I will." And then I turned to go, resisting the urge to turn back and look, trying to be cool.

Later, when learning of his misfortune, I apologized to Jaime Tate. He had expressed his innocence vehemently, but in the end, took three licks from Vice Principal Cuniff's paddle. Guilty until proven innocent, that was Bill Cuniff's policy. Jaime just shrugged it off.

"It ain't the first time. Prolly won't be the last. Don't sweat it, man."

# 28. The Park

Mary James Park was the name of record for the three-and-a-half-acre oasis in the middle of suburbia. All the regulars referred to it as the corner park or simply, the park. Had we been cognizant (we weren't cognizant of much, and there was no sign) of her official title, I imagine we would have called her Mary Jane Park.

At the corner intersection, South Haven rises slowly and heads north toward the Tennessee River. From the edge of the road, the grassy earth slopes gently down to the creek. Sidewalk divides the steeper road to the west and the hill, which scoops into a bowl behind the swings. A young boy and his companions could pass beneath McClung Avenue undetected by the traffic overhead in the tunnel, which opened the way for the creek. Many of my pre-adolescent days were spent turning rocks over in that creek in search of salamanders or crawdads. My buds and I would follow its current as it meandered through the middle of the park from the corner, past the swings, under the bridge, by the tennis courts (which were usually vacant) to the far end until it lost itself in the woods. If we were so inclined, we could follow a trail between the hardwoods leading to the playground behind Giffin Elementary School. This information became pertinent at times when in need of a quick escape route.

As asinine as the idea seems to me now, I concluded one afternoon that I could ride my bicycle down the hill underneath the arched monkey bars by the swing set. I didn't take into consideration the need to allow for head clearance. As fortune would have it, the steel bar caught me between the chin and Adam's Apple, sparing my jaw, teeth, face, and possibly my life. It's strange the things that come to mind at such times. My first thought, after I was coherent enough to stand up, was that there had been no witnesses. For that, I was relieved. P.J. Clapp[15] would have been proud to have captured the whole episode on film.

I must have been around eleven years old that summer, which would have made it 1972. Tricky Dick was in the White House. U.S. troops were dropping bombs on Hanoi. George Wallace was shot. Truman passed. One of the great humanitarians of our time gambled with his life and lost while attempting to personally deliver food and supplies to earthquake victims in Nicaragua. He was a pretty good baseball player too. You might've heard of him. His name was Roberto Clemente.

All of that was background noise. It hadn't occurred to me yet that those events were part of the real world. It all seemed so … far away. Detached. I was more likely to have paid attention when I heard *Take it Easy* on the radio for the first time. My hair was still above my ears then. Three years later, my hair hung down past my shoulders, and I parted it down the middle, constantly tucking it behind my ears.

On any given day at the park in the summer of 1975, you would likely find Crazy Jane kicking her feet up in the air in a contest with Shirley, to see who could swing the highest.

There were plenty of the local heads dropping by on any given day, as long as the sun was shining. Hurley Farmer was within walking distance, and if he had a stash, he might be there with some little skank trying to peek beneath her halter top. Just arriving from the Handy Dandy, Icee's in hand, the Mayfield sisters, might pull in with Debbie Ford. Could it get any better? Some days you'd show up, and the place would be deserted. Other times, the party would be going strong—Frisbees or footballs or joints being passed all around. Either way, if you stayed put long enough, you were certain to run into someone familiar, whether it was Eric Slater in his classic Thunderbird, complete with suicide doors and a backseat full of stoners, or just Bestsy Hyde, bopping along all by her lonesome on her return trip from Middle Earth. She swore she was a Hobbit, and quite frankly, sometimes I believed her.

If you were in the market for some Panama Red, Columbian Gold, Maui Wowie, Lebanese Blond, or even the occasional microdot, it was a pretty good place to find a hookup. When the harvest was plentiful, we'd resemble the crew from Point Place, rounding the circle in Foreman's basement. The difference being our circle assembled on the bridge, three telephone poles covered with a skin of 1x8" planks spanning the creek.

The vantage point from the bridge was by far the best. It must've been around 9:00 a.m. on a Monday. Normally, we wouldn't have been out of bed, but we had slept out in the fort the previous night, which had been a wild one. I had just parked it there with Hurley, about to light up a fat joint I had just rolled, when I spied Betsy

## The Quiet Kid

Hyde, frizzy brown hair and all, heading our way. With her Barbra Streisand nose, she wasn't likely to place first in any beauty contests, but still, she was cute enough. Rarely was she seen in shorts. I couldn't say exactly why. Maybe she just loathed shaving. Tight, faded bell-bottom Levi's exemplified her thin legs. She wore suede wallabies, like most of the guys, did, and her T-shirt clung to her like Glad Wrap pulled across the edge of a glass bowl. *I wonder if she's wearing a bra.* From that distance, I couldn't tell. By the way, she was bouncing; I was betting she wasn't.

"This is the last one I've got. Should we save it?" I looked at Hurley.

"Naw, I've got plenty."

"Maaan, you been holdin' out on me." I lit the joint.

"I'm 'bout to get me summa that." Hurley motioned Betsy our way.

"You wish." She was almost close enough to hear our conversation. "Where have you been, lookin' all cute like that?" I called out to her.

"Moria. On my way back to the Shire." She grinned as she drew closer.

"Okay. Okay. You told me about the Shire, but where the heck is Moria?"

"It's the short route beneath the Misty Mountains," she replied as if it were a matter of fact.

I could safely cash in now on the wager I made with myself when she had been further away, as the cotton fabric of her T-shirt was wearing thin. The colors of Wonderland had faded from the image of a caterpillar perched on top of a mushroom, playing a Fender Stratocaster to an audience of one bewildered Alice, barely concealing the twin protrusions which embellished what looked like—*is she stashing honeydews under there?*—and were now practically staring me in the face. Involuntarily, I followed them for a second as she sat down. Recovering quickly, I maintained eye contact.

"The Misty Mountains, eh?"

"That's right, the Misty Mountains. I'm going back that way later if you wanna come."

I had no idea what she was talking about, but not being one to pass on a convenient Zeppelin reference, I replied, "I'm packin' my bags."

"You're both crazy." Hurley shook his head at us as he passed the joint.

"You're just jealous, 'cause I didn't invite you!" Betsy shot back.

"The only place you're goin' is the loony bin, and you can bet I ain't gonna be there."

I interrupted their little dispute before it escalated. "Shut up and do somethin' with this mainline."

The joint was burning unevenly up one side. I handed it to Hurley, attempting to draw his attention away from Betsy. He spat on the forefinger of his free hand as he took it, applied the saliva where the burn was out of control and turned the excess paper to the top side, before taking a toke.

Three heads popped up and turned in unison at the sound of The Edgar Winter Group piercing the atmosphere. *Frankenstein*[16] arrived a good five seconds before Ronnie Wilson did. He had entered the park from the McClung Avenue side, descending the hill into the bowl behind the swing set. Deep, intoxicating reverberations from a moog synthesizer emitted by a portable eight-track tape player escaped around the side of the hill, sneaking up on us, arresting our attention. It was a good thing for us the cops never took a notion to use the same tactic.

"Get over here and hit this, b'fore I smoke it all," Hurley admonished Ronnie across the distance.

Never changing his stride, Ron continued toward the bridge and sat where he'd have the next turn. My thoughts wandered away from Middle Earth, back to the real world, as he said his hellos. He was Shirley's older brother. It was easy to see the family resemblance.

"Where the heck has your little sister been keepin' herself lately?" I asked him.

"She went campin' with Crazy Jane. They got back late last night. She's prob'ly still in bed."

Hurley was lighting a second joint to compensate for the additional smokers. His eyes crossed, looking down his densely freckled nose through strands of red hair as he lit it. He passed it to the right. Blowing out smoke, Hurley picked up the conversation. "Yeah, we did a little campin' last night too. Ain't that right, Scarlett?"

I knew exactly what he was referring to. Ronnie caught the look between us and asked. "So, what happened?"

Hurley was quick to fill him in. "Me and Scarlett slept out in the fort last night and went roamin' the streets in the middle of the night. 'Bout two in the mornin', we was down by the Handy Dandy when

## The Quiet Kid

'ole Scarlett decides he's gonna snatch a Coke from the machine. He's got his arm stuck halfway up in it when the cops pull up."

"So, what did you do?" Betsy asked when Hurley paused for a hardy laugh.

"When he finally got his arm loose, he hauled ass. I ran way b'fore that but stopped dead in my tracks when I saw the thicket of briars b'hind the barbershop. Now, as you can see, Scarlett ain't got on jeans like I do, but he never for a second hesitated. Cut a trail right through the middle a them briars, short pants, and all. You shoulda seen 'im."

"That explains the scratches," Betsy observed.

"It was that or juvie."

Betsy's eyes lit up as she dived headlong back into adventures in her private world of delusion, running from Orcs with wizards, outsmarting trolls, and something about a ring. Hurley argued about her sanity. Ronnie was inquisitive and defended her, antagonizing Hurley all the while. We rolled another fatty. I just laughed at them as I drifted in and out of the conversation … further away from the perils of Middle Earth…back to the park. And then away further still to Rock City Ball Park…*walking down the sidewalk, stepping over cracks…walking home from school with Shirley, intentionally lagging behind on occasion to catch a glimpse of her athletic, brown legs … muscles flexing with every step … her denim cut-offs just a tad shorter than they needed to be. She turned around to catch me in the act, laughing at me, smacking me playfully …*

"Hey! Are you gonna hit this, or what?" Hurley snapped me back to reality.

Trying to look as though I had been right there all along, I took my hit. Holding the smoke deep in my lungs, in a strained voice, I said, "Can't break the circle."

Betsy started singing.

*May the circle be unbroken …*[17]

Ronnie and I chimed in until laughing made it impossible to continue. Hurley was shaking his head, his expression saying we were lost to the world. Betsy went back to middle earth. Hurley protested. Ronnie overruled. My mind slipped away again, this time to Shirley snuggled up tight and cozy in her bed. It was time to go.

## 29. Shirley Part II

Shirley still had the *Second Helping* album I had loaned her. She dropped the vinyl disc on the turntable, placing the needle on the outer edge of the grooves. It was my newest Lynyrd Skynyrd album. Nuthin' Fancy was released in March, but with so much good music out there, it was hard to keep up.

"So, you're not a Skinny Leonard fan?" I was a bit shocked.

"Not really." She shrugged. "I like *Simple Man* and *Tuesday's Gone* and *Freebird*. That's about it."

Ron Van Zant was defending Alabama,[18] but I didn't get a chance to defend the song.

"The other stuff don't do much for me." A sheepish grin took her face over. "I guess my neck's not that red." She laughed before adding, "But I'll listen to it … for you."

Even without makeup, she was in full possession of her untamed, natural beauty. When her mouth relaxed, her lip curled up slightly, exposing her teeth. Standing there in a sleeveless T-shirt cut off above the midriff and denim shorts—the ones that were a little too short – she was showing off more than her white teeth. The muscles of her arms and legs were lean, her flat abdomen sculpted like a gymnast's. I didn't know exactly how she achieved it; she never worked out that I was aware of. Genetics, maybe. With no quick retort to her redneck remark, I pounced, tackling her gingerly, falling next to her on the bed.

I kissed her. My first impression was that she had never done it before. Her tongue overpowered mine like we were in some kind of bizarre contest, which she dominated fully. Conceding the victory, I changed the game, moving to second base and then quickly rounding third. She was leaving home plate wide open, and though she offered no resistance, something was off.

Amber would have anticipated every step as if we were partners in a choreographed dance. Everything with Shirley just seemed forced and awkward.

I wanted to score, but she seemed to be miles away. Apparently, I had deceived myself into believing I knew what I was doing. The level of excitement would've been so much higher at this stage with Amber. Now it just wasn't there. Or maybe my conscience had crawled back out to ruin my plans. I cared too much about Shirley to just drag her along for my own amusement. I threw in the towel and

## The Quiet Kid

pulled away. Taking a hard pack of cigarettes from the front pocket of my jeans, I shook out two tightly rolled joints.

"Hurley can be all right when he wants to. He sold me two for a buck. You wanna go smoke one?"

Somehow the opportunity to smoke a joint seemed to make everything less awkward.

"Yeah, sure," she said.

We walked to the former field of the TVA towers, sat on the concrete bleachers, and smoked both joints. Keeping things as light as I could, I managed to give her some constructive criticism on her kissing technique. She was a quick learner, vastly improving on our next attempt.

"Yeah, that's more like it." With my hand still behind her neck, I looked into her eyes. Her gaze was far from fixed. The brightness of the sun contracted her pupils down to a pinpoint, seeming to enlarge the brown irises as they darted back and forth like pinballs hung between bumpers in full-tilt mode, scanning my eyes as if she were searching them for the answer to some unasked question. Finally, it came.

"What happened back there?"

I said nothing. Mute. Looking back at her, afraid if I responded, it would be to the wrong question. Obviously, she knew. Something wasn't right. The thing was, I liked her—a lot. But knowing deep down inside my true motive for being there, I was having a hard time following through. Even though I wanted her, I had no desire to play her. She helped me with the answer.

"It's Amber, isn't it?"

"Busted." I pulled my hand away and hung my head, no longer able to look at her straight on.

"Look, if you still have feelings for her, then you don't need to be here with me." Shirley stood up quickly. "I like you. I really do. But I can't do this. I won't." She stood over me, waiting for a response.

I looked up and said the only thing that would come out. "Sorry."

"You're such a jerk." She huffed off, walking hastily in the direction of her house.

"Wait. Can't we still be friends?"

"I'll have to get back to you." She never looked back, but she said it loud enough to be sure I heard.

All I could do was watch her walk away. Running after her would have only made things worse. *She's right. I am a jerk.* I had screwed up royally with no one but myself to blame. I could only hope I could make it up to her somehow.

## 30. Clearwater

"That's so sweet." Mom's comment was barely audible over the drone of the highway.

From behind the wheel of the vehicle, Betty Willard returned something that sounded like "Mmm-hmm."

Cindy Willard's head was snuggled against my chest. We had fallen asleep in the backseat on the last leg of a long southbound trip. I kept my eyes closed, not wanting Mom to know I had heard and that I was now awake. I imagined eyes gazing at me in the rearview and wondered what her mom was thinking.

*This is as far as it goes, I swear.*

Cindy, a cute little blonde, was my third cousin, from what I'd been told. She was a couple of years my junior. Kelly and Foxy had been too young. As limited as it was, the scope of my conscious forbade me to violate either of them. I hoped I had learned something. There was no lasting damage in those relationships. The sting of what I had done to Shirley was what lingered. I was enjoying the warmth of this present physical contact, but I knew we were at a threshold that could not be crossed.

The late afternoon sun in my face was as intrusive as the annoying whine of the interstate. In a matter of minutes, we would be crossing the Sunshine Skyway Bridge, an event my mom felt we should all witness.

"Wake up," Mom said. "We're about to cross the bridge."

Three heads popped up, peering groggily over the backseat. Richie Barrett had been snoozing in the way back of the station wagon with Cindy's two sisters. Cindy righted herself, wiping spittle from the corner of her mouth, trying not to be obvious.

The rest of our party was in the lead car: my dad, the Willard patriarch, his two sons, Matt and Jeremy, Blaine Freeman, a friend of Matt's from school, and my boy crazy baby sister, Kristi. It was no accident she ended up riding in their car. The lead car started its ascent up a mountain of concrete, a great curving swell, like a giant behemoth heaving up from the sea. We were in awe, completely unaware of the anxiety this sight was causing for Jeremy the eldest Willard boy. Suffering from gephyrophobia—fear of bridges—he was attempting to burrow beneath the seats.

On the other side of Tampa Bay, we all let go a collective sigh of relief. Just as we did, something more annoying than the intrusive sun or the whining tires came on the radio. Freddy Fender. Cindy requested that it be turned up, and she belted out the chorus of *Before the Next Teardrop Falls*. I knew then if it wasn't clear before. I had no earthly business being with her. Still, I had to laugh and join in the next time around, changing the words to *before the next teardrop farts*.

A vacation was just what the doctor ordered. Foxy and Kelly had been innocent bystanders I had run over without regard. I had screwed up royally with Shirley. Still, I had this unquenchable thirst to drink from a cup to even some stupid score I insisted on keeping with Amber. Maybe what I really needed was a big slice of humble pie. Miraculously, Amber still wanted me. God knew I still wanted her. Things had been so easy with her. The past wasn't going to inadvertently repeat itself. Rick Brady could never unscrew her. Regardless of what I did or didn't do to keep pace with her past indiscretion, it would always exist. *In the past*, I should've reminded myself and moved on. Or more correctly, moved right back in her direction. But no, I was bound and determined to follow through with my fool-heartedness

For a brief moment, standing on Clearwater Beach, staring out at an impossibly distant horizon, the ocean washed everything clean. Cindy's age and relationship became a nonissue. My recent mistakes: Gone. The dilemma of the unleveled playing field and tying the score with Amber: Gone. The quest became irrelevant. School, girls, cigarettes, sex, drugs, and rock 'n' roll, all gone—swallowed up in the waves curling up to wash it all away in the vastness of the sea. I stood in awe at how boundless it was and how small I became standing next to it. The only thing in existence was the white sand, the azure sky, and the salty green water. I drank in the image with my eyes, endeavoring to process what would've been fatal to ingest any other way. It was life, and all life a part of it. I had stood on the ocean's shore when I was still too small to remember. Now, though it seemed like it was the first time, it was like another part of me had been there before. Déjà vu. I remembered, as if it had always been with me—had always been a part of me. The awe of the Skyway Bridge paled in comparison.

"It's beautiful." Cindy sounded as if she barely had breath to speak.

## The Quiet Kid

"Yeah," I said, "And enormous. It seems like it goes on forever."
"Ya'll can jus' stand there 'n' gawk," Blaine said. "I'm gettin' in."
He ran, sand exploding from a trail of footprints.
We all followed, crashing into the warm surf.

A chameleon raced around a palm tree like the red stripe circling a barbershop pole, eluding Blaine Freeman. Undiscouraged, he persisted. "Dammit," he said. "Almost had me one."
"Might as well hang it up, Blaine," Richie antagonized.
"I'll catch one yet. You jes' wait an' see."
"You'll be here 'til the cows come home. That thing ain't gonna wait on yer slow ass to catch up."
"Shut up, Richie!"
On our first day at the motor court, Blaine was strutting around, fluffing back his feathered brown bangs between his fingers and thumb. "We need to get back down to the beach, man, so I can swa-vay some women." He had been saying this at every stop throughout the entire road trip. I wasn't quite sure what to make of him. He had a slight overbite, and I internally questioned his swa-vaying abilities. But apparently, he did okay back home. Later, by the pool, he found an empty bottle of J&B. Lying back on a white metal lounge chair, he hammed it up for a photo, pretending to chug the bottle.
*This guy might be all right.*
"C'mon, man. Let it go." I motioned Richie away with a side nod.
Richie followed, and we strolled through the motor court.
"Did you see how much smokes are?" Richie pointed in the general direction of the vending machine situated between the coke machine and the ice maker. Behind the glass were packs stacked high above rows of metal pull-knobs—all the brand names: Pall Mall, Salem, Benson & Hedges, Winston, Marlboro, printed on placards with the price: $1.00.
Richie and I had skipped lunch for the entire last week of school after hearing rumors about the price of cigarettes in Florida. It was more than twice the forty-five cents we were used to paying. With the extra change we saved, we managed to stash away enough hard packs of Marlboro Menthols in our suitcases to get us through the week.

The streetlights warmed up as the day faded. Just as we thought we would slip away, a tiny voice caught us from behind. "Can I come with y'all?"

What choice was there now? Like it or not, my baby sister was tagging along. Still, I had to make her think it was a privilege. I set some ground rules. "Yeah, but you can't breathe a word to Mom."

"I swear."

I lit a cigarette, adding, "And no, you can't have one."

We had barely left the motor court when Richie spotted a frog. Cigarette dangling from his lips, he freed his hands to snatch it off the pavement.

Seeing them everywhere, we caught all we could get our hands on. Within a hundred yards of our motel wasn't a safe place to be if you were a frog. They weren't big, but they were abundant. We found an empty plastic gallon ice cream container, poked holes in the lid, and put Kristi in charge of it. Our hands had to be free to smoke while we caught more. After a thorough scouring of the nearby streets, the well was over half full. And then we realized we had no idea what to do with our captives.

Richie pulled one out, slinging it high into the air. We couldn't follow its flight pattern against the dark backdrop of the night sky, locating its landing spot only by the disgusting sound of the splat, accompanied by a last dying croak. We found this morbidly amusing, taking turns at launching the helpless amphibians one by one to their imminent deaths.

Richie hurled a frog in the general direction of a neighboring two-story motel. I couldn't say if it was a good shot because I didn't know what he was aiming for. What he hit was a door on the upper level. *Splat!* Certain someone would surely answer what they had perceived as a knock, we fled. Back at our swimming pool, we released the remaining evidence into the chlorinated water, threw the bucket into the dumpster, and called it a night.

Lying in bed on our last night in Clearwater, I was nursing wicked sunburn. My feet were swollen so bad I could no longer wear shoes. Mid-week we had charted a boat on a half-day, deep-sea fishing excursion out in the Gulf of Mexico. Blaine said if it weren't for the fish, he'd be catching nothing. I snagged a red grouper while the sun

## The Quiet Kid

was baking my feet. The remainder of the week, I had to wear tube socks under my flip-flops.

Drifting in and out of sleep, I replayed the week in my head. I thought about the west coasters we had met on the beach, still trying in my head to emulate their surfer speak. I was hoping to catch one last glimpse of the ocean in the morning before we left.

Instead of waking to the morning sun, a mysterious flashing red beacon stirred my slumber. The intensity of its brightness was overwhelming. I rubbed my eyes, trying to get oriented. And then one sobering detail hit me. There were no other lights on anywhere. It was downright eerie. Kristi and Richie woke up as well, and we slipped outside. The scene at the street was surreal. Complete darkness was intermittently disrupted by the flashing strobe of the red light from a police cruiser. They were taking the driver of a long, white Cadillac into custody. The Caddy had mowed completely through a power pole. Somehow, the driver had survived the impact. The car hovered a foot off the ground, mounted on top of the wooden pole like a trophy, the top section of the pole an oversized hood ornament, suspended from the power lines. It came as no surprise when we learned the driver was inebriated. It was probably the reason he came through uninjured. After all the excitement, it was difficult to fall asleep. But eventually, R.E.M. came, and the red lights faded.

# 31. Bobbi Spencer

It was late in the day. My shadow elongated, almost reaching the creek. I was sitting in a swing at the park, still thinking about Clearwater—still thinking about Shirley. Voices carried from the bridge. I knew they were smoking, or from the volume, drinking—or possibly both. I really didn't care. I hadn't come for the party. I just wanted to be by myself. Exerting little effort, I stretched my legs, pushing the swing back a few feet, and then let momentum take over, dragging my toes in the dirt as I swung forward.

I heard two voices coming closer, singing *The Ballad of Curtis Loew*,[19] in no way resembling anything remotely close to harmony.

*Mark Price.*

Even in the dim light, his blonde hair gave off plenty of feedback. He was staggering arm in arm with some girl. They were both obviously drunk. When I looked closer, I recognized the girl. She had been to my house before with Sherry.

Bobbi Spencer was a friend of my older sister's. Her reputation spread thighs wide throughout South Knoxville. In an instant, I decided. She was the one—an easy mark. She had been friendly to me already. She was cute, maybe a little slutty, but cute, and best of all, I had absolutely no interest in any kind of long-term relationship. There was only one thing I needed from her. *She's perfect.*

From somewhere behind me, the sun made one last peep for the evening. And then it started to get dark.

The shade of Laura McNeil's front porch was a good escape from the heat of July. The humidity was low, so it wasn't all that bad, but we'd worked up a sweat walking back from the river park. We had just smoked a couple of jays. "You're only with her for one thing, right?"

I knew she was talking about Bobbi. I'd done my best to skirt the subject up until then, and my first instinct was to deny it. But the idea that I wanted anything other was even more repulsive. Besides, she would've seen right through me. "Yeah."

"You could do so much better, ya know," she said.

Everyone knew Bobbi was a free pass. What could I say? I couldn't explain, even though she probably had a good idea why. I felt sure Amber had told her something. But even if she'd understood, she didn't know the obstacles I'd encountered along the way. She didn't

## The Quiet Kid

know the dead-end streets I'd been down, only to meet another brick wall. Nor could she see as clearly as I that this was the quickest, most efficient solution to my dilemma, and probably the least painful. *As long as Bobbi doesn't give me the crabs.*

I was just ready to get it over with and move on. "Maybe so."

Even Don Lance was saying I should leave it alone. But I was through wasting time. We camped out in my backyard. Sometime after 1:00 a.m., Bobbi showed up. Maybe she was sober. Maybe not. Don Lance might've been asleep or at least pretending he was. I no longer cared on either point. Bobbi crawled into my sleeping bag. "Ball me," she said. And without further ado, we did the deed. It would be the only time. I felt no need for an encore.

I scratched an imaginary itch for two weeks after, like you'd do if someone mentioned a case of head lice that was going around. It passed without the aid of penicillin, and I put it behind me.

Mission accomplished.

# 32. Control

After Bobbi Spencer, you would have thought Amber and I would be straight. The score was tied one to one. We were even. Now we could move on.

Forget about it.

It was never enough. I had learned how easy it was to leave Amber standing there holding the bridle. Once I had been set free to run wild, why should I come back into the stable? Except to be fed, stroked, and pampered.

We got back together. I still remember the date. It was one of those dates she earmarked, scribbling it down when she signed my next yearbook, making sure I would never forget. August 2nd, 1975. I knew we were getting back together. I invited her to the Mountainside Theatre to see Unto These Hills with my family.

Cherokee, North Carolina nights, even in the mountains, were warm enough to go without a jacket. Amber's eyes were highlighted powder blue in contrast to her body-hugging hot pink shirt. Even in the low light of dusk, the tight-fitting apparel did its job, exemplifying every line and exaggerating the imminent excitement around every curve. We were on the back row of the amphitheater's semi-circular seating, which stepped down to the action. While everyone else was deeply engrossed in the drama unfolding at center stage, Amber rested her head on my shoulder, whispering softly enough that only I could hear.

"I understand, babe," she said. "You did what you had to. But it's okay now."

"Then, you will?" I had asked her for a second time to "go" with me.

"Of course, I will. Ya think I've been waitin' all this time for nothin'?"

I looked at her and smiled. She smiled back, her blue eyes full of dreams.

She had me back, and things were copasetic, at least for a while. Amber had given me something I should never have had. Control. She had surrendered her will, thrown up the white flag, and said come take it all, heart, mind, body, and soul. Everything she had and everything she was belonged to me now. I wanted it all. The

## The Quiet Kid

amount of control I was given should have been unlawful. Donny Rupe had said she would do anything for me. I had no idea.

If we were in a crowd and her talking grabbed too much of someone else's attention, I cleared my throat. That was all it took. She learned quickly to pick up on my signals. If she wanted to engage in some social activity that I wasn't in compliance with, all I needed to do was pull out the "how much do you love me" card. My ace in the hole. The same card I played whenever I wanted something from her. The field was wide open for me, no longer a level field of play. I could take it whenever I wanted, while she remained on the sidelines. She always remained faithful. No individual should be allowed control over the will of another. It would turn out to be a hard habit to break.

My insecurity didn't help matters. What I was unable to achieve socially, I could now manipulate in Amber. Somehow, this secured something in me. I was the quiet kid, the one about whom everyone said: *I wish I could have gotten to know you better,* or *Maybe if we had more classes together we could have gotten closer* or, *To a really nice guy, if only you would talk more,* when they signed my yearbook. I was so self-conscious. If I tried to answer a question in class, I immediately became terrified at the sound of my own voice. It was easier for me to find an individual or two I felt comfortable with and avoid speaking in the presence of a crowd. To me, three or four people constituted a crowd. If there were more than that, I would withdraw, intimidated by—what?—The threat of judgment or scrutiny?

And then along came Amber: a cute, sweet innocent who was completely devoted, willing to do anything for me, whenever I wanted. If I was the Earth, then she was the Moon, held in orbit by the pull of my gravity. She had become my possession. My own personal puppet on a string, ready when I decided it was time to pull her out of the box to perform, waiting quietly for whenever I decided it was time to come out and play.

# 33. A Quiet Rebellion

Summer was over. I wasn't ready to be back in school yet. Something in the order of rebellion was needed to demonstrate my resistance. On a Wednesday afternoon, I rode with my Aunt Angie after school, staying at her house while Mom was still at work.

Angie and Jackie Pratt ambled as slow as humanly possible, sloths on Sunday, in no hurry, shuffling their feet with the ragged hems of their bell-bottoms sweeping the floor.

*Swish. Swish. Swish. Swish.*

Angie must've drawn some twisted pleasure from tormenting her mom (my Mamaw), making her wait. By the time we got to Angie's locker, the halls were empty. By the time we finally arrived at the rear parking lot, it was a virtual ghost town. Poor Alta Scarlett was waiting with saintly patience in her little beige AMC Gremlin.

Angie wanted to smoke a bowl of hash in her bedroom.
"Seriously?"
Dad was waiting out in the living room.
"Seriously. He'll wait. It'll only take a minute. Two hits. That's all you'll need. C'mon Michael. You know you want to."
I thought she was nuts. But I grew up playing with this girl, pretending to be monkeys in the zoo behind the metal bars of the headboard of Mamaw and Papaw's bed. Giant kosher dill pickles were our bananas. How could I not trust her? So, we opened the windows, lit some sandalwood incense, and put the fire in the hole.
On the ride home, it occurred to me that it didn't take much to fly under Dad's radar. He was either oblivious, or it just didn't matter to him.

Friday, we were once again floating on cloud nine. Angie offered to pierce my ear—a snack to feed the growling tummy of my rebellion. We had plenty of time before Dad was due. If I could conceal my bare feet under bell-bottom jeans all day long at school, I should have no problem hiding an earring from my parents underneath my long hair. Angie sterilized a sewing needle over a match flame and then poked it through my ear lobe into an ice cube, quickly replacing the needle with a gold post earring.
I got it past the old lady without incident.

## The Quiet Kid

The next morning wasn't bright or early, but when I finally rolled out of bed, I took care of only the necessary. I cooked an egg sandwich the way Sherry did: Break the yolk, salt, and pepper, flip it, a slice of American cheese melted over the top, and slap it between two slices of white bread, mayo on both sides. I scarfed it, brushed my teeth, and then set a course for the park.

I wasn't even halfway down my street when Alan Morton intercepted me. His maroon VW Beetle screeched to a halt in the intersection of Hackman and Berea. He bailed out, guitar in hand, leaving the door open and the engine puttering in park. His foot propped up on the rear bumper created a rest for the acoustic guitar. Stretched tight, the faded denim of his jeans strained to hold itself together around a bare kneecap.

"You gotta hear this, man. I just figured it out!"

I was mesmerized, watching his fingers walking the frets. Each knew where to be and exactly when they should be there. Every single hammer on and pull off flawlessly synchronized with the deftness of his picking right hand. Every note played perfectly from the rambling intro to the familiar string slapping chord progression of Pure Prairie League's, *Amie*.

"That's too cool, man. You gotta teach me sometime."

"Yeah, man. Hey. I'm headin' over to the Pratt's. You wanna come?" He did a double-clutch with his eyebrows, raising them like a precursor to a wink. "There's gonna be some killer smoke."

"Like I got somethin' better to do."

We jumped in his car and sped away with the windows down, our freak flags flying[20] in the last warm wind of late summer.

Jackie Pratt opened the door to greet us as we were climbing the stairs. "Hey, stranger," she said to me. She tucked a kinky strand of thick brown hair behind one ear, squinting at the sun, leaving only one blue eye open to see through. "C'mon in."

We entered the cosmic décor of the party room above the garage: hanging tapestries with moons, stars, and smiling ceramic suns. Janis was working on a pile of buds scattered out on a coffee table, her face hidden by long, straight curtains of strawberry blonde.

"Look what I picked up on the side of the road," Alan said.

"Oh, hey. If it isn't the little runaway." Janis was in my grade.

She smiled when she looked up through sea-green eyes. Those eyes, enormous and brooding, left no doubt she was Jackie's sister.

Janis packed a bowl attached to an apparatus that resembled a gas mask and then demonstrated its use. She torched the bowl, removing the mask promptly.

"Damn." Janis strained at the smoke she was choking back, water welling up from her eyes.

She handed the contraption to me. Her cheeks puffed out like Louis Armstrong's as she held in her hit. I strapped on the mask, lit the bowl, and found out why Janis had had to remove it so quickly. The smoke completely took over. The original design was to keep noxious gases out. The smoke wasn't lethal, but a bit overpowering.

I was holding back fine until Janis started laughing at me. I lost it, sputtering and laughing and then coughing out enough smoke to get everybody high. We were laughing at each other. Alan and Jackie were laughing at us.

Their turn was coming.

"Get this thing away from me." I was shaking my head as I handed it off to Alan.

After we'd had a few rounds, Jackie fetched a silver tray with four tall glasses of iced water. A little pile of red capsules was in the middle. "The Red Hots are the house special. Today only," she offered. Popping one in her mouth, she washed it down with big gulps.

Janis and Alan grabbed one each, so I thought *why not* and picked one off the tray, reading the tiny white letters on the coated capsule—*Placidyl*—just before I swallowed it.

Putting the gas mask away for another day, we passed a couple of joints. From there, things got a little fuzzy. Jackie went to turn the volume up on the stereo. *Jackie Blue.*[21]

She swirled around the room in a circle, a glowing streak of orange trailing her cigarette like a comet's tail.

There would have been only one way of knowing how much time had passed when I strolled by the park, and I didn't have a watch. The Placidyl was in full bloom. Observing the crowd gathered on the hillside, I had to investigate. Besides, I was in no condition to go home. So, I navigated the slope as best as I was able, planting myself in the grass when the need to go farther was no longer expedient.

Angie was there. This was yet another unusual event highlighting my day. She spotted me staggering to a near crash-landing. I parked in the grass, leaning on one elbow like I was posing.

"Steve!" She said. "Where've you been?"

I thought of looking behind me, but even in my drug-induced frame of mind, I could tell she was looking directly at me.

I just happened to be wearing a T-shirt with a Superman "S" emblem. Having yet to make the connection, I stared at her in a haze of confusion.

"Where's your shoelaces, Steve?"

Two and two finally equaled four, and I concluded that she was screwing with me. But finding it difficult to formulate a reasonable response, I looked at my shoes, and then back at her. "My shoelaces are fine. Who the heck is Steve?"

"You're Steve. Look, your initial is right there." She pointed at my shirt as if it was proof.

I looked at the "S", contemplating the legitimacy of her claim and then realizing with no uncertainty who I was, looked back at her, standing my ground (in reality, lying on it). "I'm not Steve. You know who I am." When I made this assertion, I might've been slurring my words a little. I tucked my hair behind my ears, unveiling something that had managed to remain hidden throughout the course of the day.

"You're bleeding." Angie leaned in to examine it, but I recoiled in suspicion. "No, really, your ear is bleeding," she insisted.

Instinctively, I felt the ear that had been pierced the day before. Startled at the absence of the little round post, I rubbed my thumb over the spot where it should have been until I detected an unusual swelling within the lobe of my ear. In my state of mind, the process of putting two and two together again took a little longer than it should have. But ultimately, the pieces of the equation fell into place. I had slept on my left side, and the ball of the earring had worked itself inside my earlobe while I was sleeping. Stumbling upon this revelation, I did what seemed logical. Reaching behind my ear, I located the backing and yanked the orb through the fleshy lobe. The drugs prevented any sensation of pain. I handed the earring back to its original owner.

Angie winced, reacting to the pain I should've felt. She then commenced her teasing, questioning the whereabouts of my shoelaces, and continued to refer to me as Steve. At some point, I crashed, awakening to the chatter of my peers who were still scattered about on the side of the hill next to the swings. I had no idea how long I had been out.

"Hey, look. It's sleepin' beauty. Glad to see you're still with us."

I turned my head to locate Hurley. Dusk was approaching.

"Oh, man, I should get home."

"Bad idea, Scarlett," Hurley said. "You're effed up, six ways from Sunday. Why don't you come to the house with me fer a while? You ain't in no shape fer goin' home."

I was in pretty good shape at this point, having slept off the brunt of the drug's effect. But I sensed his discretion. Plus, he winked. *He probably has weed.* He didn't want anyone else to know. Not that he was stingy. There were just too many heads.

"Can I come?" Edwina was also being discreet, having picked up on our agenda. She was petite, blonde, and way cute, so naturally, Hurley said okay, and away we went.

At Hurley's, we smoked a couple of fat doobies in the basement and then moved out to the backyard to smoke cigarettes. I started thinking about Amber, and I decided it was time to call her.

I was walking out to the road when Edwina's delicate fingers on my arm gave me a start. I hadn't realized she had followed me. "Do you really have to rush off?"

"I, um ...."

She was blunt, not leaving me much space for responding. "We should get to know each other better. Hurley said we could use the waterbed."

Caught off guard, I considered for a moment, looking her over. She was tiny, but still, she had plenty to offer. *She's got that sexy librarian thing going on.* Enticing, in gold-rimmed glasses, like something I'd seen in a magazine. I wanted to take her up on her offer. But then Amber flashed through my head, a visual of her in that tight, hot pink shirt. I thought of things we had done as recently as the past weekend. Much of it started on the very waterbed where Winna was now beckoning me. Even I was astonished at my sudden desire to do right by Amber. She was probably at home waiting by the phone.

Still, another part of me couldn't quite close the door. "I'm gonna hafta take a rain check."

Holding my breath, I turned to go, hoping she wouldn't pursue the matter further. I wasn't sure that I could say no twice. I never looked back. Edwina let it go.

When I got home, the old lady caught me red-eyed. I had forgotten the Visine. She grounded me for two weeks. Ironically, she permitted me to go to Ian's house every day for an hour. Mom trusted him. Ian hadn't reached the same conclusion as the rest of the Baptist faith. In his mind, marijuana was not the devil's weed. The hour I had been granted was plenty of time to get completely baked. Wintergreen Certs and Visine was all I needed to keep her suspicions at bay.

# 34. Grounded

Invisible beyond the reflection on the glass, I waited for Amber to open the door. Knowing her mom wouldn't drive away until she had entered the building, I backed up far enough to maintain stealth. Then we were off to the auditorium.

The week I was grounded, I spent an hour after school at Ian's and at least two on the phone with Amber. After a couple of days, the limitation of our physical contact was making me crazy. Finding a solution was only a matter of time.

My old lady had to drop me off before she went to work, so I was at school early every day. Most of the faculty didn't arrive for another half hour. Amber convinced her mom to bring her to school earlier as well.

There were no windows in the auditorium at South High School. All the lights were off. A sliver of illumination sliced the blackness, expanding over the rows of seats as we opened the back door. We only had a few seconds to see our way to the side aisle, moving quickly before the shaft of light diminished and was swallowed up on the other side of a massive *ka-chunk* when the latch hit the strike plate. Using the backs of the chairs as our only guide, we maneuvered down toward the front of the auditorium. The doors by the right side of the stage led to the main hallway via a secondary passage. By way of previous investigation, I knew those doors to be padlocked with a chain securing the handles in the middle. The double doors on the left, our destination, opened to a tiny vestibule and another set of doors which were locked to the world outside. There was no doubt we would have been alerted by the opening of the only unsecured door well before anyone could get to us or even suspect we were there. And by then, we would've been long gone, having already slipped outside. We didn't need much space. The limited confine of the tiny vestibule was enough.

This became our daily ritual, after which I often departed in search of the morning buzz. Amber stayed behind most of the time. As the year progressed and it got cold, I would meet her again, afterward, down by the shop classes where the rising heat from the radiators would lift the incriminating smell that permeated my coat.

Faithfulness had become part of our relationship once again, at least for a while. In the back of my mind, however, the thought lingered that other opportunities would present themselves down the road. But how could I not come back for more of what she was giving me? Amber was very giving. I think she took great comfort in knowing she was keeping me around for yet another day. Which begs the question: Who was really in control?

# 35. Busted on the Bus

We were in the back of the pep bus, returning to school late on a Friday after a football game. I was with Don Colter and a couple of the other village idiots. Jerry Harris, the art teacher, was our bus chaperon that night. He wasn't the only male teacher in school with hair that was almost as long as ours. Everyone had long hair. But there was something decisively different about him, and it wasn't just the mustache and the beard. The environment in his class suggested a freer spirit. When he handed out assignments, he could care less if students sat on the tables. He allowed us to listen to music. He even encouraged us to bring our own. Whatever we wanted. Where most teachers seemed to want control of our thought process until it fit into a nice, neat little package on which they could stamp their approval, Jerry seemed to thrive on the very opposite. It was almost as if he wanted us to think for ourselves, make our own choices, decide who we should be, and let the world conform to us.

Boredom in my other classes had revealed a talent I didn't know I possessed. I started sketching on notebook paper, convincing likenesses of some of my favorite rock stars: Robert Plant, Bruce Springsteen, Elton John. Prompted by this, I signed up for art class. Having Jerry as a teacher had been an unexpected bonus. He had shown great enthusiasm and encouragement at my watercolor painting of candy bar wrappers. An incorrigible case of the munchies had supplied the daily inspiration.

Having us on the back of his bus would prove to be something Jerry hadn't signed up for. We judged him to be cool and started placing bets as to whether he smoked weed. The consensus was yes. Someone got the bright idea that if we opened the windows, we could fire up a joint, and all the smoke would blow out. Wrong! It wasn't long before all the jocks on board were gagging and complaining about the smell, as if we were poisoning them with toxic gas.

Poor Harris. We had put him in quite a predicament. Having given him no other option, he told the driver to stop the bus. The joint flew out the window while we were still moving. We weren't *that* stupid.

Harris marched to the back of the bus. We had expected him to be on our side, but we had forced him into the opposing corner. "What in the world do you think you're doing?" He paused when he

## The Quiet Kid

noticed me slunk down in the seat. "And you! What are you doing with this bunch of hooligans?"

It was a rhetorical question that sent me reeling, searching at a thousand possible answers. Dumbfounded, I held my tongue.

Harris was plenty sore, and he let us know it. He stormed off the bus to hold a conference with the principal of the school, who was on the bus behind ours. We watched Edward Skye—aka Colonel Clink—and Harris conversing outside, wishing the clouds of breath in the cold would carry their voices through the foggy windows. Five or ten minutes—eternity—dragged by, and finally, they parted. Clink walked slowly back to board his bus. Harris re-boarded ours. Then we were back on the road without another word.

We were nervous as Andy Kaufman on amphetamines about what was going to happen. *What did Harris tell him? Would we get suspended? Would we be expelled?* The suspense was killing us.

In the middle of this dilemma, I barely noticed when this little skank with a red Brillo head, snuggled up to me, trying to get me to unwind. I didn't even like her. I found her about as attractive as a zit on a baboon's butt. When she took the situation in hand under the cover of my coat, I couldn't bring myself to shoo her away. That was as far as I intended to let her take it. The second the bus doors opened in the school parking lot, I bailed. Getting away from her as quickly as possible, I caught a ride with the Colter brothers. They laughed about it all the way home. Immediately following the regrettable incident, I issued myself an imaginary restraining order, which stated that I stay a minimum of fifty yards away from Brillo Red at all times.

Amber was one of those rare children who learned to share at a young age. She found the latter part of this episode amusing, although she was more than a little concerned about the possibility of me getting expelled.

When we were called into Clink's office on Monday, we thought for sure we were goners. We fully expected to be kicked out for smoking dope. But being Mr. Oblivious as he tended to be, Colonel Clink bought the story Harris had fed him, hook, line, and sinker. We were burning incense on the bus. Can you believe it? That Harris was a clever one. He made sure we were scared enough that we wouldn't be so stupid again without landing us any real trouble. We all promised it would never happen again and got off with only a warning. We're still laughing about that one.

If it hadn't been for Clink's assistant Principal Bill Cuniff and his crooked finger, which he was always pointing in our direction, the whole school would have been lined up at the gates of Hell, waiting for our hand baskets. Good ol' Cuniff. We had a little ditty we sang about him to the tune of *Folsom Prison Blues*.

*Here comes big Cuniff*
*He's comin' down the hall*
*He's got a great big paddle*
*And he's gonna bust your ...*

# 36. Halloween 1975

I was hanging out at the park with the King Brothers. Three or four other heads were there occupying the bridge. None of us had any weed. No one had alcohol. It was Halloween, and we had nothing. Zero. Zilch. Nada. Boredom levels were peaking. That's the only rational explanation for what happened next.

A single lamppost illuminated the backyard of the closest neighbor. It must have annoyed Jimmy King. He hopped the fence. It was one of those short, wire fences, barely over three feet high. Saying he hopped it was a stretch. It was more like a high step. Anyway, he proceeded to smash the globe of the lamppost. The glass shattered, extinguishing the light.

He returned, hee-hawing, so proud of himself for what he'd done. *Moron.*

Shirley Wilson wandered upon us aimlessly. Her body was in our midst, but her mind was elsewhere. She had flown to a distant planet, trailing the odor of airplane glue in her wake. None of the rest of us could reach her there, but we were all trying to help guide her back safely. That was when the worst possible scenario—outside of her permanently losing her mental cohesiveness, or worse yet, dying on us—happened.

The cops showed up. Their squad car glided straight down the hill across the grass, almost to the bridge. Everyone scattered. Shirley was completely frozen, unable to move. Being straight as an arrow at the time, I had the presence of mind to realize I had no reason to run. I had done nothing wrong. So, I stayed on the bridge with her. When the men in blue blinded us with their flashlights and their authority, I pointed them toward McClung, away from the woods, where the suspects had fled. The cops were unsuspicious of us. After all, we hadn't left the scene. The officers got in the squad car and sped away.

I remained there with Shirley, talking her down. It wasn't long before the toxic fumes from the glue loosened their grip, and she started making sensible conversation again. If ever I had carried out a heroic act, that was it. I stayed when she needed someone, and everyone else had run away. Our friendship was sealed with that deed. When Shirley had come back down to earth, she thanked me with a kiss.

Okay. I made that part up.

# 37. Blaine

Blaine Freeman had the issue of Playboy featuring a spread of Bridgett Bardot. He also possessed a link between the jocks and the freaks, fitting in with both crowds as if he was unaware there was even a difference. Maybe there wasn't. Maybe the difference existed only in the insecurities that fed our still-developing brains.

Case in point: Blaine was dating Sara Lionheart, who fell into the sect classified as jock. Sara's sister, Linda, was in a class all her own, but most definitely not the one that collected school letters on their jackets. Perhaps it was due to a sisterly spat, or maybe just a need to be righteous or, who knows? Maybe she was genuinely concerned for her sister's well-being. Whatever the case, Sara was contemplating leaking some news of dire consequences to the patriarch of the family. Linda had at that moment in time, a pound of marijuana stashed in a secret compartment underneath her waterbed. As was the case in the lives of most teenagers, there existed a need to confide matters of such importance to one's peers before the involvement of parents, who everyone knew could never be totally trusted. Sara shared her secret as well as her impending intentions with her boyfriend. Blaine, in turn, having no prior relationship with her, but having a general responsibility to the pot-smoking community at large, alerted Linda.

Linda's initial reaction to Blaine's approach had been something like this. "Whatta you want, bang boy?"

She addressed him this way due to his incessant habit of fluffing back his bangs, which were like asymmetric wings divided by the part at the center of his hair. And maybe a little because she was cynical toward the world in general, especially the part of it that had yet to prove its worthiness.

Linda's view of social status was altered when Blaine informed her of the potential narc residing underneath the same roof. Of course, Linda was eternally grateful and relocated her substantial stash to a safer haven.

I took Amber to see Black Oak Arkansas opening for Foghat. Blaine was the fifth wheel. Blaine and I were a foot taller than Amber in our six-inch platform shoes. After the show, Blaine had a close call, nearly tumbling headlong down the steep concrete steps

## The Quiet Kid

from the upper balcony of the Knoxville Civic Coliseum. As far as I knew, he hadn't been doing anything other than smoking pot. But we did smoke a lot of it.

"Whoa!" Blaine's arms flailed wildly, trying to catch his balance as he teetered forward.

Amber reached out, and calmly pulled him back by the sleeve of his jacket. She was the smart one and had only smoked a little.

"Thanks," Blaine said, stopping to fluff back his bangs.

"No problem."

"I hate to think what would'a happened if you didn't catch me." Blaine continued to lead us down the steps, taking greater care, and watching his feet.

"You'da been a bloody heap down on the floor," I quipped.

He turned around at the bottom, flashing a grin that displayed his overbite. "You got that right, brotha."

Blaine had found his way there but needed a ride home. We needed to locate an unengaged pay phone. This was often difficult after concerts, so we walked to the Hyatt Regency to call my mom. As a bonus, we could ride the glass elevators for a rush and a unique view of downtown, killing some time while we waited.

Another perk of this visit was the generous scattering of glass ashtrays with the Hyatt logo. I had noticed them before, one for every pay phone stall. I planned on picking one up this time. Sherry had gotten me started with this little endeavor into kleptomania when she brought back a couple of glass souvenirs from out west: an ashtray from Harrah's in Reno, Nevada, and another from Northstar at Tahoe. Since then, I had garnered some cheap additions from Arby's, Burger King, McDonald's, Western Sizzler, and Holiday Inn. The Gaylord Opryland Hotel ashtray was the only name of exceptional superiority in my stash. The Hyatt was about to give my little collection an upgrade.

The Hyatt Regency Hotel was directly across Hill Avenue on the south end of the coliseum. Bands that performed at the coliseum usually stayed there before being hustled away the next morning en route to their next gig.

Trudging up the grass embankment seemed an impossible task when looking up, barely seeing the tiered glass and concrete façade of the hotel beyond. I dug my feet in sideways. Amber, again the smart one in tennis shoes, tugged at my hand. Blaine followed my lead on a sidelong course and managed without the assist.

The three amigos (Amber with her two artificially elevated escorts), strolled into the outer lobby. I picked up the receiver and dropped a dime in the slot but froze before I could dial the number. A black stretch limousine pulled up outside. The chauffeur opened the door for three huge men in black suits, obviously bodyguards. They stood at attention with their hands clasped in front of their crotches, guarding the emergence of a fourth male who had a long mane of golden hair that was almost white. His white platform boots came up just under his kneecaps. His pants were also white and were extremely tight—a stretchy material which almost appeared to be painted on—obviously to enhance the package he was toting for all his swooning female fans. From a distance, he might've been mistaken for a steed-less Lady Godiva. But closer examination revealed the flatness of his bare chest and the blonde patch of hair at his breastplate.

Flanked in a triangle of walking mountains in Armani suits, he strutted through the door that was being held open for his entry.

"How ya'll doin' tonight?" he said casually, as if he knew us, his voice sounding like he had been gargling sandpaper. It was hard to imagine his voice staying in key and actually carrying a tune, but only a couple of hours earlier, that voice had indeed belted out the band's encore, accompanied by Ruby Starr. It nearly brought down the house and gave the headlining Foghat the difficult task of following them.

We stood in silence for a moment, star stuck, until at last, Blaine broke the ice. "Was that Jim Dandy?"

It was a rhetorical question. We all knew who it was.

He had strutted back and forth on stage like a Banty rooster, making a percussion instrument out of a steel washboard and thimbles, on *When Electricity Came to Arkansas*.[22] Looking wild eyed and half crazy, he made his declaration about the sanity of mankind. This drew rousing applause, accompanied by rebel yells, just before he breathed a raspy fire into *Mutants of the Monster*.[23] He had just ambled through, addressing us like we were some of his not too distant kin.

## The Quiet Kid

After I made the phone call, I pulled Amber close, securing what was mine. We made a quick ride to the top floor, snatching a souvenir for my collection along the way. Upon returning to ground level, a hotel employee approached us, politely asking the number of our room. Not bothering to answer, we walked away as quickly as we could (there was no point in trying to run in those awkward shoes) toward the front exit. Already having taken everything we needed from the establishment, there was no point in hanging around. We skated sideways, gouging our way down the hill back onto paved level ground.

Amber thought Blaine was quite the gentleman; she told me later. Where a lot of guys, even my closer friends, might have made crude remarks or unseemly jokes, Blaine always treated her with the utmost respect. In his eyes, she was a lady. He had even held the door for her on several occasions the night of the concert. Chivalry was not dead. A hint of jealousy crept in. *Why?* Maybe she was expressing something about the way she liked to be treated. Maybe I should take notes and apply what I had learned for her benefit as well as my own. Besides, Blaine was always a standup guy. I knew the respect he displayed toward Amber was genuine, without ulterior motive. I should've probably thanked him for the tip.

# 38. LSD Part II

Angie always called my buddy Joe Cool, for reasons I could never quite figure. I don't know. Maybe I was a little envious that she hadn't bequeathed the moniker to me.

Whatever. I was staying all night at Joe Cool's, and we came in late after a night of looking for the party. His brother was sprawled out on a mattress on the floor of his basement bedroom. Noogy, focused on some faraway celestial universe beyond the ceiling, was unaware we had entered the room. He sat up quickly, once alerted to our presence. The pupils of his eyes were microscopic. He was tripping.

We lit cigarettes, and he began talking to us with surprising clarity. And then suddenly, as if his sanity had punched out and departed for the bar, he began writhing on the mattress, clutching his head behind his forearms, moaning. "Noooo ... noooo ... God, please make it stop."

We tried talking sense into him, but he completely ignored us. He seemed to have disconnected from us as if we'd left the room. And then, just as suddenly as it had started, it stopped. Noogy sat up, asked for another cigarette, and carried on a civil conversation ... for a while. It happened again. Seemingly without reason, he would momentarily lose his facilities and disappear to a place we were unable to reach.

It took us long enough, but we finally pinpointed the source of his anxiety. There was music playing on the stereo. It wasn't loud but definitely audible. The album Noogy had selected to set the tone of his trip was Black Sabbath's *Paranoid*. The stereo was set to repeat. The first three songs didn't present a threat to Noogy's fragile state of reason. But every time Ozzy growled, proclaiming he was *Iron Man*, it sent Noogy into a not so beautiful oblivion. We resolved the situation by changing the music, replacing his selection with *Houses of the Holy* side one.

The knowledge that external stimulus could dictate the internal effect on a person who was under the influence of LSD was a good thing to possess the night Sherry came home late, teetering on the edge of sanity.

For all I knew, she might have been seeing rainbow colors dripping from cracks in the paneled walls that only she was privy to. But much

## The Quiet Kid

like Noogy had been, Sherry seemed to have her wits about her … until the spiders arrived. They weren't on the floor or the walls or even at her feet. The only place the annoying little arachnids seemed to be was on her arms. No matter how vehemently she swept them away, she couldn't get them off.

The only connection I could make to a physical trigger was the current of air coming out of the vents whenever the AC kicked on. If I didn't get her outside, she was sure to awaken the old lady. And then the investigation would commence. Nobody wanted that. So, as quietly as humanly possible, I slid the glass door along its tracks, and we slinked into the backyard, up the hill away from Mom and Dad's bedroom and around the carport side of the house to the street. The second I instigated the diversion, the spiders went away.

We strolled down Hackman, taking a left at Berea.

"Where we goin'?" Sherry was too distracted to be concerned about an answer. Her eyes kept getting hung up on things, mailboxes reflecting the streetlights, a yellow fire hydrant, headlights lending anthropomorphic qualities to the parked cars. *Are they on? Are they off? Are they eyeballs?*

"Why do the cars have eyeballs?"

I had to keep tugging at her elbow to steer her in a forward direction.

"Doesn't matter," I said. "We're going on a little trip."

That made her laugh. "I'm already onna little trip." In her mind, I felt sure there was some secret double—double entendre beyond the obvious pun.

I led her to the corner where Mayfair turns to slope toward Island Home, and we sat down Indian-style on the pavement in the middle of the intersection. It was after 2:00 a.m. As long as we weren't causing a disturbance, no one would be up in our neighborhood for hours.

A slight breeze kicked up. The spiders began to crawl. I wondered if she actually saw them, or if it was just the sensation—the wind raising goosebumps that felt like a thousand tiny legs having their way with her fragile psyche.

"Sherry."

She didn't respond to her name. She just kept swatting.

"Sherry!" I repeated, a little louder than I wanted. She gave me a look that was somewhere between peeved and a little confused, like she wasn't sure that was her name. But I had her attention. "Can you blow some triple smoke rings for me?"

Many nights, when I waited up for her to come home, we would stay up and talk and smoke cigarettes. Sometimes we'd slip out the back door if one of us had a joint. On one of those nights, she had demonstrated her triple smoke ring trick. She would form an oval shape with her lips and roll a thick ring of smoke out slow, letting it hang in the air. The next one would come out with a little more force, passing through the first, hovering just inches beyond as they both lingered, beginning to spread. And then she would tighten the oval, snapping her jaw, propelling the third smoldering halo inside and beyond the other two rings before they disintegrated.

"If I had a cigarette." The spiders were gone now. She looked intently to see if I had one.

She had a pack of her own, but her thoughts were scattered and fleeting. And I had her attention. I offered her one of mine, taking one for myself, and then lit both of them with my BIC.

It was enough to occupy her mind for a while. I tried, failing miserably to imitate her skill. I was doing well if I got one with good form. She never managed more than two, one passing through the other. And every time the imagined eight-legged pests returned, we smoked and blew smoke rings, talking about whatever came to mind. To her, it didn't have to make sense. It just had to flag her attention.

Fortunately, the time at which she had dropped her hit (or hits, as the case may have been) had been significantly earlier than when she came home. We'd been out there for an hour or so. Sherry began to mellow, and I was convinced she was cool to go home. My only concern now was the possibility of the old lady with her keen intuition being wide awake and waiting for our return.

Much to my relief, the sentinel wasn't standing guard at the back door when we arrived.

I crashed, leaving Sherry alone with her random thoughts. She would come down soon enough, and I would see her sometime late, late in the afternoon.

# 39. Grade 9 and Summer

We were strutting around like shameless, senseless peacocks in dual zipper jeans, which lowered a flap, a drawbridge to the castle's business, rather than the single zip-fly opening. Neither of us was wearing a shirt, flaunting our summer tans and abdominal six-packs. Randy Tucker had a black mustache, and though it might not have been as thick as a full-fledged adult male's, it was impressive for a juvenile at the age of fifteen.

We had each just downed a quart of Schlitz Malt Liquor. Look out for the bull! We were feeling pretty good. The summer perfume of freshly mowed grass arose from the plush green outfield of Rock City Ball Park.

"Oh, crap!" Randy blurted.

I spotted the patrol car, which normally wouldn't have alarmed us.

Next to it stood Kyle.

In the politically correct terms of today, he would be referred to as mentally challenged. Some might use the term handicapped. Kyle was retarded. It means slow. Look it up. We were okay with that. We liked Kyle. The problem was that he believed himself to have been deputized into the Knox County Sheriff's department, a seemingly harmless fantasy indulged by the Andy Griffiths of the local police force.

It was too late to slip away. Our only hope was that the driver would find amusement from the comfort of his front seat, not getting involved enough to bring him in proximity with the smell of alcohol on our breaths.

"C'mere, bo'." Kyle said, unintentionally omitting the 'r' sound and cutting off the 'y' at the end of boy. All of his words sounded as if they were being slashed off slightly at the end. "I gone put yo tail in jail." He already had his handcuffs out, displaying them in the slap and clasp position.

Luckily, Kyle put them away. Instead of using them, he horse-collared Randy and attempted to shove him into the open back door of the patrol car. Randy's thin, soprano, girlish laughter as he struggled created unintentional comedy. Managing to slip out of Kyle's grasp, he sprinted just far enough to be safely out of range. We had never seen Kyle run for any reason.

"Come back here, bo'. I gone put yo tail in jail."

"Sha-za-am!" Dissecting the word into three syllables, Randy sounded more like Wayne Newton with his jewels in a vice than Captain Marvel. "That was too close for comfort!"

Still laughing, we practically fell through the front door of the Family Pantry. It was time for another quart and some Wintergreen Tic Tacs—just in case.

We were on our way to Chevy's house. Chevy – just like the automobile. Chevy, tall and slender, with the Brooke Shield eyebrows.

I knew her from the ball field. I flirted with her every chance I got in between hanging numbers on the metal sign in between innings. My dad had gotten me a job keeping score for girls' softball. I was at Maynard Glen Field nearly every night. There was more to it than just hanging numbers on the board. I had to keep up with all the stats—how the girls reached base, how the outs were made, by which position, and how the runs were scored—all recorded in my book. And then there were the cute little distractions running the baselines or bending over home plate for a handful of red dirt. But the distractions were what made the job what it was. Best job on the planet.

I had taken a liking to Chevy and broke up with Amber in pursuit of her.

The Tic Tacs were about as useful as black paint on tar paper. The way Chevy's mom chained smoked, she couldn't have smelled a joint if we'd lit it right in front of her on the back porch. She was always around when we arrived. We had stopped going to the front door. A white-haired version of Chevy, her mom, was aged by the sun, and the thousand years of cigarettes she had crammed into her lifetime by chain-smoking.

*I hope Chevy never gets that wrinkled.*

"Sha-vay-lah!" She hollered into the house. "Your friends are here!"

I wondered if that was her real name—Sha-vay-lah. And if so, how was it spelled, Chevella?

I had been dropping in on Chevy for nearly a month, sometimes with Randy, sometimes alone. Mostly we hung out on the porch and watched her mom, lighting another cigarette from the still burning cherry of the last one. "These things'll kill ya," Ms. Stone said as she

## The Quiet Kid

extinguished the smoldering butt into a mountainous stack growing out of a Frisbee-sized glass ashtray. "I'm tellin' ya. Y'all better quit before ya get like me."

I had taken my best shot with Chevy, but she wasn't having it, claiming loyalty to Amber. *But we broke up.* Didn't matter. Maybe she just didn't like me that way. So now we were just hanging out.

I wasn't complaining. Her mom was good company, and she never, ever let the conversation lag.

I guess I could've gotten back together with Amber, but what was the hurry? It seemed senseless with so much of summer remaining, to get entangled with the legality of being her boyfriend. Something else might come up. Now that Amber had passed her sixteenth birthday and the test for her driver's license, everything had just gotten easier. She was still waiting by the phone, ready to drive over at a moment's notice should the need arise.

A green flame burns eternally at Greenback Industries alongside highway 411. Or at least that's what we believed as kids. Kristi and I would look for it every time we passed it on the way to Vonore to visit our cousins. In Monroe County, Vonore was the equivalent of Mayberry with a post office, a general store, and an Esso station all within the same block of what was downtown. Glance down to change the radio station as you passed through, and you would probably miss it.

The youngest Stuart, Terry, was a year older than me—stocky with a full mop of hair the color of corn husks in wintertime with bangs whacked in a straight line across his forehead just above the eyebrows. His speech was unmistakably country. "Hell far." He'd say. East Tennessee slang that meant "Hell fire."

With little else to do, we'd often shut ourselves in his bedroom and sing along with Elvis, *In the Ghetto*, or Tennessee Ernie Ford's *Sixteen Tons*. In a way, he resembled Elvis when he did that sneer with his upper lip. Terry used to sing to the tune of Johnny Cash's Wreck of the Old '97, a song which is barely printable.

> *I was going down the road, making ninety miles an hour*
> *When the chain on my bicycle broke*
> *Well, I landed in the grass with the sprocket up my—*

You get the gist.
Not to leave a bad impression, Terry was also fond of singing this:

*One, two, three, the devil's after me*
*Four, five, six, he's always throwing sticks*
*Seven, eight, nine, he misses every time*
*Hallelujah, hallelujah, Amen*

That was before he obtained a driver's license.

By the summer of 1976, *KISS Alive!* was old news. In Podunk, USA, aka Vonore, it was the interior smell of a brand-new Camaro. I was at a great advantage, knowing every guitar lick and every power chord on the entire album. In the living room of some double-wide trailer in the middle of BFE, Terry's buddy, Mike, was smitten, trying to imitate my polished air guitar thrashing. Equally, enamored was a cute little fox-faced brunette by the name of Donna. As the evening progressed, it was brought to my attention that she'd been eying me from the moment I stepped through the door.

She was, as it turned out, as shy as me. But when I went outside to smoke a cigarette, she followed. Stars adorned the black blanket of the Monroe County night, sparkling in our eyes. To us, they were nameless. Neither of us knew anything beyond the universal constellation. After we had pointed out the Big Dipper, there wasn't much else to say. I pulled her close, and we followed the course of nature, engaging the parts of us that were otherwise useless.

Back inside, we sunk into the couch as one conglomerate blob. She wedged herself into my chest. We barely spoke the rest of the night, moving only to keep from disrupting the ever-circling flow of the joint, or to get another beer, to piss or just to reposition our hands. Our fingers were interlocked when my arm wasn't behind her shoulders. Once, when the joint passed from our communal possession, we took the opportunity to seal our faces together at the lips, only to draw more attention than either of us cared for, so we reserved the smooching for an occasional smoke break, outside, under the secretive, nameless stars.

It should've been awkward, but everyone was having such a good time. We listened to the irrelevant conversation—background noise—of the other four auxiliary souls in the room, strangely comfortable in our silent little igloo, hands clasped tight, melting into the couch.

"So, are you gonna do her, or what?" Terry asked on the drive home.

I laughed. "She's a sweet girl ... and cute, but really, when will I ever see her again?"

He was driving too fast on some dirt road in the middle of what could only be nowhere. The only thing existing in my world was whatever happened to be in the short field of the headlights. I never saw the turns before he steered into them, bouncing and swaying unavoidably, a little too tipsy to bother fighting against centrifugal force. More unexpected than the last curve, both of Terry's hands flew off the wheel, covering his face as his head arched backward. "Oh, crap!" He wailed, in sync with a *thump*! Something rolled up into the undercarriage. Instinctively, I grabbed the wheel if only to hold it steady. If there had been a need to turn, it wouldn't have mattered. My reaction time at its best would've been too late. And then Terry slowed, regaining possession of his faculties and the steering wheel.

"What?! What happened?"

"A rabbit. I hit a rabbit." Terry pulled over to gather himself.

"That was messed up."

"No, kiddin'. I didn't see the little bugger until it was too late."

We both stared straight out the windshield, catching our breath as if we had been running a marathon. As the aftershock wore off, the sound of our breathlessness became suddenly comical. Laughter erupted like spontaneous combustion.

Drying the tears from our cheeks, we settled in on the stars, which refused to stay in one place.

"What's that?" I pointed to a group of slow-moving lights that didn't appear to be following a straight line.

"It don't look a plane, does it?"

"Naw ..." As I spoke, the lights took a sudden dip and then hovered just above the horizon. It might have been moving forward slowly. It could've just been sitting still. From our vantage point, we couldn't tell if it was a mile away or a hundred. Our collective state of mind, chemically influenced as it was, didn't aid our already skewed judgment. Unexpectedly, as if whatever it was had been shot out of a catapult, it launched skyward, a reverse shooting star slicing through the darkness at an impossibly steep angle. And then it was gone.

"Whattaya think that was?" I already knew the answer.

"A UFO." Terry sounded stunned, emotionless as a corpse.

"Well, I sure as hell couldn't identify it."

"Let's smoke another joint."

"Might as well. We're here."

# 40. Ted

It was June 24, 1976.

We had limped past our second anniversary. Amber was elated. To her, the break-ups counted for nothing. "We're together now. That's what matters," she said, her powder blue eyes twinkling like the stars in Monroe County. "So, what if there are some gaps?" Our time together would soon be acknowledged again when the calendar page turned to August.

My weekend in Vonore had taken us beyond the official date. The girl I had met there was just the passing of a weekend, but that didn't matter either. We were celebrating June 11, our belated second anniversary. I was taking her to the Ted Nugent concert. Wait. Let's clarify. Amber had recently gotten her driver's license; therefore, she was taking me. She drove. I bought the tickets. Ted was playing the slot between Nazareth and The Ian Gillian Band. Nazareth was okay, Ian Gillain—who knew? I didn't care much about either of them. I was a huge fan of the Nuge. It was to be the first time I would see him performing live. If I had been wise, I would've recognized the omen, and it would've been the last.

Before the concert, I scored something called Angel Dust. It was a poor man's smack. I had never done it before, or smack either for that matter. The white powder I held in my possession was really nothing more than PCP, a tranquilizer used to sedate animals.

Not knowing what to expect from the drug, I opted for a seat instead of the normal crowd-wrestling affair by the stage. I wasn't taking any chances. Amber had no objections when I explained my strategy. She popped her gum and said, "Whatever you want," with her reassuring smile. As long as I was happy, she was happy.

A head taller in six-inch platform shoes, I gazed down over her wheat brown hair, perusing her body, taking my sweet time before reconnecting with her eyes. She never seemed to mind the visual inspection. I was thinking it would be nice not to be in the thick of the masses for a change.

"Come on." Our fingers intertwined, I led her through the crowd—somewhat sparse above the pit floor—ignoring the enticement of the popcorn vendors. There was no time for viewing programs or T-shirts as we made our way into the upper balcony, picking a spot in a section on the left side of the stage.

In E section, situated behind the knee wall above the vomitory, the line of vision was clear between the seating and the stage, free from the possibility of being obstructed by someone's fat head. Even if everyone stood up, straight ahead was nothing but a short railing. From our loft, we sat and watched the freak show filing in through the haze, which was already carrying the smell of high times. A tall, skinny dude with long, frizzy hair and a David Crosby mustache followed a girl with ebony hair chopped off in straight bangs, the top of her head barely making it above his waist. Groups of boys my age wore black T-shirts with Nazareth or Ted Nugent logos. Blonde foxes in halter tops bounced along on wooden platform shoes. Some guy with his chest bared probably wasn't going to make it through the opening act, judging from the path he was weaving. A Frisbee was making the rounds, sometimes sailing into the upper seating. Huge hoop earrings, sequins, and stars, psychedelic tie-dyed shirts, leather hats, feathers, ball caps, ripped jeans, and confederate flags. When the lights went down, the tiny flames of raised lighters broadcast their presence amongst the two-fingered whistles and rebel yells.

The view was great from where we were sitting, but until that night, I never noticed how horrible the acoustics were in the Knoxville Civic Coliseum. At the floor level, you didn't experience the echo bouncing through the upper structure like a yodel in the Swiss Alps. After the opening act, I slipped off to the restroom with a rolled-up dollar bill and a make-up mirror I'd borrowed from Amber to snort lines. It was time to find out what kind of devilry was in this Angel Dust. By the middle of Ted Nugent's set, I was beyond the point of no return.

I had never felt so helpless in all my life. Even on LSD, I had held onto a thread of coherency. It might've been as frail as a spider's web, but a connection with reality, nonetheless. That strand snapped with the animation of the concrete and steel structure around me. At first, it pulsated. Then it breathed, expanding as it sucked in oxygen, exhaling, compressing, constricting my breath. Gremlins hidden behind the columns conspired against me, slipping behind the seats, melting into the walls. They plotted to bring down the house, seeking to entomb me. The outer shell began to separate from the superstructure, rivets popping loose as the concrete skin pulled away from the supports.

When it drew breath, it drained the spirit from within me. When it exhaled, I could feel its crushing pressure. The steel support columns were shifting all around me, the concrete walls sliding off like the putrid hide of some rotting animal carcass, the skeleton caving in, threatening to bury me beneath a pile of debris. The volume of its respiration grew louder and louder. The droning echo in my head was no longer audible as music. *Stranglehold* became nothing more than an amplified *wah-wah-wah-wah*, over and over and over. I wanted it to go away. If there had been a ledge with a clear shot to the escape of death, I probably would've thrown myself off. I could no longer feel my arms and legs. My entire body went numb.

I've heard of people on PCP hurling themselves off the tops of buildings, plummeting to their deaths. The theories behind these incidents are always the same: They thought they could fly. I have a different theory.

Maybe they just wanted to make it stop.

Amber knew something was amiss. She had no idea how horribly wrong it was. Whatever I said to her was marred in a haze of incoherence. I wondered if I was speaking at all. She managed to keep me sane, her voice in my ear soothing me as I began to weep. I wanted to go home, but I was unable to even think about standing much less walk. I could barely move.

Amber prayed. The whisper drifting into my ear gave me hope. When I heard the name, Jesus, my faith stood at attention, like a German Shephard hearing a dog whistle. Now, I was anchored to the Rock, to the one solid foundation in a shifting world of intangibles. I asked Amber to help me stand. She did, and we stood there unsteadily for a moment, the three of us. She helped support me as we cascaded down the steep concrete stairs. On top of six-inch platform shoes, I had no sensation of my feet making contact with the ground. It felt like I was floating. Jesus had taken my hand and led me out onto the surface of the raging sea, calming the water as we walked. The building had stopped breathing. All was calm.

Everything after that was a blur. I had no clue as to how I got home or why Mom hadn't sniffed me out in my impossibly wasted condition. Maybe my angels had covered my tracks even in that.

I had stood before the whip master and endured the punishing scourge inflicted by the drug, made my bed, and slept in the blood-soaked sheets of remorse. The One who loved me most, my Deliverer, heard my cries and rescued me.

Don Lance didn't believe it.

"I was saved last night."

"How can you be sure?"

"Jesus was there, man. I'm tellin' you."

"Maybe you just imagined it. You were pretty high."

There was no convincing him. How could anyone be convinced? No one saw Him. No one else other than Amber and me had even known what was happening. If any bystanders happened to see us traversing the stairs, they might've taken notice for a moment. We were another case of some stoner not knowing his limits, like the shirtless guy I saw before the show started. It would've barely registered to them, an event of little significance. To the casual observer, it would've appeared Amber was supporting me, helping me stay erect. But she didn't possess the strength it would've required to prevent us both from toppling down the stairs. And I wasn't helping much. She knew He was there. She felt His presence as much as I did. It could've been angels. But we had called on His name. Jesus.

*Where two or three are gathered together in my name ...*[24]

To someone that wasn't a part of our gathering, there were probably a hundred logical explanations.

Don Lance's was the simplest. *Maybe you just imagined it.*

I knew better. I knew what I knew.

We were not alone that night.

# 41. South Young

South High School as we knew it was coming to an end. At the close of the school year, 1976, it would exist only as a junior high school and a memory, a ghost lingering in the cobwebbed corridors until our lives slowed down enough to reflect upon its haunting.

Construction had been completed on the new building, which would combine South and Young. The bitter rivalry between the South High Rockets and the Young High Yellow Jackets had been alive for a quarter of a century. We were all certain violence and bloodshed would ensue. Over the summer, we wondered what our new name would be. The Tigers? The Bobcats? The Scarlet Knights? The Warriors? We didn't even get to vote. When it was all said and done, it was decided we would be the Trojans.

The Trojans! They named us after a condom! We might as well have been the Love Gloves. If it was just a ploy, designed to distract us and keep us from bashing one another's skulls in, it worked. Young gave up its orange and black. South surrendered its red and white. The Trojan Man proudly hoisted a banner of blue and silver overhead. As far as I knew, no casualties were ever recorded as a result of the once heated rivalry.

New colors weren't the only change in the air. The Vietnam War, being over (in terms of U.S. military involvement) left a hippie with little to protest. Not that I was ever involved enough to protest. I was a clueless rebel—inspiration for a future Tom Petty song.[25]

Faded blue jeans with holes in the knees were being discarded for newer, darker blue denim with a lot less bell in the bottom. Some of the new flare leg jeans had double zippers in the front for easier access. If we stood for nothing else, we were still a nation of sluts, free love, and all that, just not as sloppy in our appearance. My hair was still long, but flannel shirts gave way to polo shirts – if I felt like dressing up, pseudo silk. The girls were dressing up more. Personally, I missed halter tops.

Some of this transition had transpired earlier, about the same time when Rock 'n' Roll began caving in under the pressure of commercialization. Rock 'n' Roll, having lost its sense of direction, was being replaced by over-polished industrialized crap and choked to death by disco. Imagine that: The Gibbs brothers kicking the snot out of Jimmy Page and Robert Plant and anyone else who cared to get in line.

Is there a point to all of this? Probably not. If anything, I felt like I had lost my way, roaming aimlessly past the bright orange, red, and pink lockers lining the halls of our new school. My sole purpose for existing had become the search for euphoric Utopia via mind-altering substances. In between, it was just making it through the school day, inching closer to the day I could put it in my rear-view mirror. I stood for nothing, insistent on wandering further and further down the path to nowhere. In my white shirt with red plaid laced in strands of silver, and adorned with mother of pearl buttons, complimented by a denim vest, and matching double zipper jeans, I strutted around unmindful, dressed to kill.

The sleek design of the new building was intended to feel futuristic, with its sharp angles, round, concrete columns, and stacks of dark brick segmented between tall, skinny reflective windows. At the top of a wide splay of concrete steps, the front office was tucked away underneath a crushing slab of concrete, a cavernous design, clearly not the inspiration of a claustrophobic mind. Standing there too long, looking up at the recessed canned lighting could make a person feel like a bowling pin about to be picked up and replaced for a spare. Beyond the office on either side were grassy courtyards enclosed by the building. To the right, a covered breezeway led to the cafeteria (or commons as it was labeled by the architects.)

I had just entered the building at the far end of the hallway, about to turn at the "T" in front of the giant wooden doors of the art studio.

"Hey, Scarlett, wait up!" Dan Robbie's husky voice echoed off the lockers in the vacant hall.

Dan was a stoner in the truest sense, cruising through most days on a buzz that started before homeroom, rejuvenated at lunch, and again on his way home in the afternoon. His eyes were dark brown whenever they weren't red—if you could see them through the narrow slits. His brown hair curled, only partially covering his ears—a trend that was becoming more prominent.

I was even considering getting a trim. *Nah.* By this time, my straight locks, sandy brown in the winter, almost blonde in the summer, hung down between my shoulder blades.

Stopping to lean back with the rubber sole of one shoe against the column of block wall between the neon lockers and the doors of the art department, I waited for Dan to catch up. It had been a busy morning, and I was down to my last four joints, intending to save at least three for myself and whoever I ran into at lunch. After school, I would get more.

"You got any of those left?"

## The Quiet Kid

The blanks in his question were an easy fill. "I got a few," I said.

"Lemme get a couple, man."

"How 'bout one and I'll match you one."

"Deal." He slipped me a folded George Washington, which I palmed and tucked into my pocket.

I had been doing a home study in street economics. It broke down like this: An ounce of weed was twenty bucks, a pack of Zig-Zags, next to nothing plus tax. A decent bag without a lot of stems and seeds would yield anywhere from thirty-five to forty joints, give or take, depending on how fat you rolled. The average head didn't have five dollars to his name at any given time of the day, but almost anyone could come up with a buck. If you showed up an hour early with twenty pre-rolled joints, you could unload most of your stash at a dollar a pop before the first bell rang for homeroom. It wasn't going to earn me a living, but I normally broke even with plenty left over to smoke. And it always paid to make charitable contributions, because you were bound to get paid back.

We went straight down the hall, out the doors, past the office, and through the covered corridor toward the commons.

"Where we headed?" I asked Dan as I followed him

"Dunno yet."

As we neared the entry of the commons, Ann Karnish appeared from behind our reflection on the glass doors. "Hey ya. Where you guys goin'?"

Flickering two fingers, I motioned her our way. "Come with us." I turned down the walkway toward the back of the school. Ann shadowed us without question.

"Lemme ask you guys somethin'," Dan started.

Ann's dark hair was cut in a Dorothy Hamill style, which I didn't normally care for, but she pulled it off with an easy cuteness and spunk. "Out with it," she demanded and then laughed at her feigned seriousness.

"Without leaving campus, where's the best place to spark a doob around here?"

"There's the back corner behind art," I responded.

"Yeah, but don't you ever get the feelin' someone's gonna pop around that corner before you see 'em comin'?"

"Yep. Always."

"On the other side of the music building…if the band's not practicing," Ann offered.

By then we were descending the steps by the chorus room. We could have gone straight through the hall out the other side to the practice field, but instead, we stayed the course out into the sunlight on the wide-open backside of the school facing the main road. "What's the best way to get caught?" Dan pondered out loud.

Ann and I shrugged, waiting for Dan to give a hint.

"Look conspicuous."

About that time, I noticed some guys on the other side of the field that was often used by the band for marching practice. At the crest of a small rise, there was a minuscule amount of woods—more like shrubbery—by a cow pasture, where these guys were obviously trying to hide. "You could go where those idiots are goin'." Dan pointed them out. "What's the problem with that?"

"Too conspicuous," Ann replied.

"Bingo." Dan sat down in the middle of the sidewalk, halfway between the building and the road. "And where's the best place to look inconspicuous?"

"Right out in the open. This is perfect," I said as Ann, and I sat to join him. "We could see someone coming from a mile away."

"From any direction," Dan added.

"Way before they get here," I finished, lighting a joint and then a cigarette. "Just in case."

Dan lit a Marlboro Red. We kept the joint down low as we passed it, holding it between our forefinger and middle finger like a cigarette when we toked, as opposed to the forefinger and thumb. Halfway through the second joint, our conversation landed on rock concerts, when something Ann said threw us off-kilter.

"I just hate when those guys jam out on their guitars."

"You're kiddin' me," I said. "How can you like Rock 'n' Roll and not like the guitars?"

"Yeah, that's the best part." Dan backed me.

"No, I like the guitars, just not when they go on and on and on."

"Huh. Must be a girl thing."

It was clearly a gender issue. I remembered what Shirley had said about not liking Skynyrd all that much and wondered if I would ever figure girls out.

## The Quiet Kid

"Next subject, please." Dan had decided it wasn't worth the debate.

Ann was distracted anyway. Looking away from us, she cocked her head to one side, her eyes fixed in the distance. "Why do you think those guys are running?"

"I dunno, somebody prob'ly spotted 'em," I surmised watching them take flight.

"Better them than us," Dan observed. "Maybe we should be movin' on."

"Yeah, we gotta get to class anyway," I said.

"You ain't got no class, Scarlett," Dan quipped.

"Yeah, well." It wasn't much of a comeback, but it was all I had. I was pretty stoned.

Ann was discarding the last of the roach while Dan and I ripped ourselves loose from the concrete. Standing, we each offered her a hand, assisting her to her feet. She popped up like she was on springs.

"Ann, on the other hand, has class all day long."

"You got that right," Dan agreed.

Then we did what we did every day at that time: rushed to beat the fourth-period bell.

There seemed to be a lot of commotion as we hurried through the lower hall on the backside of the west wing. Coach Warpath and a couple of other teachers were going from door to door, gravely intent on finding a handful of students to pull out of class. The impression they were giving was that they didn't have names, but rather, they were trying to identify the perpetrators by means of recognition. We were just trying to slide by unnoticed, practically pressed against the wall when Warpath escorted Donnie Bryson down the hall by the arm with what seemed to be a little more force than necessary.

"Whoa," I said when they were far enough away.

"What do you think's going on?" Ann queried, hoping the answer wasn't what she was thinking.

I replied with another question. "Remember those idiots we saw running from the hill?"

"Ya think?"

Paranoia carried us to class early. Dan and I slumped down in our seats on the back row.

On the front row, Brian Lamar sat sniffing the air suspiciously after we passed by. Brian was a black kid, or more accurately, a chocolate brown-skinned kid with an unkempt fro. The seat across the aisle was occupied by his buddy. Peter Lennox was also black with a lighter complexion.

Brian had earned a reputation as the class comedian, a title held in close competition by none other than my good buddy, Dan. Brian sniffed the air louder and turned to Peter for confirmation. "Hey! Hey, Petey! You smell that?"

"What, man?" Petey sounded uninterested.

"Smell like reefer." Brian curled his upper lip as if it was assisting his nose and sniffed again. "Yep. Reefer. Petey, you smell it?"

Petey laughed – a low, almost inaudible laugh which resembled a muffled growl. "Huh, huh, yeah, I smell it."

My paranoia kicked into high gear. But reasoning that Ms. Tyler was not yet in the room, and the whites of my eyes were truly white thanks to Visine, I breathed easier.

On the other side of the classroom, Robin, aka Nails, arrested my attention. At the mention of the word reefer, she had turned around to check us out.

She knew.

She was model skinny with sweeping locks of auburn hair. She was by far the prettiest girl in the room. For that matter, she was the prettiest girl in most any room. I was drawn to the startling length of her cherry-red fingernails, which had earned her nickname. She smiled at me, batting her long, black Maybelline eyelashes, luring my focus to her enormous, piercing, jade green eyes. I smiled back. Oddly enough, she blushed. Her face possessed an inherent look of knowing. What exactly, I'm not sure. That we were high? No, there was more. Rumor had it she dabbled in white magic. I tried not to stare, but I was drawn to her as if she had cast a spell.

Somewhere from a distant land, I heard Brian say, "You been smokin' reefer, boy?"

I snapped out of it at Dan's high-pitched reply with an emphasis on the first syllable. "Nig-atory."

Cringing, I instantly recalled the warning issued to me by my young black acquaintance at Cal Johnson Rec Center when I was just a boy. The word Dan had implied was not acceptable for use by white people. I feared Brian might react with violent ramifications. I was relieved when

Brian copied Dan's general tone, emphasizing the first syllable with a honking sound. "Honk-atory."

And then it was on.

"Nig-atory."

"Honk-atory."

"Nig-atory."

"Honk-atory."

They were both laughing in between. Most everyone in the class seemed amused, but none as amused as those two were. Some of the students seemed a tad uncomfortable, squirming in their seats and pretending not to hear.

Ms. Tyler came into the room, bringing silence to their racial tennis match. She would not have found it even slightly amusing.

Back at school on Monday, we found out what we'd suspected to be true. A total of ten guys who had been on the hill by the band's practice field were brought into the office for questioning that afternoon. Colonel Klink brought in backup in the form of Dickie McCarter, a well-known narc from the local police department. Amongst the alledged perpetrators were Ian Bradford, Big Nasty, and Don Colter. All of them were expelled from school for smoking marijuana, all but one.

Don Colter.

I asked him later, "What exactly did you do to get out of it?"

"It's like, the man was tryin' to pin somethin' on me I knew wasn't right, askin' me if I was there." He hesitated for a second just to keep me in suspense. I was, in fact, hanging on every word.

Then he revealed his big secret. "I just told 'em, no, man. I wasn't there." That was his brilliant strategy for avoiding expulsion. By deductive reasoning, I concluded the rest of them must have admitted their guilt, most likely promised leniency.

So much for pleading the fifth.

## 42. Carrie

"Where's the Frisbee?"

"Um, wait a sec." I reached beneath my seat, locating the plastic lip without having to poke around. "Got it." A healthy scattering of unsmoked cannabis covered the surface of the upside-down disc. I handed it to Sherry. "Are you rolling another one?"

"Yeah. It's a good thing you didn't flip that."

I laughed, a low, two-syllable stoner's *huh-huh*, to acknowledge my amusement. "We already smoked ..." I tried to remember. A haze lingered in the car from the last joint. "I dunno. How many we smoked?"

"I dunno. Six maybe. Maybe seven. Who's counting?" she said, rummaging through her purse. "Where'd I put those damn papers?"

"Oops." I was suddenly aware I had stashed them in my jacket.

"Klepto." Sherry took the pack from me, shaking her head slightly with a half-smile, half-sneer. "I swear, Michael. You prob'ly got my lighter too."

Digging in the pocket of my jeans, I confessed. "Guilty."

She laughed. "Wow. I was kidding. You really are a klepto." She twisted the weed packed-cylinder between her fingers and thumbs until it began to resemble a machine-rolled cigarette.

"I know. I came home last night with three lighters."

"Somebody's gonna come after you one of these days."

"Nobody ever remembers." I clicked the ignition switch back a notch and then turned on the radio.

"Good luck, findin' somethin' decent in this town," she said in between licking the paper and putting the seal on her masterpiece.

"I'm just lookin' for the time." Twisting the knob, I searched for a D.J.

"Why don't you ask that guy?" She nodded in the direction of my window.

I spun around in haste, my heart skipping a beat at the possibility of someone sneaking up on us. No one was there. "Oh, crap! Don't do that to me."

She laughed so hard, she snorted.

My head continued spinning around involuntarily, checking both sides to be sure no one was walking over from the rear parking lot. My heart was racing. Someone approaching our car would've had

## The Quiet Kid

a specific motive. Sherry composed herself and struck a flame to the joint.

I had parked strategically behind the Capri Cinema in a spot out of the direct path. It was between the back lot and the side of the theatre, facing the wall, which was the same color of green as oxidized copper. *Maybe I Should've backed in.*

"Maybe we should go get tickets," I announced.

"Relax," she said, still holding the smoke. "We got plenty of time."

She was right. I knew it, but her little shenanigan had unnerved me. I couldn't sit still. "Um, how can you be so sure?"

"It was 3:05 when we passed the bank clock. The movie doesn't start 'til 4:20. That's an hour and fifteen minutes. There's no way we been here that long."

"Yeah, but still… What if somebody sees us?"

"Don't get paranoid on me." Sherry took another hit, waiting on me to get my head on straight. "Nobody can smell it with the windows up."

I had spotted several people in the rear-view mirror crossing the service road from the backlot at random intervals. None of them had given us a second look. I had to concede. "Yeah. You're right." I took the joint from her, inhaling my fears in an enthusiastic toke.

We were there to see "Carrie," a film based on the first published novel by Stephen King. We had purposed to be scared out of our wits. Awaiting us inside, a girl was about to have her prom dress ruined by gallons and gallons of blood. We didn't want our buzz to wear off before the fulfillment of this advertised promise. Seven joints (or was it eight?) was our insurance. As it turned out, it wasn't the blood, nor was it the violent rage of a vengeful teen's kinesis that scared the hell out of us. It was the overbearing zeal of a controlling psychotic religious fanatic of a mother hitting a little too close to home. The whole Old Testament – you sin, you die, wreaked havoc on my brain, kicking the terror into high gear. Piper Laurie—in the role of Carrie's mother – became my mom, discovering I was high and locking me away in a closet to pray lest I be damned to burn for all eternity.

On the ride home, Sherry asked, "You wanna smoke another one?"

"Um, not right now. Maybe later."

# 43. Prayer Meeting/Fall Creek Falls

Dickie McCarter had his day in the sun. And Ian Bradford did his time. Exonerated, Ian was allowed back, returning to South-Young a little wiser. Perhaps marijuana wasn't the devil's weed, but it hadn't done him any favors. It hadn't been worth the risk or the price he had to pay. He decided to focus his energies in more productive endeavors. Assisted by Mark Lee and the metal shop teacher, Mr. Davenport, Ian gained approval from the school faculty to start the first martial arts class that either South or Young had ever had. As far as we knew, it was the only existing one in any high school in the city. Ian and Mark were students of Hapkido on their own time, working their way through the colored belt ranking. I wasn't taking it as seriously, limiting my education in controlled violence to the hour-long class after school. The small group gathering in the commons consisted of mostly guys and one smoky-eyed girl named Rhonda.

Short with long, brown hair and batwing bangs, her vulgar blue eye shadow made Amber's seem tame. Rhonda's long, black eyelashes were poised for flight. She was sultry, like some barfly perched and ready to seduce anything within a twenty-five-yard radius. If I hadn't gotten to know her, I might've misinterpreted. But she was a hardcore Jesus freak and the reason I was drawn to the Bible studies at her house.

I had begun contemplating the direction I was heading, the incident at the Ted Nugent concert having not yet burned out of my short-term memory. Jesus had revealed His love for me when I was not yet seven years of age, and now He was knocking at my door. Although not quite ready to walk the straight and narrow, I knew I had been a little too close to the edge. The edge of what, I wasn't sure.

Other than Rhonda's mom, everyone—even the group leaders at the weekly Bible study in Seymour—was our age or just a few years older. It was the first time I had heard anyone expound on the scriptures and relate them to the day and age we were living in. By we, I mean my generation – the lost wandering remnants of the free love movement. Sex, drugs, and rock 'n' roll was our mantra. We needed a more powerful word to show us the way.

I did benefit somewhat from these meetings, but the biggest impact—what stuck with me—was the skewed Christian outlook

## The Quiet Kid

regarding popular music. There was a big discussion about the practice of backmasking in recorded music, which some believed was intended to deliver the devil's message. Certain rock records spun in reverse on the turntable produced eerie satanic messages about the dark lord himself.

*They can't be serious.*

My biggest question was about the sanity of the religious zealots concocting these notions. Talk about paranoia. *Some people should get a life, or better yet, get a grip.*

The main song in question got a lot of publicity due to its popularity. Viewing the lyric as recited by the zealots while listening to a portion of *Stairway to Heaven* [26] as it was played backward, a person might've been swayed by the power of suggestion to believe Robert Plant was paying homage to Satan.

We spun the fifth verse (the one about the hedgerow), in reverse.

*Oh, here's to you, my sweet Satan. The one whose little path*
*Would make me sad, whose power is Satan*
*He'll give those with him 666. There's a little tool shed*
*Where he made us suffer, sad Satan*

Deeply disturbing, especially the part about the tool shed. It was a stretch to get those words out of what was heard. Without the printed words in your face, while you were listening, you more than likely wouldn't have picked any of it out. Depending on the interpreter, the reversed lyrics varied. It was kind of like the audio version of the Rorschach inkblot test. The psychologically dysfunctional heard things which were outside the norm. Or maybe they just heard exactly what they were listening for. If any of this was done intentionally, it was probably just to screw with their heads. Maybe that was Satan's plan all along: to occupy the time of the religious. Idle hands are the devil's ... uh, something, something ... workshop! That's it! And now, maybe the tool shed thing kind of makes sense.

We also overanalyzed a song by the Eagles, concluding that the *Hotel California* [27] was Hell and that the protagonist in the song had fallen asleep at the wheel, unaware when he awakened that he had died and gone to the nether regions.

A line in the song referenced the captain and wine, stating the unavailability of that spirit (wine—in this context) since 1969. This was said to be implying that Anton LaVey (the captain)—the founder of the satanic church in California, and author of the satanic bible, written in 1969—had banished the Holy Spirit from the Hotel (Hell). This was a dangerous place from which there was no return.

The reference to killing the beast with a "steely" knife was supposedly about the antichrist, which in this instance could not be killed. In reality, the term "steely" was a nod to Steely Dan.

When the protagonist tries to escape, he finds there is no way out.

I didn't put too much stock in these theories. There was another one floating around in which the protagonist was the victim of an alien abduction. I thought the whole train of thought to be on par with the Salem Witch Trials, where the badly misguided self-righteous, blinded by their zeal, searched for their next victim, poised to burn at the stake anyone that scared them, anyone whose point of view might differ from or obstruct their own. Yeah, religion sometimes does that to people. Remember the Crusades?

The most baffling part of it all is the amount of time we squandered searching for questions with no definitive answers – hours dissecting one song like it was a biology frog. It didn't bring me any closer to the truth. I was too distracted anyway, stealing sidelong glances at Rhonda.

In the spring, Sevier Heights Baptist Church hosted a youth retreat at Fall Creek Falls. Phil Ramsey invited Mark and me to go. Phil reminded me of John Denver. Same glasses, a little younger, but that same *ah-shucks,-ain't-life-peachy* demeanor. He was at home in faded jeans, a flannel shirt, and a pair of hiking boots. He had the same boyish charm and toothy grin, and gosh darn it, you'd have to be the Grinch not to like the guy.

Mark and I weren't cardholders in the Izod social club, so we didn't quite fit in with the Sevier Heights youth. The cabins bunked four. We were the leftovers—the three amigos. That was fine by us. It didn't faze Phil.

Phil was a couple of years older. He was a devout Christian, as sincere as anyone I had ever met in my life. Adamant in his relationship with Christ, he lived his values out loud without coming across as judgmental or condescending toward those outside the faith.

## The Quiet Kid

The three of us settled in and then strapped our boots on for the hike to the falls.

The two hundred, sixty-five-foot cascade from whence the park took its name is the highest in the eastern United States. Impressive from the view at the head of the trail, it was even more spectacular once we had reached the bottom. It was too early in the spring to be warm yet. Most everyone was wearing a sweatshirt. The cool mist was enough to capture our breath as we ran behind the falls. The thunderous pounding of the water on the rocks combined with the stunning vista and sharing the experience with the energy of youth in numbers made the hike remarkable. But it wasn't the high point of the weekend.

Phil had been messing around with this little ditty, strumming the tune on his six-string. He repeated over and over, the only words he had written to his song so far.

*Western movement ... western movement.*

Everyone in camp was supposed to bring something in the way of entertainment when we gathered in the evening. All we had were Phil's three chords and the words.

*Western movement ... western movement.*

By the time night fell, we had it figured out.

At the group cabin, the time came for us to have our turn in the spotlight. Phil sat in a chair with his guitar. Mark and I bookended him with our backs turned toward the small audience. We stood up with our feet spread apart and our thumbs locked onto our belt buckles. With a big, silly grin, Phil started banging out the three chords to his song. When he came to the pause between the first and second western movement, we twisted the tops of our torsos around, facing the group as much as we were able without disrupting the position of our feet, and gave a loud *hmmmmm*. So it went:

*Western movement, (turn) Hmmmmm ...*

*Western movement, (turn) Hmmmmm ...*

Each time, Phil would sing louder, intentionally letting his voice crack a little. By the third round, he sounded deranged to the point of coming unhinged. It was almost frightening had it not been for the howling laughter which grew louder with each refrain. At the fourth go-round, we decided we should quit while we were ahead before someone realized it wasn't as funny as it had first seemed. We were a hit, but I fear this description doesn't do it justice. Location joke. You had to be there. Even so, that still wasn't the high point of the weekend.

We were outside on the last night. The only light for miles and miles radiated from the stars and the campfire, a dancing orange glow illuminating the faces around it. Other than quiet conversation, the only sounds were the crackling and popping of the flames devouring the wood, the wilderness, the drone of crickets, and an occasional *whoo, whoo* from an owl no one could see. A camp leader brought out an acoustic guitar. He didn't strum. The key of A resonated through the still night as his knuckles rapped on the face of the hollow wooden body, imitating the hammering of nails, one solid knock followed by three, decreasing in volume, fading as the A chord echoed behind the knocks. And then he picked up the rhythm, strumming as he sang *Didn't He?*[28]

I felt the pressure of the words being driven into my heart with each nail as he started knocking for the second time.

The Word became reality for me, finding its way home. At that moment, I believed again.

> *The lamb, no longer wobbling at the knees, had gained confidence. Sure-footed, he ran and ran, unaware he had left the safety of the flock until the day came when he was hopelessly lost. Bleating loudly, the shepherd heard, searching until He had found him. Carried back to where he felt secure, the lamb had forgotten his troubles, only to run headlong into the unknown, not knowing he had strayed again until it was too late. The darkness had come gradually, and he took refuge there, until at long last he heard a sweet familiar voice....*

# 44. Art

I had given correct responses to the required minimum number of questions on a written exam, plus provided adequate visual evidence by way of physical demonstration that I could maneuver an automobile around one city block without violation and park it within the limits of a painted space, thus earning myself a license, approved and endorsed by the state of Tennessee Department of Transportation, granting me the privilege of operating a motor vehicle. My copper '69 Dodge Coronet was parked outside. Some days, I could almost hear it calling my name from the second tier of the school lot. This was one of those days.

We didn't get many days quite so perfect. In East Tennessee, there were a handful of days between the ground thaw and the wave of humidity signifying the beginning of summer. That day, the humidity was inconsequential. There were a few fluffy white clouds floating lazily across the azure horizon. It was T-shirt weather. You'd have been fine in a pair of shorts, but it wasn't hot enough to be uncomfortable in blue jeans. There was only one thing missing.

"You know what we need, cuz?"

"What's that?"

"A large Mountain Dew Sno-ball." Mark seldom suggested activities which involved bending the rules. But neither of us *had* to be in fifth-period art. We had signed up for study hall at the beginning of the year and never shown up. After the first week of calling your name on the roll with no response, the teacher automatically assumed you'd dropped. We could go to art or not. Technically, we weren't in the class, so really, we'd just be tweaking the rules. We decided to take the matter into Jerry's office twenty minutes before the bell signaling the end of fourth period.

The massive wooden double doors of the art department opened to a studio displaying the most current student artwork. Framed paintings and pencil sketches hung on the walls. Sculptures and clay pots on pedestals were featured in the open space. On either side were dual working studios of equal size. Jerry normally started class in the north studio where he'd take roll and hand out new assignments, after which we were free to work in either or even outside if the weather cooperated. The potter's wheel was in the south studio. And the kiln for firing clay was behind the display room, off the hallway which connected the work studios. Also accessible from that hallway was a restroom, a janitorial/supply closet, and Jerry's office.

"Hey Harris," I started, "What would you say if I asked you ...," hesitating.

"Oh, come on, you turkeys. Out with it." Harris could tell we were up to something.

"Can we go get Icee's?"[29]

"Now whyyy," he stretched the word out, "would you ask me that?" He paused for effect. "You know I can't give you permission." And then he added, "It's easier to get forgiveness than permission."

"So, what are you sayin'?"

"I'm sayin' if you get caught, I don't know nuthin' about it."

"Cool! We'll be back in twenty."

We were already on the way out when Harris stopped us. "Oh. And one more thing."

"Yeah?"

"You gotta bring me back a Twinkie."

"Done. Thanks, Harris."

Before we could slip down the hall, away from the north studio where students were already filing in for class (it wasn't unusual for the serious artists to cut into their lunchtime to get an early start), a doe-eyed girl named Penny Marks snuck up behind us.

"Hey, Scarlett. Where you goin'?"

I was smitten for the second time that day. This time, it wasn't spring fever. It was the sweet music of her voice. When I turned to look, it was the vision of her angelic face, framed by her blonde Farrah Fawcett wings. Every time I saw her, every time she spoke to me, I was smitten. But I knew we had to hurry. "Gettin' Sno-balls. We gotta go." She gave me a look which I knew meant, *what about me?* And I was held captive for a moment. "I'll get you one." She smiled, releasing me.

I had most of my classes with Amber, three hours a day of drafting classes in the morning, and an hour of Art for sixth-period. She had scheduled the classes I wanted just to be near me. I don't know why it seemed like such a good idea, but at the time it did. Perhaps I just felt more comfortable having my possessions close enough to keep them under constant surveillance. But it would prove to be problematic,

# The Quiet Kid

interfering with my ability to seek out some strange[30] whenever she wandered onto the radar.

I took drafting as a vocational class. It was my backup plan. I had heard TVA was paying draftsmen ten bucks an hour. But I was more interested in art. I hadn't given up on the idea of being a rock star, but as an artist, I had higher aspirations.

Jerry Harris taught us about light and shadows, depth and perception, and mixing colors from a palette of the primary three: red, blue, and yellow. But more than that, he enlightened us, prompting us to consider our values, to think about things more important than algebra or biology or science or economics – things like integrity, honesty, and true friendship. He valued relationships above everything. That mattered. It made a vast difference in my perception of the world around me. This amazed me because he was the teacher. It wasn't necessary. It was his choice. Part of this learning process was his method of grading – the strangest system I had ever seen. You were required to evaluate your own work based on the amount of effort you put in. I found it impossible to cheat on his honor system, and rarely did I turn in a poor effort. I normally gave myself A's.

Jerry nicknamed me Junkie. I wasn't sure why. Because he could, I supposed. Because we had that kind of friendship where he could tease, knowing I'd never take it too seriously. It was the same way he'd tease if he'd seen you outside smoking, saying: "I saw you blowin' that fagg." He'd completely forgotten the stupid, unfortunate incident on the pep bus, or at least never mentioned it.

We had an ongoing feud as to who was better: Ted Nugent or James Taylor. Slowly, over the course of years, he would persuade me he was right—James Taylor, by virtue of depth. However, I would never admit it to him.

Jerry, as much as anyone else in the entire school, was my friend. His art room was the one place I could go where I didn't feel the need to hide. There was no need to slump down in my chair and hope nobody noticed me. I could do things there I was good at. I felt confident in them and didn't mind so much when observers passing by would take note. In the environment Harris had created, I felt at home like I could let down my hair, let it fly, and no one would be calling me freak with detrimental undertones behind my back.

On my own time, Jerry would let me paint whatever I wanted, even if it meant copying from photographs to render my favorite rock stars in watercolors. However, that would never fly when it came to gradable work. That had to be original.

I wasn't thinking about any of that as we hurried to get back with our Sno-balls. I was thinking only of Penny and her pretty blue eyes.

We slipped into the art room through the back door, eliciting protests from the entire room.

"Hey, where's mine?" "No fair." "Did you bring enough for the whole class?"

Mark handed a brown paper sack to Harris, who quickly realized there was more in it than just his Twinkies. "Hush, youngins'," he said. "They brought some for everybody." Jerry reached in for his Twinkies and then passed the bag, which was full of Bubble Yum and Tootsie Roll Pops to appease the masses.

I sat down across the table from Penny, delivering her Sno-ball as promised amidst the distraction.

"You're just in time. Harris just finished handing out today's assignment." She paused to pull a frozen line up the straw.

"Yeah, and?"

"You get to draw me while I draw you."

"How did I get so lucky?"

"I didn't have a partner. Odd man out. Harris volunteered, but I said I'd wait on you. Oh, and you better make me look pretty."

"Is there another way?"

She couldn't repress the smile. She knew it was true and barely blushed. She was probably used to hearing it. Penny Marks was in a different social class. She could've been a cheerleader. She wasn't. She could've been on the cover of a magazine. As far as I knew, she wasn't. Yet. With her face, she could've been darn near anything she wanted to be. What she was was way out of my league. I knew it. She knew it. But I didn't care. That small, glaring fact was like an ant trying to hold back a steamroller. But it wasn't going to stop me from trying. After all, she'd waited on me.

The look of concentration was too cute for her face to contain. I had to smile.

"Stop it." Penny started to giggle.

## The Quiet Kid

My smile turned into a chuckle. "What?"

She tried to straighten her face, which only made it worse. "Stop, I can't do this if you keep makin' me laugh."

"I'm makin' you laugh?"

We both lost it. Trying to stifle it to keep anyone else from noticing was like passing nitrous oxide on the down-low at a Richard Pryor show.

"Quit it, now. Be serious."

"Okay. I'm being serious now," I said.

We tried to force the corners of our mouths downward. It worked for a second or two until that in itself became too comical, and then we burst out laughing again. There were a few snickers from around the room, but most everyone was focused on their assignment, able to block us out with the help of Fleetwood Mac.

Harris moseyed by our table. "I know this can be funny, but remember, Marks has to do this for a grade."

I wasn't getting graded until the next hour's class. Knowing this, I considered the severity of what he had said. I didn't want to screw up Penny's grade. It would give her cause to be mad at me. "Okay. Okay. Look away and count to ten. Then we'll start again."

Focusing on *Dreams*,[31] I gained my composure.

For some inexplicable reason, the notion struck me that the barriers between social classes were imaginary. They simply ceased to exist. Somehow, we were above it all. Penny and I had been getting along this way for a couple of months now. We had been having a lot of fun joking and teasing on the regular. I had every reason to believe she liked me. Sure, I ran with the crowd commonly referred to as heads or freaks. Penny ran track and played basketball. But did that make her a jock? Some of her best friends were cheerleaders or members of clubs, DECA, Honor Society, and the like. But she was in a class all by herself. I didn't care. If it didn't matter to me, why should it matter to her?

In the last five minutes of class, we were putting our stuff away. That's when I made the mistake of thinking I had a shot.

"So, you wanna go catch a movie on Friday?"

"Just you and me?"

"Yeah, just you and me. We could go to Ye Olde Steak House and then go see *The Sentinel* ... or somethin' else, whatever you like."

I was thinking *The Sentinel*, envisioning her clutching my arm, snuggling for security when the scary parts came.

"Mike, I like you. I really do. But I don't think it's a good idea."

"But I...No. It's okay. I get it."

I really did. For a minute. Money was a requirement for members of Cherokee Country Club, the wall was still standing in Berlin, and girls from wealthy families on the upper rungs of the social ladder absolutely did not date heads. Period. On the other hand, Rosa Parks refused to sit at the back of the bus, and women were being admitted into West Point. So, what could happen was still anyone's guess.

Amber and I were together in a perpetual on-again, off-again kind of way. By the time the month of April rolled around, and I got my license, it was more off than on. There were just too many pretty fish in the sea, or at least one too many. I suppose if it hadn't been Penny, it would've been someone else.

Amber had always been the sole member of my most adamant fan club. One day when I'd debated with Harris over what I should be able to paint in his class, she had spoken out fervently on my behalf. Jerry kicked her out.

But now, as the end of the school year was fast approaching, there was trouble brewing I hadn't anticipated.

"Michael, I have to know. Do you love me?" Amber's gaze refused to fix on one eye.

Unable to focus, I hung my head to escape the erratic searching of her darting powder blues for a moment. Then, ignoring her wide-awake REM, I forced a stare somewhere beyond the inquiring surface. "And if I say I don't know, you're gonna go out with him?"

"Not if you don't want me to. I just don't want to throw this away if we don't have a future."

"Well, I don't want you to."

"What about you and Penny?"

"Penny? Seriously? There is no me and Penny."

"I thought you wanted to go out with her."

"It doesn't matter what I want. She doesn't want me."

"So, where does that leave us?"

"Look, I have no desire to go to Junior Prom."

## The Quiet Kid

"I don't care about that." Amber's eyes stopped, finding anchor on mine, longing for the answer I hadn't given.

We were between periods in the drafting room. Everyone else had gone out for the five-minute break. Amber needed an answer that would validate our relationship. I was in danger of losing her. Control was slipping through my fingers. I needed to tell her what she wanted to hear. It wouldn't be that difficult. For the most part, it was the truth. Though I only had a loose grasp on the true meaning of the word, my feelings for her hadn't changed.

Penny Marks' desire to be with me was zero. I had no other immediate prospects. And now some guy had taken an interest in Amber. He wanted to take her to Junior Prom. I don't think she wanted to go as much as she didn't want to be left out in the cold. Yes, even in springtime, a girl left at home alone too long can get cold. It was only a matter of seconds before drafting students would file back in before the third-period bell. The ground was coming up fast. So, I pulled the cord before it got too close.

"Why don't we go out tonight?"

"And then what?"

"I wanna get back together." Her chin was quivering, her powder blue eyes on the verge of spilling tears. I pressed my thumb to her cheek to catch them.

"You mean it?"

"Yes," I said. "And I do love you. That has never changed. I can't stand the thought of you with someone else."

And that was that. The main motivator. That guy was not going to take what was mine. She belonged to me. Somewhere deep inside, I believed we would be together one day with no one else running through the frame, blurring the dimly lit picture. *After high school, I'll be ready to settle down. For now, this will have to do.*

She smiled, the sparkle in her eyes returning. Nameless guy was already a fading memory. I supposed it wouldn't be so bad celebrating another June 11th with her. Besides, it would be nice having sex again on the regular. That would be even easier now that I was driving.

For the record, we skipped junior prom.

# 45. Watertown

Mike Stuart cultivated his love of wild things at a young age. Enticing squirrels with pieces of bread, he would lure them first onto the windowsill and eventually into his attic bedroom. Growing up in the small town of Vonore had a way of leaving him to devise his own entertainment. If there had been some old guys in rockers on the wooden plank front porch, chewing the fat about the latest town council meeting under cover of the tin roof at that general store, you might've been led to believe you had just stepped into Mayberry. The only thing missing was Floyd's barbershop. But even Sheriff Andy Taylor would've been bored after a couple of days in Vonore.

During his stint in the Navy, Mike came to stay with us whenever he was given leave. One weekend, he brought home a guest none of us could have anticipated. It was black and white, sleek like a cat, and minus her scent glands, a pet that would have left Pepé Le Pew drooling. No one else I knew, but Mike would have dreamed of owning a skunk.

It stood to reason that when he ventured out into the world, his feet would land in a place where the inhabitants were wild. He bought a hundred acres, mostly undeveloped, about forty-two miles east and slightly south of Nashville. The nearest town was nine miles away, a booming metropolis called Watertown.

The cooling system in my dad's 1961 Chevy Nova II wasn't exactly state-of-the-art. It wasn't designed for long hauls at interstate speeds. I found this out the hard way in the summer of 1977 on my way to Watertown. Twice, I had to exit I-40 to let it cool down, making for a long day. It would be the same on the return home.

The highway's monotonous hum ceased, and I loosened my grip on the wheel as the asphalt ended and the tires transitioned to unpaved road. Gravel shifted, groaning and popping beneath the rubber, and the weight of the old Chevy as I picked up momentum and the complaining found its own harmony with the singing birds, barking squirrels, and the croaking of frogs as I passed by a pond. Where thickets of innumerable nameless bushes and vines thinned out, trees parted, leaving vacant gaps into the unknown, beckoning to be explored. Shadows from the canopy spread a canvas for

## The Quiet Kid

patches of sunlight, which broke through, decorating the ground, penetrating the darkness even in the deepest parts of the forest.

Topping the hill, I arrived at a clearing where I saw the two-story rustic cabin. Constructed nearly a century ago, it had yielded to the years and was now missing a roof and many of its windows. Next to it so deep in the woods, the tiny trailer seemed out of character. But it was just as Mike had described it. I knew I was in the right place. This was home to Mike and his live-in partner until renovation of the original homestead could be completed.

The next morning, I awoke drawn to the places that had stolen my attention from the road on my way in. Over breakfast, I had Mike point me in a good direction.

Mike was the big brother I never had. The first time I had ever driven, it was behind the wheel of a truck at his place back when he lived in Pegram. He was a lady's man with an ever-present sincerity in his eyes. He was good looking, suave in a country boy way, soft-spoken and self-sufficient. Other than Alan Morton, he was the guy I most aspired to be like. If he had been a guitar player and an artist, he might have landed the number one spot.

He gave me a brief tutorial on how to use a .22 rifle and instructions about where I could and could not go. I set off into the woods to hunt rabbits. It was exclusive hunting ground. Mike owned most of the surrounding property. The main thing I had to watch for was other houses. If I saw one, I was too close to the border of Mike's acreage and should turn around.

Time moves differently outside the imprisonment of concrete and asphalt, traveling along at its own pace, moving when it decides to move. It was standing still now. When the moment came for it to move forward again, a rabbit stirred out of the invisibility of its camouflage. It ran about ten yards and stopped. Instinct told it to stay still. Frozen against the backdrop of its environment, it would have been nearly impossible to spot had I not already seen it in motion. But I locked in on its resting place, seeing it clearly.

*Boom! chaaa ...*

The .22 rifle echoed through the trees and across the hills. An easy kill.

Time was set in motion again, carried along with my forward momentum. I gathered my quarry and ventured onward, spotting movement not too far ahead. This time it wasn't the same. Even though I had seen the movement, I could barely see the tiny brown blemish. I knew it was a rabbit—only a baby. It had been separated from its mother. Perhaps she had fallen victim to the forest, eaten by a coyote, or maybe I was holding her limp carcass in my left hand.

Time stopped again. To prevent it from ticking forward too quickly, I moved as slowly as possible, not wanting to give away the slightest movement. I had to fool it, make it believe I was frozen with it, and yet still gradually progress. I had to alter the parameters, shifting within them—moving yet seemingly motionless. Within the stillness of unmoving time, I lay the rifle on the ground and the lifeless mammal next to it and then crept toward the furry infant. Its tiny heart must have been fluttering madly, wanting to flee yet following its untested instincts. It remained inert. Visible to me now were its furious rapid breaths, the only activity signifying that seconds were indeed ticking away ... as ... I ... closed ... in ... hovering ... over ... slowly ... cupping ... my ... hands ... lowering ... them ... even ... slower ... casting a shadow ... over ... the tiny ball of fur ... only inches away ... until ... I was sure ... another millimeter ... would have made it flee, and then I sprang, snatching it from the ground.

I held it close for a few minutes, stroking it gently and feeling bad about the one I had shot. There was nothing left to do but release the baby. I couldn't take it back. I let it go, watching it sprint away as fast as its tiny legs could go. Picking up the rifle and the dead rabbit, I turned back toward the trailer.

No longer interested in the hunt, my path was directed in as much of a straight line as I could manage. Maneuvering around trees, bushes, and briars made the simple task difficult. Coming with greater frequency, the trees seemed to be closing in. Soon, I landed in a thick patch of briars. Funny thing was, I had no recollection of any of this when I came in.

Time, which earlier had seemed to stand virtually motionless, now accelerated, doubling its normal pace to make up for what it had squandered. The sun, which just moments earlier had been positioned high above the clouds in the big blue sky, now dropped from its lofty perch, falling low and settling just above the horizon. I hadn't noticed its position when I first stepped into the woods.

## The Quiet Kid

Wading through a sea of thorns rising to my armpits, my arms were forced straight up over my head to keep the rabbit carcass and the rifle from getting tangled. It was difficult enough to push my way through without creating extra drag. In the midst of my struggle, a sickening reality occurred to me, filling me with dread. I had no idea where I was. Gone were the open spaces. Nothing had looked familiar for a while now. The light from the sun faded fast, time unrelenting in its quest for righting itself. In another half hour, it would be completely dark. At this pace, maybe sooner. Dread turned to despair and then quickly turned to fear. I wasn't relishing the idea of spending the night in the woods—alone. At the very least, I had to break free from the bonds of the thorny briars. There might even be snakes in the thicket.

Like the face of the Almighty—probably because I had no idea how that would actually appear—the face of Reverend Lowe came to me. Although not audibly, I could hear him in one of his more serene moments explaining how Jesus was a beacon for those who were lost. I remembered the daze and darkness of PCP and then heard the knocking on the face of a guitar in the key of A.

In desperation, I called out His name.

"Jesus." Quietly at first. And then louder.

"Jesus!"

Louder still.

"Jesus, please help me! Jesus! Help me find my way!" I knew He was the only one around for miles – the only soul who could hear me. I hoped He could hear me – that He would come to my aid.

It was only a matter of minutes when I broke free from the grasp of the thorny vines and stumbled onto a dirt road. I still had no idea which way was back, but it didn't matter. My Savior was faithful, a light to my path. He had led me to a road, all the while knowing I would lose my way again. For now, I was on a road. I knew it would lead somewhere, and eventually, I would find my way.

# 46. Valerie

Between the front office and the commons, one of the square brick columns in the breezeway appeared to be in dire need of some added support. I was doing all I could, shoring it up with my back pressed firmly against it and the sole of my left shoe assisting my balance.

School was back in session.

She emerged from beyond the mirrored front of the commons. She was svelte. Model skinny. In slow motion, her head rotated slightly, allowing the breeze to lift her long, brown locks from her shoulders as if fans were blowing to add effect for a photoshoot. She was beautiful.

I was upright, moving almost involuntarily in her direction.

She was wiggling in tight jeans, complemented by a matching denim vest, the lapel of her plaid shirt spreading out to her shoulders. Unbuttoned at the top two, a "V" opened to frame her tanned breastplate. Apparently, the third button required her immediate attention to ensure its position at the exact center.

My heartbeat was clogging my ears. More aware of it than where I was, I had to avert my eyes quickly when she looked up. The oxygen flowing between us as our eyes met wouldn't have sustained a hummingbird. She flashed a huge smile as she passed. It was all I could do not to look back over my shoulder to see if she was looking back over her shoulder.

Amber and I were about to be on another break.

She must have seen it coming. Amber never even flinched. In the grand scheme of things, she knew exactly where she stood. The unwritten ground rules had been carefully established. If I saw her at all, it had to be away from school. In public, we would speak, but only casually. The appearance of anything other than friendship would be picked up by anyone who knew our history. Any hint of genuine affection between us could be sniffed out from miles away. No one else could know. That would spoil my chances.

And she would still be there when I needed her.

"I'll still see ya this weekend?" Amber hoped.

"Maybe, but don't count on it."

She inquired about holidays, which of course, were hers, though I doubted seriously it would drag out that long. Just in case, I promised her the prom.

That was on a Wednesday.

## The Quiet Kid

It was the third week of my junior year, 1977. On Thursday, Bebe Sanders and I were slinking toward the back of Mr. Hall's fifth-period class, having just returned from a long lunch. We had been out "cruising" with Dan Robbie in his *Midnight Rambler*. The name taken from a Rolling Stones song made the vintage American Motors vehicle seem a lot cooler than it actually was. If you wanted to know where we had been, all you needed to do was trace the red roads mapping our eyeballs. Mr. Hall was already handing out a pop quiz on the latest chapter we had covered in American History.

Bebe pulled her long, frizzy hair back in a ponytail and then rummaged through her leather purse for a pencil.

*She probably studied. I'm screwed.*

Not that it mattered much. If you acted like you were paying attention in class, made an occasional comment, and above all, laughed at Mr. Hall's corny jokes, you'd probably scrape by even it was just by the skin of your teeth. Coach Hall was an okay guy. He had wire-rimmed glasses and graying hair that was thinning a little, parted to one side. He appeared to be in good physical condition, lean, but not overly muscular. Outside the classroom, he coached golf and tennis. Within the confines of four walls, he bided his time teaching American History and Health and cracking corny jokes on average of a dozen per class with a silly "cat that swallowed the canary" grin on his face. Sometimes he made profound statements such as: "All those models and people you see in movies and on television are the freaks. The rest of us are the ones who are normal." The best thing he taught us, and my personal favorite, was this: It doesn't matter if you know the answers. What's important is if you know where to look to find them."

Coach Hall found it necessary to personally hand-deliver each test sheet that day, rather than giving a stack to the front row to be passed to the back. Making his way toward us, he offered a sheet to Bebe, who was taken aback when he stopped to look at her straight on. "Are you red eye?"

Bebe shot him a goofy, uncertain smile as he turned and continued passing out the test pages with blank answers.

She looked at me with an *oh, crap he knows* face. In the next row over, Dan was trying to contain an outburst, which could only have been perceived as guilt after Coach Hall's insinuation. Gathering himself, Dan muttered low, repeating the inquiry. "Are ya red eye?"

Bebe's worry dissolved in relief. The revelation must have dawned on us simultaneously. Mr. Hall had simply asked her if she was ready (red-eye) to take the test and not red-eye, as in, *I know you've been out smoking pot before class.*

With that out of the way, Dan was looking to the future. "Tomorrow, we should be somewhere else."

"Like where?"

"Anywhere."

I agreed to skip with Dan on Friday, but I would need a written absentee note on Monday.

Thursday after school, I was looking for Linda Lionheart.

"Hey Baby, I heard you and Amber broke up again." She gave me a quick peck on the lips, a friendship kiss.

Everything about Linda was dainty—her lips, her eyes, the bones of her fingers and wrists—like a delicate porcelain doll you didn't dare handle roughly for fear it might break. But her innerworkings were steel reinforced. You could chip away the surface only to find an indestructible infrastructure. Something about her was assertive as if she always knew the score.

"Yeah, it's true."

"Who is it this time?" She knew me all too well.

"Well ... I don't really know her name yet. But I saw her yesterday afternoon outside the commons. It was just after lunch and ...."

"Wait. You don't even know her name?" Linda laughed. "You are an idiot, ya know it."

"Yeah, well."

"What does she look like?"

"She's kinda skinny, pretty..."

"Obviously."

"... tan, brown hair, feathered bangs ..."

"Does she have big tits?"

"What makes you think ...?" I became defensive just before she cut me off.

## The Quiet Kid

"Relax, sweetie. I'm kidding."

"Um, actually no, she didn't. The way she was struttin', I'm sure I would've noticed. She seems kinda cocky for a girl."

"What was she wearing?"

"Hmm ... she had on a denim vest and a white shirt, red plaid ..."

"That's Valerie."

Leave it to a girl to deduce from your conversation who you were talking about based on a description of the walk, the attitude, and a guesstimate of her cup size. And leave it to a girl to know exactly what another girl was wearing the day before.

"You know her?"

"Yeah, Valerie Van der Burke. You should be careful. I mean, I love her to death, but ... hmm ... how should I put this? She doesn't play fair. I wouldn't want to be dating her."

"Can you introduce me?"

"No, sweetie, I wouldn't do that to you. But I *can* tell you she just broke up with Kevin Swain. He's on the football team."

"Yeah, I know who he is. So, she's available?"

"Just be careful," Linda warned again. "If she breaks your heart, I won't say I told ya so, but ya prob'ly had it comin'."

The first bell rang for homeroom. We were about to part ways when I remembered to ask her about the excuse note for Monday.

She wrote the note. And for the remainder of the year, if I needed a note for being out or tardy, Linda scribed it. There were so many that even when my absence was legit, I had to discard the one from my mom in favor of the one I would ultimately get from Linda for fear the teachers might believe Mom's handwriting to be forgery.

Come Monday, I was back at the same spot where I first saw Valerie. Five days straight, I followed the same routine, every day a little bolder, at first just smiles and then "hellos," leading to small talk, and eventually: "What-cha doin' this weekend?" I got the nerve from someplace I didn't know existed and asked her out. I was still a little gun shy from Penny Marks, but there I was, asking Valerie Van der Burke on a date, even after being cautioned against it. I had read somewhere a girl will go out with a guy just to avoid being stuck at home on a Saturday night.

"I'd love to," she smiled.

The Kingston Four Cinemas was the first of its kind in Knoxville, offering four separate movie theatres under one roof. I took Valerie there for a midnight showing of *Monty Python and the Holy Grail*. The strange British humor was foreign to us, or maybe we were just too high. We left early. It was exactly the kind of thing I didn't want to happen. I was certain it would be our last date. She practically passed out on her bed when I took her home. The questions raced through my head. *Does she want to me to crawl in bed with her? Is her mom awake?* I had met her mom briefly beforehand. With dark hair and glasses, she was more than a little obese. I had found it hard to believe the beautiful, tan, slender young vision lying next to me was the product of that woman, and—I didn't want to think about it. Valerie snuggled with her pillow. I wanted to lie down next to her and see where it went. *If I move too soon, will she kick me out on my ear?* She'd never go out with me again. I had no clue as to how I should handle the situation, so I left her sleeping and let myself out.

Valarie came looking for me Monday morning before school.

"I am sooo sorry about Friday," she apologized profusely in her little mousy voice. "I was just so tired and a little stoned," she confessed with a giggle. "When my head hit the pillow, I was gone. It wasn't you. I promise. You forgive me?" She batted her eyes, and I almost had to laugh at the obvious ploy. It was patronizing, and I hated being patronized, but she was too cute not to let it slide.

"So, can we have a do-over?" My request following her apology seemed like the best angle.

"Sure can. Whatcha doin' after school today?"

"Whattaya have in mind?"

"Take a ride with me."

The final bell rang. I hit the door like a thoroughbred out of the gate at the Preakness. She followed me home, and I left my car in the driveway. We headed back out toward South Haven, took it down to the river, and made a left. It was a low traffic area and good place to smoke a joint. It was gone by the time we hit town. I added the roach to her collection in the ashtray. She made another left to avoid crossing the river, leading us back into South Knoxville.

## The Quiet Kid

I started punching buttons, trying to find something on the radio, which at times was next to impossible. Abba, *Dancing Queen*. Rose Royce, *Car Wash*, Pablo Cruise, *Whatcha Gonna Do?* The frog station was playing Waylon Jennings, *Luckenbach, Texas*. I almost left it there. I kind of liked that song, but it wasn't a good risk for the occasion. I wasn't sure what Valerie would make of it. So, I soldiered on. KC and the Sunshine Band, *I'm Your Freakin' Boogie Man!* I was getting impatient. And then I landed on Ted. *Cat Scratch Fever.*

*Perfect.*

"Crank it up!" she said.

I obeyed, pleased to know she liked Ted Nugent as much as I did.

She drove like she owned the road, blowing through the red light in front of McDonald's on Chapman Highway in the turn lane, maneuvering the bronze GTO around the right side of waiting traffic. Terrified, I thought I might claw holes in the dashboard. When we came out on the other side of the intersection unscathed, I slumped back in my seat. She was laughing. And then we were both laughing our butts off. She was probably laughing at me. I was laughing to release the terror, just glad to be alive. I couldn't decide if she was fearless or completely insane. Maybe she was just showing off. I was okay with it, either way.

"You got any cash?" Valerie had to yell to be heard over the music.

"What?"

"Gas money!"

I nodded vigorously, and she whipped into the left turn lane, pulling into the Gulf station at the corner of Woodlawn Pike. She turned the key all the way back, shutting off the engine with the music still blaring.

"I just need a couple of bucks to get home."

Wondering what she would've done had I been broke, I pulled a folded five from my front pocket. "Here. Get three and buy us some Cokes or somethin'. I'll pump," I said, hurrying around to open her door.

"Thank you. Such a gentleman." She smiled, wrinkling her petite nose at me as she got out. I unscrewed the gas cap, shoved the nozzle in, and watched her tiny butt swivel as she walked inside, feeling the vibration of Ted Nugent's guitar in my free hand through the top of the car. I wanted to give her a wolf whistle, but she had just labeled me a gentleman. I wasn't willing to take the risk.

Val peeled out of the parking lot, and we were back on the road. From my side, the needle looked like it was pegged around 80. She let off the accelerator just before we passed Lakeshore Deli, slowing a bit through Colonial Village, where she lived. We broke away from the congestion, the fast food, the Family Inn, Palace Lanes, Tennessee Valley Skate Center, out past K-Mart. The distance between businesses grew wider and wider. We passed under the bridge at John Sevier highway, and the foothills of the Great Smoky Mountains came into full view. I lit another joint. The radio accommodated us as we continued cruising south. *Breakdown.*[32a]

I imagined myself smooth like Tom Petty's vocal, suave like Mike Campbell's guitar, Valerie unable to resist. [32b]

Wondering if she was feeling the vibe, I must have looked at her with more intensity than I'd realized. She returned a defenseless smile. "What?" she said innocuously.

"Nothin'." I took the joint and peered at the curves ahead. I wanted her. She knew it. But crossing that line with her terrified me for reasons I couldn't grasp.

I liked her. I liked her cute, mousey little voice and her spunkiness. Mainly, I liked her because she was beautiful. I was so blinded by it I could have overlooked most anything else. When she dropped me off in my driveway, I was terrified at the question I was about to ask. But she had a way of making me push through the fear. After all, she'd said yes twice now. I walked around and leaned over with my forearm on her door. "You wanna go with me?"

"Mike," she started with what sounded like pity in her voice. She glanced down, but rebounded quickly, locking onto my eyes. "You're sweet, but I can't. It's not you. I just don't want to be in a relationship right now."

I didn't get it. *Why not?* I didn't say it out loud. I acted nonchalant, not wanting her to know that it bothered me. But she could probably tell it did. I looked out toward the road for a second, turning back when she wrapped her slender fingers around the back of my neck to pull me close. She kissed me and said. "Ask me out anytime. I won't say no to that."

She wanted to go out again. That was a good thing. Also, she greatly admired my sterling silver lightning bolt necklace. She wore it home.

# 47. Valerie/Ted Part II

P.T. Barnum has been credited with the well-known phrase: "There's a sucker born every minute." Although those weren't his exact words and his biographers, agree his credo was something more along the lines of, "A customer born every minute," whoever coined that infamous saying most certainly got it right. I was living proof.

Ted Nugent was coming to town again, October 13th. This time, he was headlining. If the date itself wasn't premonitory, the experience I had had the first time around should have sufficed as a warning. Nonetheless, I was determined to plunge headlong into another disaster. This time, I wanted to take Val along for the ride, never suspecting she would be the source of adversity. She would be in the driver's seat while I sat helpless on the passenger side, unable to predict what she might do next. At least on this ride, my knuckles wouldn't be white against the dashboard as she blew through a red light.

Terry White already had a ticket with her name on it; she informed me when I asked her to go. But, still wanting to go with me, she would ditch him after they got inside. Then we could meet somewhere. I was flattered she was willing to go through all that trouble for me.

Somewhere beyond the grave, P.T. Barnum was laughing hysterically.

Inside the coliseum, I was happy to find her right where she said she'd be. The show was going to be nothing short of spectacular. Finally, I would get to see the Nuge in all his hedonistic glory. I would be high this time, but not incoherent, and I was with the prettiest girl in the entire place, as far as I was concerned. Little did I know she was flying high from something she'd gotten out of Terry White's bag of goodies.

She excused herself, feigning a trip to the restroom. "I'll be right back."

She must have come down and needed a pick me up.

Thirty minutes passed. I was still alone. At long last, she wandered back.

The second time she did it, P.T. Barnum was selling tickets to the show. Even in the afterlife, he was making a killing. Third time's a charm, or so they say. "They" must've been holding front row seats at the big event.

That was it for me. Ted Nugent took the stage, the moment for which I had anxiously awaited, and I was sitting next to a vacant chair. After a while, I gave up on her and left my seat, walking around crestfallen, kicking at cigarette butts on the concrete floor. A tumultuous thunder reverberated through the pathetic acoustics of the Knoxville Civic Coliseum. The Motor City Madman dragged a pick across the strings of his hollow-body Gibson Byrdland guitar, the screeching enough to make the back hair on a mountain lion stand at attention. Normally, this would have been my favorite part of *Stranglehold*. But I was absorbed in self-pity.

Lugging my still breathing carcass past the front row of the rear balcony, an arm reached out and stopped me in my tracks. Valerie. She had ditched Terry White and had been looking for me. And now she was seated next to a familiar face. I hesitated for a second. Quickly glancing past Val, I locked eyes with Linda Lionheart. She mouthed, "I'm so sorry." I knew she meant it. I could read it in her eyes. It wasn't her fault. I should've listened to her.

Val wanted to talk. I couldn't make out what she was saying. Lost in the thunder, it really didn't matter anymore. I shook my arm free and bolted for the exit.

*Show's over. The clown is going home.* Not willing to shell out a refund, P.T. Barnum had already left the building.

"You have every right to be mad, sweetie," Linda Lionheart let me know she was on my side before hitting me with the full truth. "But on the other hand, you kind of had it comin'. I mean, you knew what you were getting into."

"Yeah, I know. I shoulda listened to you."

"You have my permission not to forgive her, but if you decide you want to, she really does wanta make it up to you."

We were coming into school past the corner of the building, where the brick wall juts out at an acute angle. It was Friday morning. Just as we approached the double-doors, I could see her beyond my reflection in the glass. She was lingering in the hall in front of the art department. I hesitated. She couldn't see me yet.

Linda gave pause, watching for my reaction. "See. She's waiting for you."

I opened the door, and Valerie looked up anxiously. She gave me a little wave like she wanted me to see her but wanted to hide all at the same time.

## The Quiet Kid

"Hey, girl," Linda greeted her.

"Heya."

"I'll catch up to you later."

"K. See ya." Immediately Val redirected her attention to me. She was hanging her head slightly, looking up at me with puppy dog eyes, her shoulders slumped with arms straight in front of her skinny frame as she twisted her hands, one turned inside the other. "I am sooo sorry."

We were standing in the "T" where the hallways intersected in front of the art room. She continued apologized profusely, explaining her obligation to Terry because he'd bought her ticket and all.

I couldn't forgive her immediately. I let my angst build, finally releasing it by executing what was supposed to be a near-miss reverse spinning round kick inches from her face. Learning the move in martial arts class, I had done it a thousand times. There was no reason for misjudging the distance. I could've done it in my sleep. It was some kind of psychosomatic meltdown, a Freudian slip of sorts perhaps. Badly miscalculating, I clipped the end of her pretty little nose. *Whap!*

She covered her face with both hands. All I could see was her eyes. I wanted to run and hide, but she held me there, staring back at me in—I couldn't be sure, horror or disbelief—for a brief, painful moment. Or maybe it was shock. Now the shoe was on the other foot. The fit was far from comfortable.

"I am so sorry." Because what else could I say? "I did not mean to do that. I was just goofin' I didn't mean to–"

"You're an asshole."

"I know."

"There's no blood. It didn't really hurt—just my pride. I don't know why, but I forgive you if you forgive me. But we are not even," she said. "You owe me one."

Other than Amber, Val was the only girl I'd had in my bedroom for a long time. From the floor to the ceiling, the walls of my room were one giant collage—every square inch plastered with photographs. Three oversized posters, Led Zeppelin, Queen, and Pink Floyd, were the main focal points, along with 24x36 pin-ups of Kiss, Jimi Hendrix, Farrah Fawcett (the one in the orange, one-piece bathing suit), Cheryl Tiegs, a blacklight poster of Aurora Borealis, and one of the Dallas Cowboy Cheerleaders. A panel on the closet door displayed a larger-than-life Susan Anton. In between, the spaces had been filled with poster board and covered in 8x10 photos of scenery from various magazines, the backdrop for layers and layers of rock stars, scantily clad (or partially naked) women, fast machines, and other random fare. Each cut out and strategically overlapped to eliminate the hard vertical and horizontal lines. I'd done my best to camouflage bare breasts to avoid the wrath of Mom. It was one those Playmates basking in the sun, reclining against a coconut tree that caught Valerie's eye.

"What does your mom think about this?"

I was crunching through a riff from *Train Kept a Rollin'* on my electric imitation Stratocaster (white like Jimi's), hoping to impress. I stopped to look up as she pointed out the object in question. Shrugging my shoulders, I replied, "What can she say?" Trying to seem as if it were no concern of mine as if I was too cool to be worried with such trivial concerns, hoping to make her swoon at my aloofness. Turning back the volume a bit to kill the feedback, I picked out the opening progression of *Stairway to Heaven*, which drew her attention away from the colorful scenes on the wall and back in my direction.

"I love the way your hair looks hangin' down like that." She drifted across the room to run her fingers through it. "You look like a rock star." Wrapping the fingers of her left hand around the back of my neck, she pulled our lips together, the chords playing softly to the twisting rhythm of our tongues until my concentration was shattered, and I had to pull her closer. The music ended, and that's pretty much where we ended. It was the last time we were together. We were as close as we'd ever be, physically. Emotionally, there was nothing.

I couldn't figure her out. What made her tick? What was it she wanted out of the relationship? Did we even have a relationship? She was always taking my stuff. There had to be more to it than that. I didn't have much stuff, and I certainly didn't have any money. I didn't even have a cool car. She didn't want to go steady. *Does she even really like me?* For some reason, I was way too intimidated by her to make a move, even after the closeness in my bedroom. The lack of intimacy was an aura surrounding her like an invisible, impregnable force field. I couldn't turn it off. Maybe I was just afraid she would take me halfway and leave me hanging in frustration. It was time to call it quits. Besides, Amber was much less complicated.

One movie, one concert, a sterling silver necklace, a Good Times Deli T-shirt, and we were officially through. She could keep the stuff. She'd never have my heart.

I deserved Valerie Vander Burke after all the crap I'd put Amber through.

# 48. Skynyrd

Friday, October twenty-first, I was sitting in my car before school. Stunned. Devastated. Like I'd been gut-punched and was still trying to get my wind back. I drew another breath and let it back out. It was the only thing I was capable of. Anything else would've required a conscious effort. I didn't have it in me. Staring blankly into the illuminated face of the radio as the mournful guitar wailed the opening bars of *Freebird*,[33] I waited for the voice to come back and tell me it was untrue. Everything the D.J. had just said was a terrible misunderstanding. Surely there was some mistake. Still, in denial, I switched the radio off before the vocal gave way to blistering dual guitar leads. I stepped out of the car. The sullen faces I encountered on the way in the building confirmed the truth.

A chartered Convair 240 plane had crashed near McComb, Mississippi. The lead singer of Lynyrd Skynyrd, Ronnie Van Zant, was dead, along with lead guitarist Steven Gaines, and his sister Cassie, a back-up vocalist for the group. Gary Rossington, Alan Collins, and Artimus Pyle had miraculously survived – although not without severe injuries—along with the rest of the band and crew.

The world was off-kilter. Tipped off its axis, it wobbled out of control. We were all vulnerable.[7]

Suddenly, it was plausible.

The power of our music exemplified our lifestyles. In part, it defined who we were. Now, without perceivable cause or warning, our world came crashing to the ground. The sky was falling. The party, it seemed, was not going to go on forever. I was too numb to go to class, but what else was could be done? So, I went through the motions in body only, sitting stupefied in homeroom and the morning classes. Having followed the band since first hearing *Freebird* (now commonly known as the redneck national anthem), I knew nearly every song on every album, knew most of the words and had seen the band live on three occasions. At their concerts, I was hyper-aware of the danger, poised to duck for flying whiskey bottles. I had retreated to the dungeon of my bedroom, cranking the volume as *Don't Ask Me No Questions*[34] did the talking for me when my old lady pried a little too much. *Freebird* was my alibi every time I walked out on Amber, hopping the fence only to realize the grass was just as green where I had already been.

## The Quiet Kid

Ronnie Van Zandt had gone toe-to-toe with a legend. He had stood his ground with Neil Young on behalf of the *Southern Man*.[35] Rumor had it that the two of them sat down with a peace pipe to put the matter to bed. Ronnie sometimes wore a Neil Young shirt while performing live to signify the end of their civil disagreement. He had worn the shirt when they shot the cover of their latest album: *Street Survivors*. The Irony. They survived the game, the hustle on the street, the drugs, the rockstar trappings, working for MCA. *That Smell*[36] from the new material was about that. The plane went down in some farmer's field smack dab in the middle of BFE.

I already had the new album. On the cover, Ron Van Zant and Steven Gaines appeared as if they were being burned by flames that served as a backdrop for the group. Steven Gaines' head was engulfed in the flames. It was only a matter of days before the album would be re-released with a different cover.

This event launched the most ambitious undertaking of my academic career. It was my only real accomplishment to speak of up to that point. Before I had always fulfilled obligations for assignments, occasionally lucking into a nice piece of work.

Jerry Harris never liked the idea of me drawing and painting pictures from photographs. "Unless you take the pictures yourself, it's the same as plagiarism," he'd always remind me. He let me slide on my own time, but never for a grade. But knowing how the tragic plane crash had affected me and many of the kids who were in his art class, he gave me a wall in the gallery to display whatever I wanted, as a memorial to the band.

The memorial consisted of two watercolor paintings, one of Steven Gaines playing guitar, the other of Ronnie Van Zant on stage clutching his microphone stand with Steven Gaines behind him. The latter bore a caption at the bottom: FREEBIRDS? I wondered. A pencil sketch centered between the two paintings displayed the headline from the Knoxville News Sentinel. It doesn't sound like much, but I was proud of that display. I hoped it would make everyone else feel a little better and maybe prompt them to consider, as I had, their own mortality.

The whole world recalls the death of Elvis that year. But you could have asked any of my peers, and they would've set you straight. Elvis was not the King.

# 49. Wheeler

Amber tried. She really did, but she could never go unnoticed. She was being propositioned in her fifth-period class by a guy named Jeb Wheeler. Tall and gangly, Jeb was a bit of a dork. He had been passing notes in class, telling Amber how cute she was. And for some, reason he felt at liberty to tell her the things he wanted to do with her.

I was having none of it.

"Tell him you want to meet him in the stairwell after class." Amber listened carefully to my instructions. "But don't let on. He has to think you're really interested."

"What're you gonna do? You won't hurt him, will you?" Amber's blue eyes pleaded for mercy even though she was elated to be wearing the Scarlett trademark again. She believed it was in me to tear Jeb limb from limb if I wanted to.

Though not enrolled in any formal instruction, I had learned a little about self-defense in the martial arts class meeting twice a week after school in the commons. After much training with Mark and Ian at home, stretching out, doing forms, and sparring, my muscle tone was solid. My abs were hard as rock. At school, we sparred as well (sometimes blindfolded), so I was no stranger to hand-to-hand combat, although I had yet to be in an actual fight. They had taught me the basics—a fighting stance to make yourself a more elusive target, how to use your body weight to back your punches and kicks with power, how to get your opponent off guard, how to use your opponent's weight against him, and perhaps the most important: how to inflict the most damage, rendering your opponent defenseless and unable to continue in a fight. Once I was past his guard, I wouldn't hesitate to lay Jeb out with an elbow to the face.

Jacob Mac had witnessed me unleashing my frustrations, delivering the full power of my kicks on a punching dummy one afternoon in the school weight room. "I wouldn't want to piss him off," he had reported to Amber, who had later relayed it back to me.

"Don't worry; I won't kill him." I exuded confidence to Amber, but on the inside, I wasn't as solid. Jeb was taller, which meant he had the reach on me. And even though I knew in my head what to do to keep him at bay and how to open him up for the kill, there was the nagging, *What if?* How humiliating would it be if he turned the tables by kicking my ass? The one thing I was confident of was that no matter what the outcome, it wouldn't change how Amber felt about me, and she would still be mine. Nothing he could do could ever change that. And the thought of where he'd said he wanted to put his hands infuriated me. I had to do this for her.

"You don't have to do this," Amber said. "I can just tell him I'm not interested."

"And if he doesn't get the message? I won't stand by and let him think he can get away with sayin' those things to you. He needs to learn some respect."

It was on. I waited in the stairwell. Just like we had talked about, Amber told him in her sweetest voice she wanted to meet him after class. In his mind, she was going to give him everything he had dreamed about. He didn't have a clue. Poor sucker wouldn't know what hit him.

I tried to clear my anxiety, remembering the way I'd seen Randy Townes dismantle a bully earlier in the year. Randy was an average height, average weight, band geek. He had been taking Karate classes and was up to his green belt on the day Merle Britton, a below-average height persecutor—cocky in this opportunity to prove his manliness by selecting what he had believed to be a weak member of the herd —accosted Randy on the walk home from school.

"C'mon, punk." Merle took the first swing.

Mark and I had been walking twenty feet behind them when it started. Randy had done nothing to provoke it, ignoring the taunting Merle had been hurling at him well before we had crossed South Haven by the park.

The first swing never connected. Randy backed Merle up with a solid sidekick to the shin. Randy had clearly followed his instructor's advice. *Don't try to be Bruce Lee. Why try to kick your opponent in the head when a low kick will be just as effective.* An obvious look of surprise widened Merle's eyes. His brain must have convinced him it was just a fluke. There was no way Merle Britton could be outdone by a band geek. Resolve, anger, and stupidity registered simultaneously on Merle's face as he went back in again, absent this time of the smack talk. Again, Randy backed him up with another sidekick to the shin. An air of calm was on Randy, who didn't wait for Merle to strike a third time. Instead, Randy went on the offensive, delivering another swift kick to the shin before Merle had a chance to think. Reacting to the blow, both of Merle's clenched fists dropped down to waist level. He was open, defenseless for what came next. Randy landed a straight jab and bloodied Merle's nose.

"You broke it," Merle surmised, muffled underneath his fingers, both hands flattened out to protect the rest of his face. "You broke my nose," he said again, his brain convincing his ego of the fact it couldn't accept.

The bell rang. I snapped back to the present, trying to channel Randy's calm as I waited for eternity to pass before the first *ka-chunk* of the opening door echoed in the stairwell. It was Amber. Good. She had hurried to get there first.

"Stand where he can see you." I was off to one side of the door, just out of sight.

*Ka-chunk!* This time it was him. "Hey, pretty girl." Jeb sang it as he stepped through, oblivious of my presence.

I cut him off, stepping quickly between him and Amber. "Do you know who I am?" I said in a tone implying he should. He gave me an empty stare, saying nothing, unmindful that he had to peer down slightly to make eye contact. "Amber is my girlfriend," I said, establishing dominance.

Just then, the door opened again. Jeb's eyes diverted to see who it was. Mine stayed fixed. I only saw Lin Holloway in my peripheral. His eyes opened almost as wide as Jeb's when I said, "I would just a soon kick your ass as look at you."

Jeb flinched slightly even though I never moved. Lin froze in his tracks, still holding the door open as several students filtered in and stood in anticipation.

Jeb was trembling visibly despite the height advantage. I was doing my best to contain the shaking rush of adrenaline coursing through my veins. Adrenaline could've caused one of two things. 1) An unleashing of devastating, unholy fury, which might have been hard to call off before I did some serious damage to Jeb's face. This also could have included some grave disciplinary recourse had the wrong person stepped through the opened door or if someone decided to squeal. 2) Complete and utter humiliation had Jeb managed to defend himself long enough to get the upper hand. In an instant, I had to decide. *Is it worth the risk?* Several witnesses heard what I had said, and Jeb seemed to be in no mood to retaliate. My mission was accomplished already. Jeb Wheeler had received the message, loud and clear.

"Get outta here before I change my mind," I reasserted myself. He made no attempt to walk around, but rather turned away, hurrying back to leave through the door where he had entered.

The message was clear to everyone. Amber Barrett belonged to me.

# 50. Molly Chambers

It was early May. Already, it was hot, 85°F. The sun didn't care. It continued to punish us. Never-ending diamonds of chain link fence whizzed by in a blur. White lines ahead formed lanes, merging into the curve and vanishing to the right. The only change in view was the occasional passing of bodies between us and the fence. "Track," they would say as the patter of feet bore down on us, signaling their approach. Shifting quickly, we moved to the outside lane, just before the odor of perspiration smacked us in the face. We were sprinters, not much for the long haul. We weren't passing anyone.

Clark had stretched the sleeves of his sweatsuit all the way out over the joints of his cocoa brown wrists. His afro normally would have added six inches to his stature, but it was pressed down under his hood. *Why? He's got to be roasting.* I let the thought pass by with the next group of distance runners.

"I must be ... completely insane," I declared in between breaths and the steady rhythm of rubber thumping the asphalt.

"How's that?" Clark asked obligatorily.

"I was smokin' ... almost a pack ... a day before ... I started this."

"Yeah ... but you ... quit ... right?"

"First day ... cold turkey ... no effort."

"So why ... you sayin' ... you crazy?"

"Then there ... was ... the shin splints."

"And they ... went away ... eventually."

"True."

"So ... what then?"

I was talking way off the subject, not quite sure how to say what I wanted to say, or if I should even say it at all.

"What? Come on, man ... spit it ... don't leave me ... hangin'."

"Penny Marks."

"What about ... Penny Marks?"

"She's the reason ... I started this. It's just ... we've been ... talkin' ... a lot ... lately ... in art ... and ..."

"Man ... you don't ... want that," Clark cut me off.

"You think she's ... outta my league." I sounded offended, even though I knew it was true.

I had managed to get in the same art class with Penny again. I was still foolishly hanging on to the idea. I thought running track would somehow ease me into her crowd, doing something athletic in a school uniform.

We passed the starting mark for the twelfth and final time. Three miles. With hands on hips, we kicked our heads back and walked. Seizing the opportunity to breathe, our conversation was put on hold. When it resumed, I thought it better to change the subject.

"Why you wearin' those sweats, man? You gotta be burnin' up," I laughed.

"I can't stand the sun beatin' down on my skin, man. Besides, you wouldn't want a brotha to get sunburned." He grinned wide.

"You're not serious. You can't get sunburned?" It sounded like a question.

"Yeah, man. Whatchoo think? A black man can't get sunburn?"

"I never knew that."

"See whatchoo can learn when you keep yo' mind open." His face suggested he was kidding. But still, I knew he meant it.

"I thought you and Molly had sumpin' goin' on," he changed the subject back.

"Molly Chambers?" The idea was a mild electric shock, freezing my thought for a second, but as I processed it, I had to admit: the possibility of me with Molly was a lot more likely than Penny ever giving me anything more than the time of day.

From day one of spring track, Molly and I had been together almost every day. After track, we'd go to Lakeside Deli for hoagies. She liked hers the same way I did, mustard on the meat side, mayo on the cheese. Satiated, we'd ride around smoking joints, often ending up at her house. To my downfall, I had already filled her ears with talk about Penny. She'd had her fill, rolling her eyes at the mention of the name. And then she would remind me what an idiot I was.

"We're just friends," I concluded to Clark, convincing myself in the process.

"Yeah, well, don't misunderstand. Penny's a great girl but—here comes Walt. Let him tell you what he thinks about Penny."

Looking over my shoulder, I saw his wavy, blonde locks blowing back as he quickened his stride to catch up. He'd been walking behind us closer than I'd realized and had overheard part of our conversation, Walt pulled up beside us with a big, goofy grin.

"No doubt about it—Molly Chambers would be a lot more fun."

"What about Penny?"

"What a prude," Walt expounded. "I'm in the weight room, right? In the middle of an overhead press," he explained. "So, I've got both arms in the air. Completely vulnerable. Ring-dinger[37] sneaks up behind me ... the red-headed bastard pantsed me. Not just my shorts. He gets my jockstrap too. I'm standing there, completely exposed. Helpless. Right on cue, in walks Penny. Can you imagine the humiliation? As if that wasn't enough, she goes, 'Ew, Gross!' Jus' like that. Man. Talk about deflating a guy's ego. But hey, if you wanna take a crack at 'er, by all means. Don't let me stop ya."

Walt's tale did little to dissuade me. Penny's reaction was probably just a reaction. I mean, who'd want to see that hanging out there in public like that? They were probably right about one thing: My chances were slim and no-way-in-Hell. But I couldn't help thinking about all the times I'd made her laugh in art class. We had been having so much fun together. *Just maybe* ... I wasn't throwing in the towel just yet.

After a trip to Lakeside Deli, Molly and I headed back to the school parking lot. It was a good place to smoke. Inconspicuous. The parking lot was almost vacant, but not completely desolate. The risk factor was minimal, especially down in the lower forty. But the long-distance guys were still down there. Coming in from the northeast side, I turned left against the one way.

"You know why we're goin' this way?"

Molly knew but never got tired of humoring me. "Why?"

"Because it's against the rules." She said it with me in near-perfect sync, and then I added. "You know what I always say about rules."

"They were *made* to be broken."

"You know it. Or at least bent a little."

As if the Dodge had a mind of its own, it cut through the middle of the lot. The third tier was far enough from the building. If someone happened to exit, we could see them well in advance. Still driving, I produced a matchbook from my right pocket. Holding it with one hand, I tucked a single match underneath, folded the head around to the backside of the book, and thumbed it across the strike pad. A bright orange flame burst from the sulfur. "Just a little trick I learned in the Army."

Molly laughed, the way she always did at my stupid jokes. Poking at my shoulder with the tips of her fingers, she informed me. "You're not old enough to be in the Army, crazy boy. Now pass me that joint."

I couldn't help myself. It didn't matter how corny or random I was, the playful glimmer in Molly's green eyes was awakened, provoking a gentle nudge or poke or squeeze of my arm. She was light as the breeze drifting through the dogwoods in April. Talk came easy when I was with her, whether we were high or not. When we had been standing in line at the deli, she had had something so urgent to say which no one else was privy to. She leaned against me, her wrist resting on my shoulder, letting her fingers dangle as the whisper tickled my ear. This was what I enjoyed the most, the effortlessness, the casual playfulness in our conversation, the laughter. To take it to the next level would surely extinguish it. Even with as much affection as we had displayed between us with our eyes and our occasional seemingly innocent touches, I refrained myself from kissing her. There might've been a smoldering fire underneath our outward nonchalantness. I wasn't about to feed it oxygen. There was too much at stake to risk it. Instead, I continued in the delusion, thinking someone like me had reason to believe they belonged with someone like Penny. If I would have removed my head from my hindquarters for a minute or two, I might have taken stock in the very real possibility right in front of my face (not to mention the one I'd left on the backburner).

"So, what is it about me that keeps her from saying yes?"

The joint was gone, and I had randomly started on the subject again. Molly knew without asking who I was talking about.

"Why do you even care? You can do better than Penny. The problem isn't why she won't go out with you. It's why you shouldn't want to go out with her." Molly expected me to get it. She'd given me the same lecture, in one form or another, countless times – how she thought I was a great guy, followed by the attributes any girl would want in a guy.

"For starters, you listen when I talk, and you actually give a crap about what I have to say. You're a nice guy, a little on the bad side. Even with that warped—uhm, I mean, good sense of humor. And you're such a stud," she laughed. "Penny is too blind to see. She's the one who's missing out. And I'll tell you what else. She thinks she's too good for you. You don't need that."

"Yeah, well, I'm still not givin' up just yet."

"I knew you wouldn't. You're such a dumb ass." She slugged me on the shoulder and gave me a look of disappointment, changing to sympathy before giving way to a smile of unconditional acceptance. "You just don't know when to quit. But that's one more thing to like about you, I guess."

Molly told me in no uncertain terms I should forget about Penny. But I was too stupid to hear it. I was bound and determined to go after the one thing I couldn't have and to pass by the best thing that had crossed my path in a long time. The grass is always greener on the other side, or so they say.

Molly, her nose dotted with delicate freckles, was so sweet and funny and cute. She was just fun to be with, but I couldn't block out the sound of the train in the distance, letting the girl that would have been good for me slip like sand between my fingers.

Whenever I'd tire from chasing the train to Arrowhead (where Penny lived), I'd end up at Amber's. She didn't mind being second fiddle to whomever I was pursuing at the time. She was too good for me, as well. I didn't deserve her or Molly. I was getting *exactly* what I deserved: The constant rejection I was tolerating from Penny Marks. I was Kevin Bacon trying out for the upcoming role in Animal House, grabbing my ankles for the fraternity hazing. "Thank you, sir. May I have another?" Penny was Niedermeyer, dark and sinister underneath the cloak and hood, looking like the grim reaper, only a lot prettier.

# 51. Penny Marks

It was a desperate, if not pathetic move, but I had become so depressed obsessing over the one unattainable desire—like Hemingway's big fish.[38] It was so big that you couldn't get it in the boat. It was destined, if you caught it (spoiler alert), to be devoured by sharks before you could haul it to shore.

I could have driven, but I was hoping Penny would be impressed after I had pedaled seven miles to her house in the grueling heat just to see her. Plus, I didn't want my car to be visible from the street.

The houses in the Arrowhead subdivision weren't mansions by any stretch of the imagination, but they were at least twice the size of any in my neighborhood. Most of the houses were two stories. Some were ranchers, and all of them brick. As I turned my bike down the road that led in through the brick entrance signs, I had the overwhelming sensation that I didn't belong there, like I was a wolf about to sneak in through the back gate to invade the hen house. I stopped pedaling and coasted down to Penny's house. I recognized her Volkswagen Thing in front of the two-story brick house. *This must be the place.*

She had some idea I might show up. I had spoken with her on the phone before I left.

"It's not a good idea," she had said, adding, "Rick would be pissed."

Rick was her six foot-something boyfriend. Broad as well, he outweighed me by at least sixty pounds.

"I don't care. I'll see you in a few," I said firmly, just before hanging up.

Dismounting, I walked my bike into the shade and dropped the kickstand to park it by a gate which opened to the sunlit back yard. My heart was pounding in my ears. Butterflies, fluttering violently, ascended into my throat. I swallowed hard, tasting the hot, dusty scales of their orange wings and took a deep breath. Exhaling slowly, I passed through the gate and made my way across the sidewalk to the back corner of the house.

The yard was plush and green with neatly trimmed hedges around the perimeter and an eight-foot swath of broom-finished concrete around the swimming pool. But I saw only her, lounging on her back, less than twenty yards away. All my anxiety left, as I was mesmerized by the vision. She hadn't heard me as I approached. The radio was blaring Hall and Oates.

*Rich Girl. How appropriate.*[39]

Apparently, she hadn't believed I would come, or she didn't care. Either way, no special precaution had been taken. She was completely exposed to the brightness of the big yellow sun, covered only in the absolute necessary places by the tiniest white string bikini. I took full advantage of the opportunity handed to me. Slightly behind her, I crept around slowly to get a better view.

Her toenails, painted white to match, tugged at my attention, unable to hold it, as I followed the length of her legs, which were parted slightly, up to the neat white triangle. I lingered there, but only for a second. I couldn't help myself. Scattered across her flat bronzed abdomen, minuscule beads of sweat glistened, reflecting rays of the sun as they danced off the water. Thin white strings stretched across her hip bones, resting at the peaks in neatly tied bows. Blonde hair, delicate like fuzz on peaches, luminescent against her golden-brown skin, trailed up to her navel and along her dainty arms. The weight of her breasts was slight, but enough to create moderate tension on the strings crossing her clavicles and disappearing behind her neck. Her blonde hair was feathered back and spread out like angel wings lightly touching her softly rounded shoulders—the face of an angel. Tiny freckles, drawn out by the sun, popped up on her elegant little nose. *She's perfect.*

Behind her eyelids were irises blue as the sky. My shadow passed in front of them, and the angel awoke, startled. She bolted upright.

"When did you get here?"

"Just now." Which was true. I had only been there a matter of seconds.

"I can't believe you showed up." She looked concerned, but not totally disappointed. Whether she was interested in me or not, it had to boost her ego. Not that she needed it.

"I told you I would."

"Yeah, well, it's good to see you and all, but if Rick shows up, he will kill you."

Rick was on the football team, defensive line. I knew he could.

"He'll have to catch me!" I laughed.

"You are crazy, you know." She turned loose a smile.

"Yeah, I know. But that's why you like me, isn't it?"

"How can I not? Even if you are dumb as rocks."

"Yeah, well, you still invited me here."

"I did not invite you. I told you not to come. And yet, here you are."

"Yeah, well, you're not complainin'."

"No. No, I guess not. It is nice to have some company." Penny got up and wrapped a towel around her. She picked up a brush from a nearby table and sat back down, stroking her long blonde hair. "You want somethin' to drink? My dad has beer."

"Water would be nice. And also, you really didn't have to cover up. I promise I won't stare." I was lying, of course, watching her hips wiggle as she got up to go in the back door.

"Even if I believed that I'd still do it for your protection." She paused at the door, looking over her shoulder before going inside. "Your odds of living increase ever so slightly if Rick does show up, and I'm wearing the towel."

"I'd rather take my chances," I called out as the door closed behind her.

She did like me; I got her to admit that much, just not the way I wanted her to. We kept the conversation light and flirty for a while, but eventually, it became more serious. I had to know if I really had a chance. If not, I had decided I would accept her reasoning, whatever it might be, and leave her alone. "It could never work," she explained, although she could never quite say exactly why, always steering the subject back to Rick. Concerning him, I never got a straight answer. Did she love him or even really care about him? It was comfortable for her. Being with him worked. She was safe and secure and cared for. But was she happy?

"I really think you should go now," was the answer I got to the question.

I finally gave up and said goodbye, adding, "But if you ever change your mind …."

I could've called Penny the one that got away. Truth be told, I never even had her on the hook. She was too clever for that, nibbling away at the bait, playing with it, teasing me with the occasional tugging of my line. But she was only biding her time, waiting for a more expensive lure to drop. If it came along and was attractive enough, sparkling enough, and the timing was just right, then she would take it hook, line, and sinker. She might even pretend to put up a fight. In the end, the guy with the most to invest in his tackle would reel her in. Even so, if his boat wasn't big enough, there would always be the sharks.

# 52. Watertown Part II

Tires crunched over gravel, spitting them out into the dust trail behind the rumbling of Benny's busted truck muffler.

He was coming.

Mark and I were already awake, even though the sun had not yet made its appearance on the Middle Tennessee horizon. Farrah, the Ferret, made sure of that. She was part of our morning ritual, announcing her presence early, nibbling at our faces and ears or whatever she could find unprotected by the covers. If we had forgotten in our sleep that we were in Watertown, Mike Stuart's favorite pet made sure we remembered. Also, Farrah wanted to remind us of the thrilling rollercoaster ride we were once again about to embark upon. We looked forward to it with excruciating anticipation.

Benny was two bricks shy of a load. He drove his truck like a winged blind rat making its escape from the depths of Hades. Every weekday morning, we found ourselves being slung from side to side in the cab as the truck careened recklessly, fishtailing in the gravel around ridiculously tight curves which seemed to lead nowhere, knowing all the while it would get only slightly better once we reached the main road.

We were installing fence, mostly chain link, for Mike Stuart's company, Orchard Fence. As far as jobs go, this was the most strenuous I had done. Aside from mowing grass, I had spent a summer in a reading program for underprivileged kids at the Boys Club in Vestal, and keeping score for girls' softball at Maynard Glen Field. Those summers were cake compared to the physical labor required to erect chain link fencing.

One morning, Benny was slaving away, plunging posthole diggers into the ground, oblivious to the fact he had cut himself and was bleeding. The guy was a machine. He was programmed every day for the job at hand by his father, Lenny, who possessed a full load of bricks and was also sometimes our boss.

When Lenny wasn't our boss, we worked under Daryl, who we heartlessly nicknamed no-neck Daryl, for obvious reasons. He had no neck. And I don't mean he was so bulked up that his muscles ran straight up to his head. No. It wasn't like that. He had a physical deformity. The guy literally had no neck.

Honestly, kids can be so cruel. No-neck got pissed at Mark and me one afternoon when it was unbearably hot, and he caught us hiding out in the shade of the truck (my idea). He got over it after he found out we were only getting a hundred bucks a week—a hundred bucks a week plus free room and board. Room and board consisted of a spot on the floor of a trailer with free wake-up service and home-cooked meals compliments of Mike's latest live-in girlfriend.

We caught a break midway through the summer when Mike used Mark and me as grunt labor for the roofers he had hired. The hundred-year-old, two-story log cabin was being restored on the property next to the trailer for the most part in the shade of trees. The head knocker, whose name escapes me, worked hard, but he always had plenty of time for cutting up, if it didn't slow down the process. Whenever he would crack a good-natured joke, usually at our expense, he would cackle like the Wicked Witch of the West. The downside was we got split up during that stretch. Mike only needed one of us on the roof, so he alternated us between the roof and the fences. Still, it gave us plenty to talk about in the evening.

There was nothing out there at night except the stars. They seemed to multiply magnificently out there miles away from the light pollution. Mark and I would finish supper and lie on the hood of my '69 Dodge and talk, mostly about girls and rock 'n' roll bands, or whatever excitement might have transpired that day. It was good to be spending time with Mark again. We had never parted ways, really. After all, our mothers had raised us right next door to one another. But he had wisely chosen not to spend his days in the fog of a marijuana haze and had often been with a different crowd.

Underneath the brilliant stars, we talked of an upcoming event. Mike was letting us off mid-week to see Alice Cooper in concert. That was excitement enough, but on top of that, we had dates lined up. He was taking his girlfriend, Brenda. I was taking Bebe Sanders.

The trip home was normally around two and a half hours, or a little longer, depending on traffic. We made it that Wednesday in two flat. I must have averaged ninety miles an hour, and at one point, crossing the Cumberland Plateau, the needle hit the speedometer's max of a hundred and ten. The worst part for Mark was when we reached Knoxville city limits. Seventy-five miles an hour, zigzagging steadily through rush hour traffic had him white-knuckling the dashboard.

## The Quiet Kid

Bebe Sanders was the last pick-up before we went to the show. She had me pull off at the Gulf station on Chapman Highway, saying she had a little surprise for me. Bebe laid out two lines of white powder on her make-up mirror. "MDA," she said. I had never heard of such an animal. It was supposedly a mixture of heroin and cocaine, and God only knows what else. According to Bebe, the third ingredient was something called Crystal T, a crystallized concentration of THC—the active ingredient in Marijuana. It was added for its hallucinogenic properties. I had my doubts, especially in light of what had happened at the first Ted Nugent show. Bebe had already done the same amount she was presenting to me. "I'm feelin' fine," she assured me with a goofy grin. I set my fears aside and lined my nose and brain with the white crystalline powder.

When we arrived at the coliseum, I was flying high, until I almost drowned in what would have been the most colossally stupid drowning ever recorded in the history of colossally stupid drowning accidents. They say that a person can drown in six inches of water if the conditions are right. I almost accomplished this feat with less than an inch of water, scooped into the palm of my hand from the water fountain, and snorted directly up my nose. It was a complete shock to the system. I recognized my mistake instantly, but it was too late to reverse the consequences. Gagging and coughing for a good five minutes, I was finally able to rid my body of the unwanted $H_2O$. The human body is composed of somewhere between 50-65 percent water, and yet, there is zero-tolerance for it anywhere that oxygen is being processed. Still, I survived the night without further incident. Alice Cooper put on a superb theatrical performance.

I wrote an incredibly corny letter to Bebe. I was trying to be romantic. I was trying to be sincere. We would spend a day in the mountains together when I was back in Knoxville. I told her how much I missed her. It wasn't true, but I wanted it to be. I'm not sure why. I liked Bebe, but the reality was, I was still looking for a replacement for Amber, trying to see if I could survive without her in my life.

The trip to the Great Smoky Mountains with Bebe was going to be epic. Except it wasn't. It didn't live up to the hype. We smoked some joints and did the drive-by. A handful of words passed between us all day. Awkward. We never even got out of the car.

I didn't write anymore more letters to Bebe. We didn't see each other until school started back.

For the remainder of the summer, Mark and I worked on our tans and our lats. The day in and day out usage of posthole diggers affected our latissimus dorsi muscles in a way that caused a noticeable swelling, which we didn't really mind. It looked good with the tan.

# 53. Blaine Part II

Most of the things Coach Hall said were purely for the entertainment value. Like the time he told us about a group of thugs driving behind him, harassing him, making obscene gestures, and trying to get him to pull over. They tailed him, he said, until they realized they had followed him into the parking lot of the downtown Knoxville Police Department. The thugs disappeared in a hurry.

When he got around to the subject of us being near the end of our junior year and having newly acquired driver's licenses, what he said left us all solemn as Catholic Priests on Ash Wednesday. It was one of the rare statements he had made of an extremely serious nature. He was exhorting with a word of caution: "Statistics have proven to be very accurate. Take a good look around you. If not from this room, then from one of your other classes, but mark it down: At least one of you will not be with us for graduation next spring."

The Gulf station at the corner of Chapman Highway and Woodlawn was a popular teenage hang-out. Nothing was special about the place other than the convenience of location. Concrete picnic tables on the Woodlawn side were out of management's line of vision. We were spending a fair amount of money there, especially on weekends. Some of us would drop by and hang around until it was a party. To keep the numbers down, small groups would come and go, driving off to burn one and inevitably coming back with the munchies or to top of the tank. We ushered in our share of business.

It was July. The humidity in the air draped over me like a dank towel in a sauna. No one else was around, which was unusual even for a Wednesday night. I figured it would change soon enough and sat down to light a Saratoga Menthol, wondering why the hell I'd started back.

I didn't have to reach back very far to recall the event: an overnight trip to Cherokee Lake on the 129 side with some buddies. Greg Willis was one of them. We sat down in a hole someone had dug for a fire pit, taking slugs from a quart bottle of Smirnoff, passing a half-gallon of orange juice for a chaser. We made no attempt at crawling out of the hole until the bottle was dry. Taking a leak, or rather standing to take a leak, was a challenge. Walking a straight line was next to impossible. Somewhere in the blur, I got a nicotine craving.

"Just one won't make you start back," Greg Willis advised.

The next morning, I wanted nothing more than to puke, but I could heave up nothing except traces of foul-tasting bile. All I could do was pray, promising God I would never do it again.

*I should kick Greg's ass.* But it had been my own, drunken choice. I took another drag off the skinny cigarette.

A bronze GTO turned on its blinker and pulled into the station. Valerie Van der Burke coasted up to pump #4. I didn't bother getting up. We weren't exactly on friendly terms. It wasn't like we weren't speaking, but we had avoided each other like an impending dental appointment for the better part of the year. I wouldn't have minded finding a remedy for the situation. I hated being on anyone's bad side. Unsure about which way my luck had just turned, I stayed put.

Val exploded out of the car, looking flustered. In a flurry of noticeably quick, jerky, almost disoriented motion, she yanked the gas hose from its station and shoved it into place, fighting the apparatus as if the pump and the hose were in a conspiracy to prevent her from accomplishing her mission. Lost in the comical display, I hadn't noticed Linda Lionheart exiting from the passenger's side. She headed straight in my direction.

"Have you seen Blaine?" Linda's voice rang with urgency. She wasn't her usual, level self, and her voice might've been a little shaky.

"No. Why? What's up?"

My question didn't register. She asked another. "Have you been here long?"

"Prob'ly close to an hour. Why?"

This time she responded. "Valerie and Blaine had a big blowup, and now she can't find him. She's called everyone she can think of." She paused, her gaze miles down the highway, and then she locked on my eyes with penetrating concern.

"We've looked everywhere, Mikey. Everywhere."

*Big surprise. She's finally run him off.* Blaine and Valerie had been shacking up for a while now. I knew it was only a matter of time. I was glad later. I hadn't said it out loud.

Linda stared at the pavement, digging for another question, searching for another rock to overturn. Hoping for something they'd missed. Waiting for an answer, she knew I didn't have. After a few seconds, she realized I couldn't help. She looked up and forced

## The Quiet Kid

a smile. "Thanks anyway, sweetie. Gotta run." She turned away, hurrying inside to pay for the gas. I watched her jog back out to the already running car. Valerie laid down a black mark as she screeched away from the pumps, tires still spinning when they fishtailed onto Chapman Highway.

I hung out for another hour or so, wondering if they would come back by. They didn't. Nobody did. After a while, I gave up on the night and drove home.

Blaine died, alone, in the early morning hours of July 27, 1978. He was found in his car, which—driven at a high rate of speed—had run underneath the rear bumper of a road construction truck on Chapman Highway less than a mile south of where I had encountered Linda and Valerie. There had been no visible indication of an attempt to stop or even slow down. No skid marks were found. I imagined (though I tried not to) that it wasn't a pretty scene. Blaine had fallen from his high wire, lost his balance there in the darkness in the middle of the long night. He had been heavily sedated. Various drugs were found in his system. It was impossible to know if his actions were intentional. That was the hardest part for everyone who had made his acquaintance. Some surmised he had done it intentionally. If Blaine, the high wire artist, had found no reason to go on living, what chance did any of the rest of us have? Anyone who really knew him knew he hadn't meant to do it. Most likely, he had fallen asleep at the wheel and never saw it coming.

There were droves of kids with hollow faces at Blaine's funeral, wandering lost, searching for answers. The clergy at the Berry's Funeral Home attempted to offer much-needed comfort, but they were ill-equipped—through no fault of their own—to provide the kind of answers needed. The way would have to be sought out and discovered by individuals, one by one. But it would be found only by those who desired to bask in its light, hungered to be fed, turned over rocks yearning to uncover the truth. If Blaine's death had accomplished nothing else, it left at least one individual searching.

Some of the regular crew gathered at the Gulf station the night after Blaine's funeral. "Let's get high," they said. "That's the way he would've wanted it." And, "We'll do it in honor of Blaine."

I wasn't feeling it. I doubted their logic. How could anyone on earth possibly know what Blaine would or wouldn't have wanted? What advice would he have bestowed upon us had he been able to speak on his own behalf? I wanted to punch their faces—ball up my fist and bloody their presumptuous noses. It was just another lame excuse for those who scarcely knew him to do what they were going to do anyway. Get wasted. *No, thank you. Not right now.* I refrained myself. One thing I felt sure about was that Blaine wouldn't have advised starting a stupid fight over something that couldn't possibly be undone.

"No thanks," I said politely. With no reason to stay, I plunged my hands into my pockets, kicking rocks as I walked to my car. I got in and drove home to the refuge of my bedroom to find some more tears to shed for my friend, who was never coming back.

In the solitude of my bedroom, I stared at a poster of Ted Nugent, noticing something about it I had never seen before. Just over his left bicep was an image, superimposed and nearly invisible. The weird thing was this: Once I had seen it, it was impossible to un-see. I was no expert on the subject, but the only thing it resembled was the head of a demon. A chill ran down my spine. The words of *Stranglehold*[40] flashed through my brain. The part where he implies something along the lines of never having to die. *Liar!*

I never said it out loud, but in my head, I was screaming at the top of my lungs. With tears streaming off my cheeks, I ripped the poster from the wall, shredding it into tiny, unrecognizable pieces.

# 54. Senior Year

I tried to imagine my fellow students in their underwear, but it didn't seem to be working. My vain attempts did nothing to conceal the trembling in my voice as I recited my chosen verses of poetry for oral interpretation.

Fear of public speaking ranks above fear of death for most people, or so they say. I was beginning to think "they" may be a reliable source. The words I formed came out sounding hollow and meaningless, as I struggled to remember them. I was just trying to get through. It shouldn't have been that hard. I scanned the room and found Cindy Robbie's smiling face and focused on it, blocking out everyone else. Dan's little sister was one of the bright spots in this unfamiliar territory.

Drama.

Taking drama meant I wouldn't have to take senior English. On an experimental basis, drama was being offered as a substitute for the otherwise inescapable required subject. I had survived by the skin of my teeth, getting through the final in Mrs. Brown's Junior English class.

*There is a God in heaven.*

Mark took advantage of this little miracle from above as well. We were in a mixed grade class where we befriended Cindy and Linda Fitzmaurice, who were both sophomores. They were both as cute as sixth-period is long.

Jerry had persuaded me to attend the University of Tennessee in the fall. My schedule was loaded with Drama, Geometry, and Algebra I. I was taking Algebra I a second time to bring my GPA up because I had done so poorly the first time around (I had gotten a "D" in the class because I refused to take a book home). I was still carrying an extra hour of Art-instead-of-study-hall for my fourth-period class.

It hadn't been the first time I'd had an extra hour of Art. The way I'd stumbled into it had been a combination of sheer genius and dumb luck. A student's name was called to no response for the first week of study hall. After the first week, the teacher just assumed the student had dropped. I had heard Coach Ogle mumbling "must've dropped." So, I figured it was worth the risk, signing up but not showing up. My unofficial fourth-period class was lunch. If nothing better was going on, I hung out in the art room, partaking in their assignments or painting watercolors of rock stars.

All in all, I had it pretty good. But it wasn't feeling that way.

Linda Lionheart had graduated. I rarely saw her. Opting not to go out for track again, I lost touch with Molly Chambers. I passed her in the halls every now and again, but with no shared classes, we just lost touch.

Amber Barrett had graduated as well and had a full-time job. We were still seeing each other on occasion and talking on the phone several times a week. At this point, there was no label on our relationship status. She was always by the phone, ready to go. Sherry always referred to Amber as "my old standby."

If I had stopped to evaluate what my future held and all I had going for me—college, a possible career in the arts, and a girl waiting in the wings—I would've realized how good I had it. But I didn't. My focus was on the things eluding me: Penny Marks, for one. The fact I had spent the last four years fooling around on the guitar and gotten nowhere was another. I hadn't written the first line to one decent song or learned to play anything past some basic chords. So much for being a rock star.

The Drama class was taught by Mr. Jacobson. His thinning blonde hair looked like combed cotton candy with sideburns. Plaid polyester pants and a pullover sweater, a little weird on the surface, but who wasn't? *He's okay, I guess.*

Indubitably better than Senior English, Drama wasn't without its hurdles, namely the dramatic interpretation of poetry in the close confines of the classroom. It hadn't been a walk in the park for anyone. The latest class assignment was a little less intimidating. We had to come up with an invention and then sell it to the class. But at least we didn't have to do this alone.

Mark Lee and I pitched the concept for our product —The Phone-A-Clone—to Cindy Robbie, Linda Fitzmaurice, and the brain of the group, Chris Grady. The product would enable the consumer to conjure a clone of themselves through the telephone line using any ordinary phone, say, a public phone booth. Simple enough. It never would've taken wings had it not been for the ingenuity of Chris Grady.

Chris had an uncanny ability of explaining things in technical terms, sounding as if they made perfect sense. But he went so far over everyone's head that no knew exactly what he was talking about. Therefore, no one would be able to shoot down the plain and simple fact that we had no earthly idea how it worked.

The details of the Phone-A-Clone project were subject to a certain amount of scrutiny and discussion between Chris and me at Maynard Glen Field. Chris' older brother tagged along to give his input and to spark our creativity with his stash. We already had the basics down. A couple of joints couldn't hurt anything at this stage in the planning.

To look at Steve and Chris, side by side, you'd never guess they were even related, much less brothers. Chris was tall and lanky with sandy blonde hair and a certain air of sophistication in his mannerisms. Steve was shorter and thicker with dark hair and the beginnings of a beard. He bore a strange resemblance to a young Stephen King. In the weeks I had known Steve, he talked incessantly about his tenure in a mental institution. His favorite topic was of a certain deranged individual he had met there by the name of Kenny Schrader.

It had become apparent the Phone-A-Clone discussion had gone about as far as Chris and I could take it without further input from our group. We let it go. Steve was now deep in his ramblings.

"Did I ever tell you—he's schizo!" It was more of a proclamation than a question. Steve waited for a reply, nonetheless.

"Um, no. You mean, schizophrenic?"

"Uh, huh. Yeah, man. One minute, he'd been the sanest person you ever met in your life, and the next, he'd be goin' on and on about guys in leather uniforms with gas masks chasin' after him. He'd lock himself in his room, hide under the bed. Or he'd just run away. The interns would have to chase him down and tranquilize him." Steve was off again, ranting about the antics of Kenny Schrader until we had lost all sense of time. Chris was about to light a joint – the third, or maybe the fourth. I'd lost count.

I interrupted. "So whatever happened to the guy?"

"Oh, they managed to get everything under control with medication. I'm all right now."

"What?"

Steve looked right through me, his eyes glassy and red. He had changed, a deranged grin pasted across his face. Even though physically, he appeared the same, there was something different. I couldn't put my finger on it. "Wha'd you say?"

The grin morphed from deranged to complete silliness, more of a Charlie Brown after he'd kissed the little red-haired girl kind of smile. Even with the scraggly facial hair, Steve looked like a little kid. "I'm Kenny." He said, staring at a point in space a million miles away, a place I could never have gone even if I'd wanted to. What he said was one hundred percent true. I was sure of it. The transformation took place right in front of my eyes. I could almost pinpoint exactly when it had happened. Steve was no longer there. Kenny had taken his place.

A shiver ran the length of my spine.

Heart released their fourth album in October of 1978. I was quite taken by Ann Wilson's ethereal eyes. Those eyes—so far away and dreamy—pierced my soul like a bullet clad in full metal jacket, penetrating flesh without regard for what was in the way. In the same manner, her powerful vocals sliced right to my core.

When Heart brought their show to the Civic Coliseum, I was there wielding a 35 mm camera equipped with a 70-200 mm zoom lens I'd borrowed from Mike Stuart. Positioned on the first row of the balcony, flanking the left side of the stage, I was almost eye-level with the band. Ann Wilson prowled the platform like a jungle cat. She made an about-face at the far side, strutting back across, heading in my direction. With my forearm and an elbow braced on the railing, I was poised for the shot. She came close enough to fill the viewfinder. In the same instant, she saw me. The reflex mirror, condenser lens, and optical glass between us were no match for the power of her gaze. She looked right through them and right through me. A smile creeping up from either side of the microphone rendered me defenseless. I dropped back into my seat, blown away, without snapping off a single frame.

But enough about my boyish obsession.

"Steve Grady is certifiable Looney Tunes." I passed the joint to Linda Fitzmaurice, who was riding shotgun.

The pronounced "M" shape of her upper lip left the impression of a perpetual pout. "Chris's brother?" She looked perplexed for a

## The Quiet Kid

second, and then her eyes crossed as she focused on the joint. She hit it and then turned to pass it to the back seat.

"No, thank you." Cindy never smoked, but Fitz offered anyway.

Fitz passed back to me and turned down the radio. A thin braid dangled by the left side of her face as she tilted her head forward slightly. She fixed her large amber eyes to study my face. "What do you mean?"

"His elevator doesn't reach the top floor. He's mad." I paused for a hit. "Nutzo." I said, my voice straining to hold the smoke. Fitz was looking at me like her question had still gone unanswered. I continued. "He's out of his gourd, cuckoo."

"Aren't we all?" she stated evenly.

"No. No really. He thinks he's Kenny Schrader." I proceeded to give them the complete rundown.

The Phone-A-Clone project was a huge success. Cindy and Fitz suggested using a refrigerator box for a phone booth, which turned out to be brilliant. After the openings were cut away, we covered the cardboard with aluminum foil to give it a metallic effect. Next, to sell the illusion that Mark was my clone, we painted our faces like Alice Cooper, our invented spokesperson. Neither of us looked like Alice. Nor did we resemble one another. But with the make-up, a little imagination took us a long way. After pontificating to the class for fifteen minutes, Chris had them eating out of our hands. They would've bought whatever we had to sell.

When grades were given for our presentations, we passed with flying colors. Mr. Jacobson suggested we work Phone-A-Clone in as a skit for the senior play, which was to be presented at the end of the year. The class voted unanimously to his motion. Mark and I weren't completely convinced we wanted to do it in front of the whole school, but Jacobson encouraged us to stretch beyond what we thought we were capable of because he believed we could be even more. He was turning out to be a great teacher and an all-around nice guy. He was all right in my book.

# 55. Janet

Janet was a breath of fresh air. She was just what I needed to break free from what's-her-name. Maybe for good this time. The control had lost its adrenaline. *Amber needs to be cut loose, to date or whoever.*[41] I said it in my head but wasn't totally convinced.

I let it go the second I saw Janet in the hall.

She poked out her lower lip in a mock pout. And then she flashed her Ultra-Brite smile. Her tiny teeth were extremely white in contrast to her skin, brown and silky as chocolate milk. It was still February, and she appeared as though she'd been basking in the sun. "I guess you heard," she said with an unmistakable drawl.

*She's so South Knoxville.*

"Lemme guess. You broke up." I tried not to sound too overjoyed. I leaned one hand against the locker adjacent to hers and took the book she handed me while she stacked the ones she didn't need back on the top shelf.

"Yep. It's official. Me and Jake Mac are history." Her smile was a weak façade. The fake pouting had been closer to accurate. She was a cheerleader. She knew how to put on a good front.

"You okay?" I was genuinely concerned.

"I'm fine. It's been a long time comin'."

"But you knew it was comin'."

"Yeah ... I knew it was comin'." Now the hurt was seeping out.

I wanted to give her a big hug, but our relationship wasn't there yet.

"Anything I can do?" I turned to follow her down the hall.

"Nuh-uh, just walk me to class." Janet wrapped her fingers in the crook of my elbow as if I was her escort, and she was the homecoming queen. "We needed a clean break," she said. "An' at least there was no fightin'. We just agreed it was time to move on."

She filled me in on the details as we walked. All too soon, we arrived at the door of her next class.

"Thanks for list'nin'," she said. "And fer bein' there for me." She started through the open door, turning back before entering the room. Leaning on the jamb, she crossed the toe of one saddle oxford behind her other ankle, adding, "An' for just bein' you." She gave me a wink and slipped inside.

I thought about her all afternoon, not aware of much else, except for fleeting moments when I forced myself to muddle through the

## The Quiet Kid

pointless assignments. Replaying the image, I saw her standing in the doorway, her short cheerleader's skirt revealing her brown thighs. She was petite with a tight, compact body. Her full, cinnamon hair with natural honey blonde highlights swept back to reveal her face. She was hard to define. Cheerleader pretty didn't cover it. Unique, exotic—the mold was broken when God made her.

Cindy Robbie smiled, pleased as punch at the results of our pictures from the Valentine dance. "These are so good. For us, not being a couple, we make a cute couple."

I looked over her shoulder to re-examine the photo I'd gotten in homeroom.

She was skinny, skinnier than me even, wearing dark, straight-legged jeans with a matching vest which opened to a long-sleeved, buttoned-down white shirt. Her shoes were wallabies. I had on flared-legged jeans, dark also, with cuffs turned up at the bottom. My shirt was brown and orange plaid, unbuttoned enough to reveal the shark's tooth on a choker made from a single strand of leather. My light brown vest, borrowed from the only suit I owned, was buttoned up. The leather belt I was wearing was the same one I'd had for nearly five years. (In the back of the belt was a section of braiding, obviously not visible in the picture.) My shoes were soft leather, similar to hers, and my hair was close to the same length. She sported "Farrah Fawcett" feathered bangs. I had trimmed my long, straight mane to give it some shape, feathering my bangs, but not to the same extreme.

From behind, it would've been difficult to tell which one of us was the guy, except I was broader at the shoulders and slightly taller. The pose was casual but close with a comfortable amount of touching, which confirmed the status of our relationship. My right arm was around her waist, her left elbow resting on my shoulder with her fingers hanging free. Pulled toward my midsection, her right hand was loosely clinched as if she was holding something fragile. She made the slightest contact, not holding on to my vest, just touching lightly—close, but not too close. She was Dan's sister. Even I trusted me with her.

I sat back down next to her, and we divvied up the pictures. We were supposed to be discussing plans for the end of the year

Drama production, but for the most part, we knew what we were doing already. Mr. Jacobson was pretty laid-back about our social exchanges.

"I got you something." She handed me a small box with a card Scotch-taped to it.

Inside the box was a hairbrush. "Not that you need it," she said. "I just wanted to cheer you up." She knew the moods I was prone to. Much of our conversation at the dance had been about Janet and the whole—*I just don't know if she'd be interested in someone like me*—thing. It felt right, though – like she might say yes. But I was struggling to find the courage. I wasn't ready to face the possibility of more rejection.

I thanked Cindy and pulled the card from the envelope. On it was an illustration of a kitten on her back playing with a ball of yarn. A black and tan puppy dominated the kitten, straddling her as if he was plotting his plan of attack. The sex of the animals, of course, was not graphically depicted. Their genders had been determined by Cindy. She had penciled in 'Janet' by the kitten and 'Mike' by the puppy. Inside the card, she had written: *Be stern.*

"There's only one way to find out," Cindy said. "Ask her."

Again, I was playing out of my league. But this time, it seemed different. This wasn't just a whim. Janet and I had been talking a lot, and there seemed to be some genuine chemistry between us. I was almost sure she liked me in the same way.

I took Cindy's advice—*be stern* and strutted up to Janet with purpose. *She likes you. Whatta ya worried about?*

I wasn't taking no for an answer.

*Unless she says no, in which case I'll have to rethink my strategy.*

She was rummaging through her locker, looking down. In one swift motion, she slammed the door and turned to go. I was standing so close; if she had been taller, our lips might have accidenty met. As it was, she nearly planted her nose in my chest. She jumped back. "Oh!" She raised a hand to her heart, laughing. "You scared me."

"Sorry. I just wanted to get close to you."

It was a Thursday afternoon, so she wasn't sporting her short skirt. Jeans and a casual sweater. But still, she looked fantastic. She could've rocked anything. She looked up with a twinkle in her brown eyes. "If you wanted to get closer, all you had to do was ask."

"Okay. I will then." I hesitated only a second. *Don't look. Just jump.* "We should go out sometime. I'd really like to get to know you better."

"I'd like that, Mike. Ya know. I feel like I'm startin' to know you already. But I'm sure there's plenty more I don't know. Besides, I'm always talkin' 'bout me and my stupid problems. It'd be nice for us to talk about somethin' else for a change."

"So the answer's, yes?"

"Well you gotta ask me first, sweetheart."

"Um, oh yeah, well..." I hadn't really thought it all the way through. All I wanted was a yes from her. I guess I had assumed I'd figure out the rest when the time came.

Janet laughed. "That's what I like about you. Sometimes you just jump in with both feet without even lookin' first. So where you takin' me?"

"There's one little problem."

"You're not backin' out on me already?"

"No. No. It's just ... I've got this thing comin' up this weekend."

"Should I be jealous?"

I laughed nervously at her comment, wondering if she secretly suspected I was still seeing Amber. I wasn't. This time I had really cut her loose. "No. It's with my dad. Tennessee is in the SEC tournament in Birmingham this weekend and, well, he said I'd have to miss school tomorrow if I wanted to go." I shrugged with my palms up. "How could I refuse?"

"That's cool. Spendin' quality time with your dad. We'll figure it out when you get back."

"Um, how 'bout next Friday? Ye Olde Steak House?" I blurted out, not wanting to wait another second to secure a date with her. She could change her mind either way, but at least a spoken commitment increased my odds.

"Now, you're talkin'. A movie after?"

"Sure, whatever you like."

"It's a date then." She smiled. "Call me when you get back."

I didn't have her number. She asked if I had a pen. Luckily, I did. She scribbled her digits in the palm of my hand. "Don't lose it," she said. I wanted to seal the deal with a kiss, but the busy halls of S-Y were not the place for our first time. Janet was special. And whatever came out of this was going to be special. I could feel it.

I had played it right this time. My only recent contact with Amber had been over the phone. When I learned she'd had a visit from Jacob Mac, I let it ride, and didn't issue an ultimatum demanding a cease and desist on all further visitations. If I really wanted this thing with Janet to work, I had to let go completely and let whatever happened with Amber happen. Relinquish control. She was no longer mine. If she decided to see someone—Jake maybe—I'd have to be okay with that. Before Janet came along, I had been sure I would one day marry Amber. Janet had changed my mind. *She could be the one.* I was moving in a different direction now, and there was no longer room in the car for Amber.

Every time I thought about calling Amber, the thought vanished quickly as new ones filled my head. I could start over with Janet. A clean slate. The possibilities of this new relationship were endless. I could walk the high wire, crossing over into her world. Some of the people in her crowd I had grown up with had classes in grammar school, played pee-wee ball with, and roomed with on the safety field trip. Some of them had been my best friends.

More than that, with Janet, whatever our pasts had been would remain our pasts. We wouldn't have to share the messy details. And even if we decided to, that would be okay too. We had both been with other people. But we wouldn't let it have its way with us … wouldn't let it sneak in and muck things up.

The weekend turned out to be more fun than I had anticipated, even without the aid of mind-altering substances. Absorbed in collegiate basketball, I was drawn into the drama of the Ernie and Bernie show,[42] anticipating the challenge they would face against Kyle Macy and the Kentucky Wildcats in the final game. The boys in orange and white pulled off the big win, taking the SEC title back to Knoxville.

Back at our motel, I watched Socky Jenkins get ripped on a couple of beers. It didn't take much. Dad told me he had alcohol allergies, so the buzz kicked in pretty much with the first one.

Socky, Dad's buddy and business partner in their floor-covering business, was also Lily Jenkins' dad.

I went to school with Lily. She lived right around the corner from us on Berea. At one time, she had been Janet's best friend.

## The Quiet Kid

Later that night, while we were still savoring the taste of victory, a phone call came from Knoxville. It was Mrs. Jenkins. There had been an accident. Janet was in the turn lane at Berry's when a station wagon skidded in the rain, crashing into her. Witnesses said she had been coherent, even joking when they loaded her into the ambulance. She had internal injuries.

She didn't make it.

The Volunteers had wrangled victory away from the claws of the Wildcats.

Janet was dead.

Socky could get loaded on two beers.

Janet was gone.

Mr. Hall's damned stupid statistics had claimed another victim.

*Janet's dead.*

There would be no first date at Ye Olde Steakhouse. I would never know if she liked her steak rare. I would never know anything more about her than what I did at that moment. She had consumed my thoughts for the last few months while I worked my nerve up to ask her out. Cindy finally convinced me. And now she was gone. Forever. I wanted to feel sorry for her families' loss, but I couldn't. I was selfish. I only felt bad for me and all we had missed out on ... a possible future together. Were we compatible? I would never know. I couldn't be sad anymore. My anger wouldn't allow it. *Why did You have to take her? Why now? Why?*

How weak, how inadequate are words, how vain the attempt, trying with words to express the devastation of losing someone you care about so deeply?

Berry's Funeral Home was packed with confused, weeping teenagers—much the way it had been in July when Blaine left us. I don't remember much except the blur of tears and that guy singing *Wildflower*.[43]

Linda was there. We hugged each other's neck and bawled like babies. but the healing wasn't coming for a while. Time would have to have its way. And time was in no hurry.

The good Lord giveth and the good Lord taketh away.

That didn't mean I had to be happy about it. I couldn't shake it. Gloom covered me like clods of dirt, adding another layer to the bottom of the grave. The weight was almost comforting. *Why don't I just crawl down there and join my departed friends? What good am I to anyone here?*

Why not? Now was as good a time as any. I wanted to throw a punch in death's face, tempt him. *You think you can take me? Let's find out.*

I scored some valium, ten of the blue ones—one hundred milligrams. I took them all and washed them down with a quart of Schlitz Malt Liquor just to kick it in. Then I climbed back into the driver's seat of my dad's Oldsmobile Delta 88. It was a barge on rubber wheels. Mark was riding shotgun, having come along to look out for me. The full effect of one hundred milligrams of Diazepam didn't take long to catch up. Sped along by the charging bull, it hit me. I was flattened like Wiley Coyote under the steam roller.

We were on some back road in Vestal. All I remember was feeling the bump. When I came to, I was looking up at the still-moving car in front of us. I had just delivered a love tap to its rear bumper. It pulled off just ahead. In the separation, I spied a road to the right and quickly ducked onto it, stomping the accelerator. The adrenaline and the sound of the four-barrel revitalized me. I was fully awake on the drive home. There was no other choice. I couldn't stay out on the road in my condition.

Mark covered for me, got me inside, telling Mom I wasn't feeling well as I fell into bed and into a deep, deep sleep. That was on a Sunday afternoon.

When I finally awoke, some fourteen hours later, I looked up to see an angelic little smiling face. Cindy Robbie was kneeling at the bedside, with her chin propped into the crook of her elbow. "Welcome back," she said. "I'm so glad you decided not to leave us."

"How long was I out?" I said, rubbing the confusion out of my eyes.

"Too long. It's Monday. School's out." Cindy stroked my hair and raked the tips of her fingernails delicately across my face, neck, and arms. She talked. I listened.

"What were you thinking? This can't bring Janet back. And you being gone would just make it that much harder on the rest of us." She took a long pause, looking deeply into my eyes as if she might

## The Quiet Kid

jump in and swim around awhile. She wanted to make sure I was all there and that I was paying attention. "I will always be here for you. But don't ever do anything like this again. *Ever.*" She stressed the last word with sternness.

"Um … okay." I said, weakly.

"Promise me."

"You're so sweet."

"Miike." She stretched the "i," sounding like someone's mom. "Promise me."

Her concern forced a smile. "Okay. I promise."

# 56. Cameron

Cameron shot out of the pack like a stone launched from a sling. Her left skate dragging behind her, the toe stop skipped on the hardwood, slowing her down as she approached the railing.

"Hey! What're you doin' here?" She sounded exuberant as always, maybe even more so.

I hadn't been to the skating rink in years, a tidbit I had disclosed earlier, and she was surprised to see me. Rays of light projected at a giant mirrored sphere, reflecting a myriad of illuminate specs, swirling, and spinning recklessly as they searched in vain for a place to rest. *How Deep Is Your Love* was playing loud enough to drown out the growl of polyurethane wheels on the hardwood. I hated the Bees Gees. Somehow the curious look on Cameron's face lessened the suffering imposed upon my defenseless eardrums by their shrill voices.

It was the start of all couples' skate.

I wasn't wearing skates. "I came to see you."

"How sweet. And what a nice surprise," she said. "You skating?"

"I haven't in … I don't know how long."

"It's just like ridin' a bike. Once you've done it …."

"Nah. I don't think so."

"Oh, come on. Ya came all this way. The least you could do is skate with me. You can lean on me. I'll hold ya up."

Cameron had become just that for me—someone I could lean on.

I was thoroughly depressed, stranded in the middle of the woods with no sense of direction, having forgotten my God, forgotten how He came to lead me out of the armpit-deep thicket. He had visited often: the Ted Nugent concert when I was on PCP, Fall Creek Falls, and the Bible studies in Seymour. I had experienced His presence time and time again: special events at the coliseum, Billy Graham, and the Sammy Hall crusade.

Some guy had been at our school recently. Having recovered from a wicked drug addiction, he found strength in Jesus Christ. He had painted a dark and harrowing picture of a sordid past before bringing his story to a close—an ending full of light and hope at the foot of a bloody wooden cross. I thought of Blaine and Janet and hoped they had made their peace before the end came. And then I thought more about the drug addict—how his life had turned around in such a way that the horrible experience he survived was turned into something

God could use as a tool to open the hearts and minds of those who would listen. What did I have to offer? Nothing. I wanted to be that guy. I forget, for a moment, the potential tragedy averted the day I had taken too many Valium and rear-ended some poor innocent bystander. I wanted to wander down a dim, unexplored alleyway into the underworld, dive from a ship into the Bermuda Triangle, and flirt with misfortune to see who would emerge the victor. Then maybe I would be somebody. My self-worth had plunged to the bottom of the Mariana Trench. I figured I might as well tag along.

Whenever I talked to Cameron, she always seemed to pull me out of the funk. She encouraged me, never failing to make me smile, and she always reminded me that God had not left. I was the one who moved. He was just one prayer away.

"See. I told ya it would come back to ya." Cameron was still holding onto my arm, just above the elbow.

I wasn't completely convinced. My balance seemed precarious at best. My innocence, having eluded me for a while, seemed to return when I was with her. *Thunder Island* boomed in over the PA system. Jay Ferguson wasn't exactly the Stones, but he was a little easier on the ears. Well, at least better than the lousy Bee Gees. Close to finding my backside on the floor, we circled the rink until I started to feel at ease. By then, it was time to go home. Her mom was picking her up at 11.

Free from the heavy skates, my feet felt as if they were floating weightless. I must've have been staring at Cameron as she tied bows in the laces of her chucks.

"What?" she said, looking up. A smile crept onto her face.

"Nothin'. It's just ..." *Deer in headlights.* I couldn't get out of the way.

"What? C'mon, out with it."

She was a year my junior with guileless, pale blue eyes. I was really just admiring how cute she was. *I can't just say it, can I?* I considered asking her out on a date but thought better of it. "I just really like you. That's all."

The closeness had been nice—the contact of her holding my arm to keep me from falling. But I knew taking our relationship to the next level would require one of two things. The first would have been easy. I could've denied any lingering relationship and feelings for Amber Barrett as I'd done so often in the past. Piece of cake, right? The second wasn't so easy, but a lot less complicated.

I told Cameron the truth. All of it. Every gory detail about my relationship with Amber B. from June 11th, 1974 to the present, and all of the liaisons in between—the deceptive web I had weaved over the eyes of the unsuspecting insects: Shirley, Bobbi Spencer, Kelly, and Valerie. Okay, maybe Val didn't really care all that much. The common thread running through it all was this: They had all believed I was unattached —that I was emotionally available—when all along, my heart had been given to another who held it in a locket close to her own.

Even with Janet, I hadn't completely let go of Amber, though I'd convinced myself otherwise. In the darkest recesses of my brain, she would still be there waiting, I imagined, if all else failed. And all along, I had been trying unsuccessfully to give it away, because I had no clue about what I really wanted. I was too afraid, too insecure to let go of what I knew might've been the best thing in my life. And yet, I still insisted on searching for something better.

Sitting in the commons, unmindful of the ever-present lunchtime din, I was barely cognizant of the empathy in Cameron's eyes. "What's eatin' you, kiddo?" It was a strange thing for her to call me kiddo, seeing she was a year younger, but somehow, it worked for her.

I had been fixated on a spot somewhere in oblivion, un-engaging to meet her gaze. Her thick, brown hair was cropped just above the shoulders, giving her an almost boyish appearance. The compassion she was giving could have swallowed my troubles with one gulp. Truth be told, I couldn't pinpoint the source of my problems.

"I ... I don't really know. I mean, I've got everything going in the right direction, it seems. I've quit smoking weed, at least at school. My grades are up. I'm going to college next year. Can you believe it? I mean, the future looks bright, but I don't know. Maybe it's Janet." I paused.

"Or?" She said, sensing something else.

"Maybe ... maybe it's Amber. She's just over there waitin' for me to commit ... and I can't."

"If you love her, you should go after her with all your heart. If not ... if you're unsure, you should let her go. Set her free. See what

## The Quiet Kid

happens. God has someone special out there for you, if not her," she said.

"I guess. I really haven't been very sociable with the Man Upstairs lately."

"Well, there you go! Right there's your problem. I can listen to your troubles all day long, but I can't solve 'em. Only He can do that. He really does care about you, ya know? You should talk to Him. Don't be a stranger."

I knew she was right and took comfort in her words. My spirits lifted, and I gave her a big smile.

"That's what I wanna see. Whew! For a second there, I thought I was going to have to call Howdy Dowdy," Cameron laughed.

Howdy Dowdy was the nickname she had given Mark Lee. She knew the mere mention of it usually made me laugh.

I revealed the album I had under my notebook. "Oh, by the way ... You should give this a listen."

A huge grin filled her face. "Is this the legendary Ann Wilson?"

Cameron, I had recently discovered, had a set of pipes on her. With that revelation, I had been filling her head with my latest obsession, raving on and on about Ann Wilson. She agreed to take my *Dog and Butterfly* album home and give it a listen. I wasn't sure what she'd make of it. She was more of a *Send in the Clowns* kind of girl.

# 57. Hannah

Sometimes, I honestly didn't know what Kristi was thinking. She spent most of the school year somewhere else. Mom found out the hard way, unable to obtain a final report card for Kristi's seventh-grade tenure. The following year, Kristi was enrolled at Harrison Chilhowee Baptist Academy, a privately-funded school where Mom was working.

I was just glad it wasn't me.

I couldn't imagine having my daily lessons shoved down my throat with a side of scripture by some overzealous Baptist teacher every day of my life. That was Kristi's dilemma. I wasn't complaining. She was bringing home a fresh new face almost every weekend. All of them would become jailbait the minute I turned eighteen. Some of the girls were cute, others, not so much. None of them worth the risk.

Hannah Waters was the exception to the rule, which, like all rules were written to be broken—or at least bent a little. She was five nothing, five-six in platform shoes, all giggles and kinky brown hair spilling off her high, rounded forehead, her lips full and pouting, innocence masking seductive brown eyes—a cherub's face with rosy cheeks. At fourteen, her too young body was stacked like walls of brick in an over-engineered outhouse. The words of a Commodore song come to mind.[44]

Age was just a number. I had to keep reminding myself of that after Hannah became my girlfriend, squeezing Amber, just out of the picture's frame. Joey Keely was quick to dub her my daughter, a term he used for our relationship because girlfriend just didn't fly.

She inspired me. Not long after meeting her, I wrote the beginnings of this song.

*I thought she was sweet as honeysuckle*
*And then she grabbed me by the belt buckle*
*She said "I got somethin' to show to you"*
*I said, "Yeah babe, I wanna see it too"*
*There's only one thing that's left to do*
*Now let's ... fall in love*

## The Quiet Kid

Okay, I wasn't that inspired. I never finished it. And now you know why I never became a famous rock star.

It was April of my senior year. Another birthday was just around the corner. On paper, it put four years of separation between Hannah and me. She didn't even have a learner's permit. But she knew how to get what she wanted. She persuaded me (easily, I might add) to give her a driving lesson. We were in the Coronet on our way to smoke, and I pulled over to let her slide behind the wheel, figuring we were cool. The Valium we had taken wouldn't kick in for at least twenty minutes.

Failure to come to a complete stop drew the attention of one of Knoxville's finest. Hannah pulled over in the parking lot of the Family Pantry, followed by flashing blue and red lights. Having in my possession the only valid driver's license, I would be held responsible. Fortunately, the officer didn't search to see what else I had in my possession. The car was my dad's, I quickly explained. And, of course, I would be in so much trouble. He had to smile at the amusing predicament this brown-eyed little vixen had wheedled me into. And it didn't hurt that she kept batting those big innocent Maybellines which could not have possibly distracted him from noticing the dangerous curves just below her neckline.

He let us off with a firm warning.

Hannah, combined with an assortment of drugs, alcohol, and Mary Jane, was having a mind-numbing effect. Memories of Janet were fading in my rearview mirror, lagging behind, struggling to keep up with the rate of speed at which we were traveling. We were into a little of everything. We dropped acid in my bedroom late one night, flying under Mom's radar into the early morning light. (Dad's radar was switched off, or focused on whatever sports were on the TV.)

Hannah was waiting for me in Gatlinburg.

Beyond the Brickhouse,[45] Chapman Highway became a sidewinder. The belly of the snake arced as I bounced from its underside to its back, shortening the distance, switching lanes back and forth, in and out, belly to back. This enabled me to maintain a healthy top speed, thriving on the thrill of passing cars on the inside whenever the opportunity presented itself. The heater in the old Coronet had gone on the fritz, refusing to shut off, which forced me to travel with the windows rolled down. *Whoosh.* I whizzed by the blurring silhouettes of cars as if they were anchored to the pavement. Sometimes in rapid succession, they would manifest in staggered formation, to the inside and then to the outside. The adrenaline pumped madly as I bounced around, riding high on the humped back of the slithering asphalt, scaring life into the oncoming traffic mere inches away. I would dive swiftly into the gut to slip past another, belly, back, belly, back. *Whoosh. Whoosh. Whoosh. Whoosh.*

All the while, visions of her body, curvaceous and dangerous as the road passed through my head faster than the last Pontiac, disappearing beyond the bend in my rearview. Seeing her, breathing her in, touching her, had become essential. Like air compelling the effort of my lungs, every endeavor of my being surrendered to desire, propelling me forward. Up ahead, the road straightened out. I saw the magnificent brick courthouse on my right and knew I had just cruised into Dolly's old stompin' grounds.[46]

Her parents were home, but after she introduced me to her mom, we were left to our own devices.

She shut the door. Her bedroom had a loft. We were lying on the bed when I asked, "You wanna go somewhere and smoke?"

She looked at me, amused. Her brown eyes twinkled, a smile broadening her face. "Baby, we can do whatever we want right here."

I had a pre-rolled joint stashed in a pack of Saratoga Menthols. I proceeded to light it, cupping my hands around the flame of the BIC out of habit, like I was shielding it from the wind.

"You like the Cars?" Hannah was shuffling through a stack of LP's.

"You kiddin' me? Next to Van Halen, they're prob'ly my favorite band right now."

"Cool," she said and dropped the vinyl on the turntable.

The languid rhythm kicked in, a guitar screeching like bad brakes, dropping into the backbeat like Chinese water torture.

*Let the Good Times Roll* ...[47]

We smoked the joint. I rolled another, passing it as Ric Ocasek lamented about his best friend's girl. And then Ben Orr declared the essence of our relationship with *Just What I Needed*.[48]

We got out our guitars. She showed me how to play *Seasons of Wither*. I was too high. I got the gist of it but kept over-thinking the simple progression, flubbing up the flow of Steven Tyler's haunting Aerosmith classic on every third or fourth cycle.

"You'll get it, baby. Just keep practicing," she encouraged.

I left late, still nursing the fourth beer from our second sixer. Passing through Pigeon Forge after 1:00 a.m., I saw flashing red and blue lights in my rearview mirror. I was a little past tipsy, but I had the presence of mind to stash the last two beers, tethered by plastic rings, under the passenger seat. I placed the one I was drinking discreetly between my feet, pushing it back as far as I could. Silently, I prayed I wouldn't be asked to step out of the car. Compounding my predicament, I had recently turned eighteen and was sure I was about to be introduced to one of the many privileges of adulthood—jail. My license was already out when the officer stepped up to my open window.

"Are you aware you have no taillights?" he said.

"No, sir." It was true. I had no idea, so there was no acting involved.

"Where you headed at this hour?" He asked as he studied my picture, probably sizing me up to confirm my age.

"Home, to Knoxville, sir." I exhibited all the politeness and respect I could muster.

"What brings you this way so late?"

"Girlfriend," I said, trying not to smile too wide.

He chuckled to himself. "Sit tight while I run this."

He took my license back to call it in. The brightness of the flashing lights took me back to Clearwater and the drunk that had mowed down the power lines. I was trying to stay positive, congratulating myself for using Visine, focusing on anything but the probability of a night behind bars. The static from his radio disrupted the quiet. There wasn't much traffic. I counted cars whenever they whizzed by. *One ... two ... three ...*, I imagined the drivers laughing at my folly. I cracked my knuckles, pushing each finger flat against my palm to produce a loud *pop* from the upper joint and then folding each digit onto itself to release a less impressive click from the lower one. When I got to the thumbs, I straightened them out, pressing each one to the inside of my folded wrist. *Snap. Crackle. Pop.* He was gone for a long time. Or at least it seemed that way. It was probably less than five minutes.

After running my license, the officer advised me to try my emergency flashers.

"Yep. They're working," he observed, coming back around to my side.

*At least there's that.* I was starting to sweat.

"Leave those on for your drive home. At least it'll keep you from getting rear-ended. And get that taken care of first thing tomorrow. Top priority." He said, adding," Before you do anything else."

"Yessir."

With that, he turned away, walking toward his patrol car. Before I could put it in gear, he started back.

*Crap! What now?*

"I'll warn my buddies up ahead you'll be coming through with your flashers on. You shouldn't have any trouble getting home."

"Thank you, sir."

I eased back onto the highway, and he followed for a bit. I wasn't too worried at that point. I wasn't seeing a double line in the middle of the road. And even if I was, closing one eye always solved the problem. I was overly confident of my ability behind the wheel, having convinced myself my driving skills exceeded my ability to walk a straight line.

As I crossed the line into Sevierville, the officer turned around, heading back to his jurisdiction. I waited until I was on the other side of town and back out on the open road before downing the rest of my beer.

# 58. Keely

Joey Keely worked at Hillcrest Nursing Home, a job providing personal care for patients who were mostly invalids. Escorting lame, old people to dialysis in wheelchairs, lifting them out of bed to change their sheets, emptying bedpans was admirable work. I had a hard time imagining myself doing it in his stead. I didn't ask a lot of questions, and he really didn't talk about it much. Until he got involved with a patient named Mike Hutch.

Mike had one of those March of Dimes diseases—MS or MD or something. I could never remember. Anyway, it wasn't good. He was permanently confined to a wheelchair, was unable to use his arms and legs, and required assistance for daily activities taken for granted by the average person. He couldn't even brush his own teeth. The most devastating part in all of this, to me, at least, was his age. It didn't seem fitting for someone that young to have permanent residency at a nursing home. The name nursing home reeked of an open invitation to the dark, hooded one who carried the great sickle. Mike was barely older than we were, barely old enough to vote, barely old enough to drink, and barely old enough to be drafted into the service of the United States Military. The latter was never going to be a threat to him, which was probably the only upside to his condition. He would never be forced into the unwilling position that might require the killing of another human being.

Mike enjoyed some of the same indulgences we did. He grew his hair long. He listened to Rock 'n' Roll. Had he been able, I'm sure he wouldn't have minded strapping on a six-string, trying his hand at a few riffs. Or maybe he would've enjoyed tossing a Frisbee with us in the parking lot. One thing his condition didn't prevent (with assistance) was partaking in the smoking of a plant cultivated for one of the favorite pastimes of American youth in the 1970s.

In his off-hours, Joey would often go to Hillcrest and wheel Mike out to the parking lot to get him high. I went with him once, waiting in the car while Joey went inside. Ten minutes later, out came Joey, wheeling Mike (looking as though he'd swallowed the Cheshire cat and couldn't quite digest the grin) out the back door and down the ramp.

There was nothing behind the nursing home except a parking lot, a Dempster Dumpster, and a patch of woods. There was no reason for anyone other than the kitchen help, who really didn't care, to make an appearance until the end of their shift.

To Mike, that scrap of pavement with white divider lines represented freedom. For an hour or so, he could just hang with us and be part of something other than a bed, and four walls and a big picture of someplace he normally didn't get to go, because, really, that was all the oversized window stood for.

Joey rolled down the window in his Oldsmobile and cranked Skynyrd loud enough for us to hear, but not so loud as to raise eyebrows from anyone inside. I imagined *Freebird* held a meaning for Mike we didn't quite grasp. Joey was so attentive to Mike's needs, holding the cup so Mike could sip Coke from a straw and holding the joint every time it was Mike's turn.

The sun must've been exquisite on Mike's face after hours and hours on end under the sickly artificial fluorescent lighting. Outside, he was transformed into something real, something tangible. He tipped his head back to let the breeze catch his hair, lifting it from his lifeless shoulders, making him more alive somehow. Joey offered the second joint to Mike, who refused it, saying, "shotgun," and then he laughed a silly, infectious laugh.

Bending down to Mike's level, Joey turned the joint around in his mouth and blew a rivulet of white smoke at Mike. Signaling when it was time to stop, Mike tapped his forefinger on Joey's wrist and made a snorting sound, holding back the smoke until he could hold it no longer. He erupted into a fit of coughing, followed by the infectious laughter, reminding us how good it was to be among the living and how good it was to breathe the fresh warm air outside.

It came as little surprise when Joey got it in his head to do something a little more ambitious. To break Mike out of his private prison for a more extended period of time, Joey asked for and was granted permission to take Mike on a field trip to the Knoxville Civic Coliseum for his very first live rock 'n' roll show.

Joey was probably the most selfless person I knew. Beyond that, he was just an average head with long, frizzy hair who spoke with a nasally, stoner monotone.

We only had one direction in life: forward. "Never straight, always forward," we'd say. We were tight that year. Keelywinkle. That's what I called him. He returned the favor by dubbing me, O'Hara.

## The Quiet Kid

In November, we had made a weekend trek to Johnson City to see Heart a second time because we had heard the acoustics were so much better at Freedom Hall. They were. Firefall was the opening act. After the show, it began snowing, but not so much that we couldn't get around. We cruised around town, smoking joints, and looking at the beautiful, white landscape. It was just enough to prompt us to phone our parents and tell them we couldn't get home. We were snowed in. My folks wired us the money for another night at the fleabag motel. The room didn't matter. We were snow-bound with Jack Daniels and a few good buds.

# 59. Hannah Part II

Hannah was riding shotgun. We met Keelywinkle in the parking lot of the old South High School after scoring some weed. We headed back to my house to ditch his car in my driveway before heading out to smoke.

"Beat ya' there." Joey grinned as he jumped in his Oldsmobile. He squealed the tires, laying down long, black stripes that skipped over the speed bump.

I pitched a sideways glance at Hannah and smiled. Her feet were propped up on the dash. Her short legs parted slightly in an inviting manner. She returned the smile. I could *not* allow myself to be shown up by Joey. *Not today.*

Cramming the shifter into drive, I chased the Olds out to Moody Avenue, pausing, but not stopping. The coast was clear. Keely had established a gap. I closed it by the time he made a right at the Pantry. I was on him like white on rice when he navigated the "Y" at Sevier, staying glued to his bumper as we headed down McClung. My dilemma was finding a place to pass. There was none. The road was too narrow, with too many oncoming cars. As we crested the hill, sloping down toward South Haven, I saw my opportunity. I backed off to give myself some space. Both directions on South Haven were clear. Nothing was coming from either direction. I knew he would stop for that stupid red octagon. I pressed the pedal to the floor and blew through the stop sign, passing on the left, slowing up just enough to see the look of astonishment when Hannah flipped him double birds. She was laughing hysterically as we flew by. He tromped on the gas, giving chase up the opposing hill. Hannah was still laughing, stomping her feet on the floorboard with gleeful fury, as I screeched around the turn onto Hackman Street.

"Baby, you're the best," she said, dizzy with adrenaline when we came to a complete stop in the driveway. Before I could throw it in park, she jumped on me. Wedging her petite body between me and the steering wheel, she straddled me, wrapping both arms around my neck. She was still kissing me furiously when Keely walked up next to the Coronet. He made a dismissing gesture, waving downward with his left hand as he strolled by, circling back after weighing his options. Out of one eye, I saw an arm extend to open the door, and he let himself in.

## 60. Cameron II

Backstage, the finishing touches were being applied to the set of the big production—our fifteen minutes of fame.

Dave Weir furrowed his orange eyebrows, channeling his vision down through luminescent eyelashes overseeing his slick fretwork on the red hollow-body Gibson ES, the top of his head glowing bright as an orange slushy. He threw his head back, laughing, the sound of it masked by the volume. He rambled away from the rehearsed number into an improvised lead, and Mitch Hensley followed.

*That should've been me.* I was so undisciplined. How was I ever going to play in a band? Never having applied myself enough to learn anything beyond the basic chords, some song intros, and a few assorted riffs, I had missed the boat. Now Mitch Hensley was keeping pace with a talent sure to be short-changed by the structured numbers they would play in our upcoming presentation. *I didn't even know Mitch could play.* Dave was probably the best-undiscovered talent around.

"So, what're you doin' when you get out?" Barbara Criswell never looked away from the brushstrokes she was applying. She was thin and pretty with a delicate nose and auburn hair. The pronounced white knob of her wrist bone drew my attention as I studied the moving tendons of her forearm.

"School. You?"

"I'm still deciding. Where you goin'?"

"U.T."

"You better be studying art. You're really good, ya know?" Taking a break from her work, she turned to let me see her seriousness. "I mean it."

There was way too much time available behind the curtains for thinking as I helped Barbara, painting the green parts of the backdrop while she painted the brown. The end of the year was approaching like an unexpected train, leaving me frozen in the middle of the trestle. I hadn't been paying attention and wasn't sure which way to run or if I should just jump.

My lines for the Phone-A-Clone segment were well-rehearsed. I could recite them in my sleep, probably backward. It was less than twenty-four hours away. The end of the school year had once seemed like it was never going to come. Now it was bearing down like an ominous green sky before a storm. I felt like I was standing in the tornado's eye. I wasn't ready for all of this to end just yet. I was prepared for college, having done well in all of my classes, but I wasn't ready. The uncertainty just around the next bend was unavoidable. And it was coming fast. I wanted to crawl into a hole and hide.

I was feeling fragile. When it came right down to it, I was thinking more about the end of time than the end of school. *How do you prepare for that?* The second coming. The book of Revelation. A seven-headed dragon and the mark of the beast. For the first time in my life, I was aware. If it all started tomorrow, I might not make it.[7]

I didn't want to die.

I had no clue what I wanted. How was I supposed to tell Cameron? Since Amber had first unearthed her dark secret, my time and energy had been spent trying to even the score and then trying to one-up her. And after I succeeded, I completely lost my sense of direction. Was I looking for her replacement? A virgin, maybe? Did I want to move on? Did I actually expect to find someone who could make me feel the way she did? With Amber, I could be myself, comfortable in my own skin. There was no pretending. The lack of intimacy I felt with other girls had kept me from going the distance with every single one of them, except Bobbi. That had been out of absolute necessity, and sheer will. It had been completely mechanical. I had gone through the motions and felt nothing. The saddest part of the whole ordeal was that I walked away, not caring one iota about how she felt. It was the coldest feeling I had had in my entire young life. Every single time with Amber was still a thrill.

Penny Marks had been a challenge, one I could do nothing to win. The ball had always been in her court. She never returned it. Even if she had, it never would've worked. I was too busy holding on to Amber with one hand.

Janet had been different. With her, I had been ready to let go, to close my eyes and jump off the highest cliff into the deepest water. I had felt she was worth the risk. What we had was rare. There was a connection between us like static electricity waiting to be released with a single touch. I liked to believe we had both felt it. But it didn't matter anymore. It wasn't meant to be. And no matter how many nights I lay in bed wondering what might've been, I couldn't have it back. She was gone forever. *See you in the next life.*

Then there was Hannah.

"Hannah has changed everything."

Cameron gave me a dubious look. "And yet you still have feelings for Amber?"

"Well ya, but …."

She cut me off. "She won't wait around forever, kiddo."

"I know. I know. But I'm having too much fun with Waters to stop right now."

Cameron chuckled. "You have been more upbeat lately." She observed, her smile revealing oversized canines. Her smile faded into a look of grave concern. "But I'm worried about you."

"Why?"

"All the stuff you're into with her…" She let it trail off, selecting her next words carefully. "It's drivin' you further away from the Man Upstairs."

"Believe it or not, we've agreed to lay off everything … except the occasional joint. We're goin' to Van Halen completely straight."

"Really? Whew! That's a relief."

Mark opened our variety show production with an imitation Chevy Chase announcement and a pratfall down a flight of stairs. The Phone-A-Clone bit had been worked in as an ode to Saturday Night Live-style commercials. When the curtain went up, I was inexplicably less nervous than when I'd recited poetry to the class earlier in the year. The blinding spotlight was a distraction from the audience, which was the entire school—over six hundred students. There was a moment of confusion when Mark had difficultly lighting the fuse for the smoke bomb, but it brought a roar of laughter, the response we were going for anyway. We recovered quickly, emerging miraculously from the phone booth and a cloud of smoke to nail our synchronized lines right down to the phone number.

"Get your Phone-A-Clone today by dialing this toll-free number: 1-800-555-1234." In unison, we repeated the number, not once, but twice, in the Ronco[49] tradition, the curtain dropping in front of us, seemingly cutting us off during the third annoying repetition of the digits. Just as the laughter subsided, two heads poked through the curtains, Mark crawling between my legs to achieve the full effect.

One head floating above the other. "That number again: One, eight-hundred, five, five, five, one, two, three, four." With that, we brought down the house.

It was our finest moment at South-Young High.

Cameron led me down the sidewalk under the shadow of the concrete canopy, our reflections interrupted by columns of brick as we passed in front of the commons. Our fingers were intertwined at the knuckles. We weren't concerned with who might be looking out to see us. It was okay now. Having nothing else to declare, no uncertainty hung between us. These innocuous gestures were safe.

We spilled down the concrete stairs like they were a continuation of the sidewalk and then entered the building through the impossibly tall glass doors to our right. I tugged at one of the floor-to-ceiling wooden double doors to the first room on the left and held it open for Cameron. She scurried inside, flipping the switch to dispel the darkness in the sterile interior of the windowless chorus room. She was giddy with excitement—the very definition of schoolgirl.

Once again, she extended her hand. I took it. She pulled me in the direction of the grand piano, slowing to catch her breath. She was suddenly serious. Directing me to sit on the bench as if I were about to receive lessons, she slid in on the other side. She gave me a smile, suggesting she was about to give me something I would never forget. "Ready?" she said.

Then she looked away, closed her eyes, and inhaled deeply, drawing in every last particle of oxygen. When she let it go, her fingers began to move, and the piano came to life, transforming into part of her essence. And then her unmistakable voice followed, giving back everything she had taken from the room as she sang *Dog and Butterfly*.[50]

... a voice with such power ...
... such passion ...
... such sweet conviction ...
... peeling away every layer, she reached deep, deep inside ...

If Ann Wilson had been there, she would've been content to walk away knowing she'd left the torch in good hands.

The reverberation of the final chord lingered in the air. I was speechless.

## The Quiet Kid

She looked right through me the way Ann Wilson had done when she had used her X-ray vision to penetrate the shield of my camera. Only I had no place to fall back. I was already sitting down. Goosebumps lingered on my arms.

Her eyes longed for my approval. "Well?"

"I ..." I tried to wrap my head around what I'd just experienced, unable to deliver the message to my tongue. "Wow. I ..., just wow. I don't know what to say."

"Was I that bad?" She doubted herself. The look on her face said so.

That made me laugh. "No. No. Are you kiddin' me? That was fantastic—for lack of a better word. That, that, that was amazing, freakin' amazing. The most amazing thing I've ever heard.'" I stuttered around for the next five minutes, convincing her I meant every inadequate word. By the time I was through, she believed me. And we were both laughing at the comedy of me trying to express my stunned gratitude.

I felt like we'd just made love. Only all our clothes were still on, and our innocence remained intact. I had never been privy to a musical performance like that one—a private concert for one. Her gift changed me in ways I couldn't fathom in the moment. I would always and forever crave that intimacy and innocence, transient of words.

# 61. Hannah Part III

Van Halen was a good test for us. The innovative meanderings of Eddie Van Halen's rampaging guitar improvisations were a blazing fury of string stretching, hammer-ons, pull-offs, and finger tapping. It boggled the mind. Witnessing up close his demonstration of skills was something not to be missed. Hannah and I had made a pact. We wouldn't smoke, drink, or ingest anything to alter our perception or memories of the night.

We had made a similar agreement regarding prom night. She had been radiant in a poufy, pale yellow dress, a foot shorter than me in my tan tuxedo with matching fedora and six-inch platform shoes. After passing her off as a junior from Gatlinburg-Pittman to all my classmates (except for Keely and Mark, who knew better), it was hard to tell who was more envious—the girls or the guys. She turned plenty of heads. But the whole affair had been pretty dull, and we snatched the first opportunity to leave, eradicating the night from our short-term memories with the help of our old friend Mary Jane.

For Van Halen, we stayed true to our commitment, showing up on the steps of the coliseum at four in the afternoon. Mark brought his girlfriend Brenda, and the four of us sat cross-legged in front of the entryway until the doors were opened at around six-thirty. We ran, ignoring the vendors, trying to stay ahead of the pressing crowd, rushing past their offerings of posters and programs and black Van Halen T-shirts, hot dogs, popcorn, and especially Cokes. Our young bladders were in full control, but any attempt to wrestle our way out to the restroom would've resulted in a permanent loss of the spots we had secured front and center by the stage. It was another torturous hour and a half before the first band hit the stage. An unenthusiastic response by the crowd ensured the unmemorable Granati Brothers only played the required forty-five minutes. Instead of yelling "encore," we were chanting "Van Halen! Van Halen! Van Halen!" which gave way to the much simpler "Ed-die! Ed-die! Ed-die!" just minutes after the first, already forgotten band walked off the stage. Then there was the set-up time in between.

At long last, the quantum quartet took the stage, erupting in a fit of hedonistic, violent rock and roll. Edward Lodewijk Van Halen assaulted the neck of his homemade Frankenstein guitar. From the already classics, *Eruption* and *Ice Cream Man*, to the new additions like *Bottoms Up!* and *Beautiful Girls*, it was non-stop showmanship at its pinnacle. At one point, Eddie reached around from behind and assisted Michael Anthony (as if he needed help) in playing the bass, Michael fretting while Eddie thumped the strings. As if sheer musicianship wasn't adequate, the antics of David Lee Roth entertained those who were not fortunate enough to share our proximity. Roth ascended a mountain of Marshall Amplifiers, toting an open fifth of Jack Daniels whiskey. Seated on top, he reared his head back, taking a giant swig before pretending to hand the bottle down to a roadie. Just before the guy could get his hand on the bottle, Roth pulled it away, taking another swig. Again, Roth teased the roadie, handing the bottle down just to yank it away at the last second for one more gulp. This enthralled the already captive audience, eliciting a roar of applause and approval demonstrated by the raising of tiny flames from BIC lighters.

The Van Halen show marked the first time since Wet Willie and Dr. John that I had been completely and voluntarily straight at a concert. The dividends of that choice were well worth the small sacrifice—the vivid memory and details of the event Hannah and I would hang onto for a long time.

Waters and I took a walk to Maynard Glen Field. Knowing our relationship was nearing the end, I felt obligated to tell her about the things Almighty God had placed in my heart—His enduring mercy, and the way He had lifted me up out of a pit, time after time, whenever I had called upon Him. She needed to know His Son. If something ever happened to her, and I hadn't told her, I couldn't live with the guilt. I cared about her, even though I knew I would soon be going back to iron things out with Amber.

Hannah's response was puzzling. "I can't be saved. I'm Catholic."
She was serious.
Her remark was stranger even than, "I'm a Presbyterian." It left me completely confused and uncertain about which way the conversation should turn. Not sure how to reply to her odd proclamation, I prayed, silently asking God to show evidence of His power. Within minutes, the sky began to darken—sinister, gray clouds rolling in out of nowhere. We sat down on a bank of grass. Hannah hunkered in close as the thunder clapped, announcing the

arrival of the storm. I myself was taken aback at the speed of its entrance. *He actually heard.* The booming reverberation drew closer and closer, louder and louder, building until it was on top of us. The time elapsing between violent, molar-rattling thunder was closing in like contractions, travailing birth pains.

My face displayed concern. But inside, I was smiling.

"Okay. Okay, baby," she pleaded with the next-in-line face of a victim trapped in some slasher film. "I believe. I believe already. Now, make it stop!"

I tried my best not to laugh. "I'm not doing anything. How can I make it stop?"

"Can we go home now?"

Once again, He was true to His word. "Where two or three are gathered together in My name…"

Hannah was unaware of any gathering. Jesus had gotten the memo.

When we got to my house, the back door opened to an empty kitchen; a house discovered to be void of parental supervision. A place where salvation could be squandered, spent on an afternoon of unbridled wantonness. Leave it to me to throw away a good thing. I blew it, tossing aside every shred of conviction, thinking only of the brick house.

"Let's take a shower," she suggested.

I couldn't help myself. The Promised Land seemed a million miles away. And she was standing right there in front of me, making an offer I didn't want to refuse.

In the wee hours of the morning, Hannah was at home, and I was lying in the bed I'd made. A ménage-a-trois of insomnia and regret. *This relationship is taxing my soul.*

It wasn't her fault. This was all on me.

No one was calling *Ollie, Ollie oxen free.* I would have to make a run for it, and soon.

It was going to be okay. Amber had been faithfully following her convictions for a while now.

*Together, we can get this right ….*

# 62. The Breakup

I fled to Watertown. The refuge of Mike Stuart's was the perfect place to clear my head. Hannah and I could never work. I'd known it all along, never even kidding myself. I knew it was time to quit playing games. We'd had our share of laughs, but when the drugs wore off, it left only us. Something about only us never sat right. If she saw the real me and knew what really went on inside my head, she'd just say, "I can't. I'm Catholic." Or maybe she'd just run away. The only way I could let her go now was by putting some miles between us. The road from Knoxville to Gatlinburg wasn't long enough, even if I could've straightened out all the curves. I had to get my life headed in the right direction.

I needed to be myself. I wasn't even sure who that was. With Hannah, it felt like I was always pretending. I was trying to be what I thought she wanted. But I wanted to spend my life with someone who knew the real me, someone who wouldn't be repulsed by the skin I resided in. I knew who that someone was, and I was feeling like I could finally commit. There could be no others. Only her. Only me. Amber already knew my deep, dark secrets—probably some I didn't know myself. I was ready. It was time.

I just needed a couple of days. And when I was done, I would be sure. I would call her. Tell her that things were going to change. Tell her she could have what she'd been waiting for through all those June elevenths. A year from now would be number six. We could seal the deal with a walk down the aisle, a ring, a kiss, a promise. Forever.

Things started well. Mike had a semi-permanent house guest, Russell, who was working full-time for Orchard Fence Company. We threw back a few beers and argued over the chord progression of *Proud Mary*. I finally conceded, and then we moved on to the subject of frog gigging. He bet me five bucks I couldn't hit a frog with a .22 caliber rifle in the dark.

"You'll never be able to sight it in," he said.

Between us, we had a .22 caliber rifle, a frog gig, two flashlights, and two pillowcases when we hoofed it down the gravel road to the nearest pond. The decibels of their croaking neared a deafening level until we stepped out of the underbrush with the pond in sight.

The sound of a pin dropping would've been absorbed in the mud; otherwise, you could have heard it. We split up, dividing the pond for the spoils.

I came upon my first victim. *That thing has legs like a mother hen.* Holding the flashlight flush against the side of the barrel with my left hand, I squeezed the trigger. Pop! And then I found another. Sighting them in was not a problem. But sometimes, the velocity of the slug buried the body too deep to find it.

We curtailed our excitement, refraining from announcing each time we plugged another one. The frogs remained mute. The only sounds for the next forty minutes were the *pop* from the .22 and the swish of the gig sinking in the muddy bank. Eventually, we worked our way around to meet again.

"How many?" Russell wondered aloud.

"Fourteen, not counting the ones I lost in the mud. You?"

"I got you beat by two," he said with smug satisfaction.

"Yeah, but the bet wasn't how many," I reminded him.

"I know. I know," he complained as we started back.

On the wooden front porch of Mike's old cabin, Russell drew a frog out of his sack, demonstrating how to slice its belly and peel away the skin. "It's just like takin' off a pair of pants."

I got the hang of it quickly. My third one was still kicking when I pulled it from the pillowcase.

"Sometimes they're only stunned when you think they're dead," Russell pointed out. "Here. Use this." He handed me his knife, which was a good deal larger than the one I'd been using.

My quizzical look said I still wasn't sure what to do with it.

"Knock 'em out with the handle," he said with a silly grin that divided his thick facial hair.

It seemed gruesome at first, but after a while, it was nothing short of good ole back wood entertainment. Saturday morning, we ate like kings ... if kings ate frog legs and fried eggs.

It was a Saturday night. June 11th had come and gone. But not without notice, I couldn't stop thinking about her. *I should call her.* I could get back on the straight and narrow, and Amber could help.

I called. It went nothing liked I had planned. She was going to do something she hadn't in a long, long time. Amber had been talking to a guy in her Sunday school class at Immanuel Baptist. She was going on a date with him. There was no talking her out of it. No amount of persuasion was going to work, no matter how much I begged and pleaded, trying to convince her there would never again be anyone else but her. I had allowed too much space between us. It was too late. "We're over." She informed me.

I never saw it coming. I was flat on my back, viewing the world from a new angle. The view wasn't pretty. There was nothing left but picking myself up off the floor. And learn to duck next time.

I listened to *Helplessly Hoping*[51] too many times as I packed my stuff to go home that night. Maybe I could still change her mind if she saw me in the flesh.

"Women are like that," Mike Stuart consoled me. "You wake up one day, and they just change, like they're somebody else." He was the expert on these matters.

It was almost comical, me playing the victim.

It made no difference. I could've stood outside her house at midnight and howled at the moon. Amber had made up her mind and fully intended to stand her ground. My whole world – the world in which I once had total control – was now drunk, spinning out of control. Holding onto the edge of the bed with one foot on the floor did nothing to slow it down.

I had to run away.

Don Lance had told me once of his adventures hitch-hiking to California, about going through a place called Needles, about seeing amazing and unimaginable landscapes, nothing like I'd ever seen in the east. Pictures didn't do it justice. Only the real thing was the real thing.

I made up my mind. Maybe I could find work there and just stay—see if my East Tennessee drawl could get muddled in West Coast surfer-speak. I stuffed some clothes in a backpack. *I'll need my guitar.*

Mom was beside herself, trying to talk me out of it. But what reason did I have to stay? Finally, she convinced me to spend the night at Tennessee School for the Deaf with Ian Bradford before I hit the road.

Ian was attending a Bible study at the school.

"Suit yourself," he said, closing the door behind him after I declined his invitation. Left in the solitude of the dorm room, there was little else to do but mess around on my guitar or listen to his Christian rock albums. I hadn't been in the mood for a dissecting of my soul. But I could always listen to some Larry Norman. So I pulled the black vinyl disc from the sleeve of *Only Visiting This Planet* and dropped it on the turntable, watching the needle slip into the spinning grooves. I made it as far as *The Outlaw*.[52]

And then I broke down.

*Again, the lamb had wandered, far, far away this time, much further than even he had intended. But the sound of the master's voice called him back. And though the sound of it seemed far away, it came to him distinctly. It was but a whisper, but he heard it loud and clear as if the master had been shouting, calling him by name.*

He had been searching for me all along. I knew it was time to go home.

Over the summer, I endeavored to draw closer to God, first withdrawing to the seclusion of the Smoky Mountains doing volunteer work in the kitchen at Camp Wesley Woods. When I returned home to Knoxville, I joined the Bible study at TSD and became a member at Sevier Heights Baptist Church. The Bible Studies were most enlightening for me. I got down in the trenches with my peers, and we examined the scriptures while being real about our lives, and who we were. I learned more there than I had in all my years of pew-sitting.

I did get closer to God. I had a real, meaningful relationship with Him that was getting deeper, but I wasn't through being stupid, losing my way was a hard habit to break. I became confused by religion, disillusioned by the quarrels of men, and defeated when I was less than perfect. I would walk away again for a while. But He is true to his word. *If we are unfaithful, He remains faithful, for He cannot deny who He is* (2 Timothy 2:13).

He wasn't finished with me yet.

To be continued …

# Epilogue

So, if you're still here, you've witnessed first-hand, the truth about me. I am not a good person. Like the rest of you, I have faults—a lot of them. I can be really stupid sometimes, especially in regard to the people around me. I am insecure and self-absorbed. And that's the shortlist. I only want what's best for me, often at the expense of others.

Remember that guy Jesus? You know, the One who showed up early on in my life, calling me out by name. God, the creator of all living things, is His Father, and He sent Jesus with a message for me. He said He would never leave nor forsake me.

Guess what?

He never has. To this day, He remains faithful, true to His word.

No matter how many times I walked away in pursuit of my own desires, my own things, my own happiness (which I could never quite find on my own), He kept coming around, showing up every time I'd dug myself into another hole. In reality, He didn't just come around. He was there the whole time. Waiting.

He knew. He knew from the beginning what I would do. In fact, He knew me before the beginning. Before I was knit in my mother's womb, He knew me. So, He waited on me. With great patience and mercy, He stood by and watched as I made yet another mess of my life. And every time I called out to Him, He answered. He was and still is always there for me.

King David of Israel once wrote: "If I ascend into heaven, You are there. If I make my bed in hell, behold, You are there" (Psalm 139:8).

He is always there. No matter what I've done, or what I do, He simply will *not* give up on me.

Guess what else?

He has made me a new person. Not just a better version of me. A new me.

Don't you want a friend like that?

Think about this for a minute. If God, the creator of the universe, wanted to have a relationship with you, how would He achieve this? I mean, He is God, the Almighty. He is Holy. How could He even begin to understand what you're going through?

He came to earth in the form of sinful, weak flesh—as a man. He was subject to all the same trials, tribulations, and temptations that we experience, and yet He did it all without sin, without messing up. Not once. He never gave in to whatever allure Mary Magdalene might have held for Him as a man. Then He made a choice to lay down His life. He took the sins of every person on earth and carried them to the cross, where He died to make Himself the ultimate sacrifice. More than that, He came back to life three days later and walked out of the tomb. He defeated death so that you and I could live. Not just live, but live life to the fullest. Life to the max. Life x infinity! A life that is way better than anything I was ever able to obtain through sex, drugs, and rock 'n' roll!

Now, the ball's in your court.

Just believe in Him. Call on His Name.

He is there.

Waiting.

# Endnotes

My original intent in most cases was to use song lyrics in such a way as to enhance the scene. The lyrics often go hand in hand with what is transpiring at the time, which was true of my life as a teenager. The task of gaining permission to reprint these lyrics, however, turned out to be a greater endeavor than I had anticipated. What I have done in the footnotes is to cite the author of the lyrics, and then point you, the reader, to what was intended for the story. (The lyrics are usually easy enough to find with a quick Google search, or heck, just find the song and listen to it.) If you care to look up the lyrics and insert them where noted, I believe it will bring more life to the story, but that choice I will leave up to you.

## 6. Summer – 1972

[1] *Spinning Wheel* – David Clayton-Thomas. Performed by: Blood, Sweat & Tears from *Blood, Sweat & Tears*.
[1a] Verse 1, lines 1 &2.
[1b] Last 2 lines of the song.

## 10. Seventh Grade

[2] The school system was different in those days. Elementary school was grades 1-6th; junior high grades: 7-8th and high school: 9-12. South High School was junior high and senior high combined.

## 11. Early 1974

[3] *Space Oddity* - David Bowie. Performed by: David Bowie. The first six lines with the countdown should be inserted in between the lines of continuation … starting before and ending after.
[4] "Keep on Smilin'"—Lewis Maxwell Ross, Maurice Richard Hirsch, John David Anthony, James Robert Hall, Jack Virgil Hall Jr. Performed by: Wet Willie from *Keep on Smilin'*.

## 12. Summer 1974

[5] The first Baby Rocket team was a Minor Pee Wee football team, formed in 1966 by Jim Pierce and Ray Jones. In 1968 a grasscutter football team was formed by Gene Scarlett and Ben Mary. Source: the 1972 Baby Rockets Sports Annual. My dad began coaching because I wanted to play. The team coached

by Jim Pierce and Ray Jones was at capacity, so Dad did what was necessary. Because there was nowhere to play or practice in South Knoxville, he and Joe Maloy approached City Council, and turned over a rock hiding a nugget of gold. The TVA tower field was leased at a cost of $1.00 a year to the Baby Rockets organization. I quit playing football after half a season, but the organization thrived in the community for many, many years. (Thanks, Dad. You're the best).

### 13. Summer 1974 Part II
[6] *Rock Candy* – Sammy Hagar, Ronnie Montrose, Bill Church, Denny Carmassi. Performed by: Montrose from *Montrose*.

### 14. Summer 1974 Part III
[7] *My Generation* – Pete Townsend. Performed by: The Who from *My Generation*. Fourth line, first verse. (This one is important because it will be coming up more than once).

### 16. End of the Innocence Part I
[8] *End of the Innocence* – Don Henley, Bruce Hornsby. Performed by: Don Henley, Bruce Hornsby from *The End of the Innocence*.

### 17. LSD
[9] *Time* – Roger Waters. Performed by: Pink Floyd from Dark Side of the Moon. Second verse, 4 lines.

### 20. End of the Innocence Part III
[10] *Thank You* – Robert Plant. First 4 lines.

### 22. Reason to Believe
[11] *Reason to Believe* – Rod Stewart. First 5 lines.
[12] *Friends* – Season 3, Episodes 15 & 16.

### 27. Shirley
[13] Baptist Hospital on the South Bank of the Tennessee River – demolished 2014.
[14] Byrum Townsend Grocery, home of the Mighty Millie (the best cheeseburger south of the river) – Torn down for road construction before the 1982 World's Fair.

## 28. The Park
[15] P.J. Clapp aka Johnny Knoxville. Before his rise to MTV fame on *Jackass*, my dad coached him in Pee Wee football.
[16] Frankenstein – The Edgar Winter Group.
[17] "Will the Circle Be Unbroken?" – Ada R. Habershon 1907

## 29. Shirley Part II
[18] *Sweet Home Alabama* – Ed King, Gary Rossington, Ron Van Zant Lynyrd Skynyrd Side One of *Second Helping*.

## 31. Bobbi Spencer
[19] *The Ballad of Curtis Loew* – Allen Collins, Ron Van Zant. Performed by: Lynyrd Skynyrd from *Second Helping*.

## 33. A Quiet Rebellion
[20] A nod to *Almost Cut My Hair* – David Crosby
Performed by: Crosby, Stills, Nash & Young: from *Déjà Vu*.
[21] *Jackie Blue* – Steve Cash, Larry Lee. Performed by: Ozark Mountain Daredevils from *It'll Shine When It Shines*.

## 37. Blaine
[22] *When Electricity Came to Arkansas* – Black Oak Arkansas. Performed by: Black Oak Arkansas from *Black Oak Arkansas*.
[23] *Mutants of the Monster* - Black Oak Arkansas. Performed by: Black Oak Arkansas from *If an Angel Came to See You Would You Make Her Feel at Home?*.

## 40. Ted
[24] Matthew 13:48: "Where two or three are gathered in my name, there I am in the midst of them."

## 41. South Young
[25] *Into the Great Wide Open* – Tom Petty, Jeff Lynne. Performed by: Tom Petty and the Heartbreakers from *Into the Great Wide Open*. Last line of the chorus.

## 43. Prayer Meeting/Fall Creek Falls
[26] *Stairway to Heaven* – Robert Plant, Jimmy Page. Performed by: Led Zeppelin from *Led Zeppelin IV* (sometimes referred to as ZOSO).

[27]*Hotel California* – Don Henley, Don Felder, Glen Frey. Performed by: Eagles from *Hotel California*.

[28]*Didn't He* – Randy Matthews. Just go find the song and listen to it.

## 44. Art

[29]In East Tennessee, Icee is interchangeable with Sno-ball, just like Coke is acceptable for most any variety of soda, or pop, or whatever you call it wherever you're from.

[30]*Strange* – Any female outside of a relationship classified as monogamous through means of either legal or verbal commitment. (Not necessarily odd or weird) Proverbs 5:20 – And why wilt thou, my son, be ravished with a strange women, and embrace the bosom of a stranger? See also: Proverbs 2:16; 5:3; 6:24; 7:5; 20:16; 22:14; 23:27; 23:23 & 27:13.

[31]*Dreams* – Stevie Nicks. Performed by: Fleetwood Mac from *Rumours*. The chorus should go here.

## 46. Valerie

[32]*Breakdown* – Tom Petty. Performed by: Tom Petty and the Heartbreakers from *Tom Petty and the Heartbreakers*.

## 48. Skynyrd

[33]*Freebird* – Ronnie Van Zant, Allen Collins. Performed by: Lynyrd Skynyrd from pronounced "Leh-'nerd Skin-'nerd).

[7]*My Generation* - Pete Townsend. Performed by: The Who from *My Generation*.

[34]*Don't Ask Me No Questions* – Ronnie Van Zant, Gary Rossington. Performed by: Lynyrd Skynyrd from *Second Helping*.

[35]*Southern Man* – Neil Young. Performed by: Neil Young from *After the Gold Rush Alabama* – Neil Young from *Harvest, Sweet Home Alabama* – Ronnie Van Zant (See note 18).

[36]*That Smell* – Ronnie Van Zant, Allen Collins. Performed by: Lynyrd Skynyrd from *Street Survivors*.

## 50. Molly Chambers

[37]Ring-dinger was a nickname for Jerry Ridinger who also happened to be Coach Ridinger's son. (See chapter 17. LSD)

## 51. Penny Marks

[38] *The Old Man and the Sea* – Ernest Hemingway.

[39] *Rich Girl* – Daryl Hall, John Oates. Performed by: Hall and Oates from *Bigger than Both of Us*.

## 53. Blaine Part II

[40] *Stranglehold* – Ted Nugent, Rob Grange. Performed by: Ted Nugent from *Ted Nugent*. The last 4 lines before the repetitive part.

## 55. Janet

[41] I debated this with Linda Lionheart. (in my head) She corrected whoever to whomever, however, in my head where this conversation was taking place (at the time), I would've said it incorrectly, so I left it as whoever.

[42] "The Ernie and Bernie Show" – Ernie Grunfeld and Bernard King were the driving force behind UT's success that season.

[43] *Wildflower* – Doug Edwards, David Richardson. Performed by: Skylark from *Skylark*.

## 57. Hannah

[44] *Brick House* – Shirley Hanna-King, Lionel Richie, Milan Williams, Walter Orange, Ronald La Pread, Thomas McClary, William King. Performed by: Commodores from *Commodores*.

[45] The Brickhouse – An establishment on Chapman Highway that sold cheap, cold beer.

[46] Dolly Parton - A native of Sevierville, TN.

[47] *Let the Good Times Roll* – Ric Ocasek. Performed by: The Cars from *The Cars*.

[48] *Just What I Needed* – Ric Ocasek. Performed by: The Cars from *The Cars*. First verse.

## 60. Cameron II

[49] Ronco – a popular advertising agency promoting new, must-have inventions on television.

[50] *Dog and Butterfly* – Ann Wilson, Nancy Wilson, Sue Ennis Performed by: Heart from *Dog and Butterfly* (and Cameron) The whole song. (She performed it brilliantly).

## 62. The Breakup

[51] *Helplessly Hoping* – Stephen Stills. Performed by: Crosby, Stills & Nash from *Crosby, Stills & Nash*. The chorus.

[52] *The Outlaw* – Larry Norman. Performed by: Larry Norman from *Only Visiting This Planet*. Last verse.

# Thanks

I would like to thank everyone who has helped me believe that I could do this.

- *Brittany Murphy*, you laughed loud enough to encourage me during the early going, overlooking the crudeness, which I eventually realized needed to be cleaned up a bit before going out in public.
- *Jerry Harris* for prodding me into describing my characters a little, and just for being there. You were always my favorite mentor.
- *Lisa Belknap*, you convinced me—when I wasn't so sure—that I might be a writer.
- *Lauren Hundley*, I will be forever grateful for your insight and constructive criticism, which I found to be encouraging and most necessary.
- *Lindsay Morris*, my editor, for doing a great job and for helping me through the next steps.
- *Brad Smith*, thank you for the fantastic cover art.
- And last, but certainly not least, *Amy*, my wife, and lifelong companion, for putting up with me all these years, especially while I endeavored to bring this labor of love to completion.

## About the Author

Michael Scarlett was raised in Knoxville, Tennessee. A graduate of South-Young High School, he attended the University of Tennessee, studying art. He is presently employed in Nashville, Tennessee, and resides in Hendersonville with his wife. You can contact him at *thequietkid777@gmail.com*.

www.ingramcontent.com/pod-product-compliance
Lightning Source LLC
Chambersburg PA
CBHW062158080426
42734CB00010B/1745